MAKING A DIFFERENCE WITH CHILDREN AND FAMILIES

MAKING A DIFFERENCE WITH CHILDREN AND FAMILIES

RE-IMAGINING THE ROLE OF THE PRACTITIONER

ALISON PROWLE

ANGELA HODGKINS

First published 2020 by
RED GLOBE PRESS

Red Globe Press in the UK is an imprint of Macmillan Education Limited, registered in England, company number 01755588, of 4 Crinan Street, London, N1 9XW.

Red Globe Press® is a registered trademark in the United States, the United Kingdom, Europe and other countries.

ISBN 978-1-352-01016-9 (paperback)

This book is printed on paper suitable for recycling and made from fully managed and sustained forest sources. Logging, pulping and manufacturing processes are expected to conform to the environmental regulations of the country of origin.

A catalogue record for this book is available from the British Library.

A catalog record for this book is available from the Library of Congress.

This book is dedicated to our children:
Gareth, Megan, Caitlin and Lowri

ACKNOWLEDGEMENTS

This book has been a genuine collaboration from beginning to end. We would like to thank everyone who has so generously given their time and experience to provide case studies, bringing the chapters to life. You have reminded us how talented and inspiring our workforce truly is. We are so proud to be a part of it!

Thank you to Jackie Musgrave, our valued friend and colleague, who is steadfast in her generous support and professional challenge. Your foreword captures perfectly the essence of this book and what we wanted to achieve.

Thank you to Caitlin Prowle for her hard work, attention to detail and synonym advice! You brightened up our writing retreat with your humour, anecdotes and remarkable ability to keep us on track.

We would also like to extend our thanks to Peter Hooper and Hannah Watson from Red Globe Press for their guidance and encouragement throughout this process.

We would like to thank our husbands, Shaun and Malcolm, and families for their endless patience whilst this book has taken over our lives!

Finally, we would like to thank each other. It is always a risk to mix business and pleasure, but our friendship has more than survived the process – it has thrived! We look forward to future collaborations and writing retreats to Blacksmith's Cottage.

BRIEF CONTENTS

TABLE OF CONTENTS

LIST OF FIGURES

LIST OF TABLES

LIST OF ABBREVIATIONS

ADCS   Association of Directors of Children's Services
CAMHS   Child and Adolescent Mental Health Services
CBT   Cognitive Behaviour Therapy
CHIPS   Children in Hospital Improvement Partner Service
CoP   Communities of Practice
CPD   Continuing Professional Development
CYPF   Children, Young People and Families
DCSF   Department for Children, Schools and Families
DfE   Department for Education
DoH   Department of Health
EI/EQ   Emotional Intelligence/Emotional Quotient
EMDR   Eye Movement Desensitisation and Reprocessing
EYFS   Early Years Foundation Stage
HSE   Health and Safety Executive
INSET   In Service Training
NCB   National Children's Bureau
NICE   National Institute for Health and Care Excellence
NNEB   National Nursery Examination Board
NSPCC   National Society for the Prevention of Cruelty to Children
PGCE   Post Graduate Certificate in Education
PSHE   Personal, Social, Health and Economic Education
SEN   Special Educational Needs
SGO   Special Guardianship Order
SLT   Speech and Language Therapist
TED   Technology, Education and Design
UNCRC   United Nations Convention on the Rights of the Child
UNICEF   United Nations International Children's Emergency Fund

FOREWORD

Having read this book, I feel like a better human being. This is because the messages within the book are life-affirming and brimming with positivity. We live in an extraordinarily complex world at a time of uncertainty and austerity, and the future may be of great concern to many students and practitioners working with children, young people and families. The pressures and workload of the modern world can make us doubt our purpose and ability to be able to make a difference to children and their families. However, the content of this book is aimed at enabling readers to consider how to approach life so that it is more manageable. The modern parable by Eisley in the Introduction sets the scene for this book, meaning that each one of us can make a difference and focusing on just the one makes our task achievable.

The messages conveyed in this book are aimed at developing the skills that are needed to work in many professional contexts, not only working with children and families. It draws on some of the best research and experiences from a range of disciplines. For example, the '6 Cs' of nursing are applicable to any professional role that involves working with human beings.

A strength of the book is how the content makes clear links between theory and practice, as well as exploring how practice can be improved by understanding theory. The content conveys a can-do approach and foregrounds reality that leadership is an achievable aim for all of us. The message that leadership is something that introverts can 'do', and not only extroverts, will speak to many readers.

The notion of encouraging practitioners to develop professional bravery is an inspiring aim and much needed in a work environment that is increasingly regulated. However, such bravery needs to be informed by knowledge and understanding of the complex issues, and this book does increase knowledge and understanding of such complexities.

The book gets to the heart of humanity, and urging us to 'look for the human behind everything' is pertinent in our increasingly digital and remote world.

This book is not only a valuable resource for professionals who work with children and families, but it is also a resource that can be used to help the professionals to be kinder to themselves and in doing so, achieve even greater things in the quest to make a positive difference to the lives of our youngest citizens. This book should be a core reading text for students as well as a useful resource for continuing development for practitioners.

Jackie Musgrave
Programme Leader, Early Childhood & Primary Education
Open University
Milton Keynes, UK

INTRODUCTION: A CHANGING CHILDREN AND FAMILIES LANDSCAPE

This chapter introduces the themes of the book. It explores the rich, diverse, challenging and continually changing professional landscape that makes up the children and families' workforce. Moreover, we consider the evidence that the individual practitioner **can** and **does** make a real difference to the families that they work with and can also have a positive impact on the organisations and professional networks that they operate within. This chapter also considers the qualities of an effective practitioner, arguing that how you apply these qualities is at least as important as *what* you do within your job role. Finally, the chapter provides signposts to the remaining sections of the book.

Introduction

In a famous modern parable, Loren Eisley (1969) tells the story of a man walking on the beach. He noticed a child picking up objects and gently throwing them into the sea. The man was intrigued and, approaching the child, he asked him what he was doing. The little boy explained that the surf was high, and the tide was going out, leaving the starfish stranded on the shore. He was returning the fish to the ocean so that they would not die. The man was incredulous and pointed out the miles and miles of beach littered with starfish. It was impossible to save them all. It was impossible to make a difference. After listening politely to what the man had to say, the boy picked up another starfish and returned it to the sea. He looked at the man, smiled and said, 'I made a difference to that one!' The central premise of this book is that as a practitioner working with children, young people and families, you can and do make a difference. Our actions as practitioners are important, but equally vital are the ways in which we build positive relationships with those we work with and the respectful way that we conduct those relationships. As practitioners, having a good knowledge base, understanding the issues and having the necessary skills to support others are all imperative. However, often it is our personal qualities and our ways of interacting with others that can make such a difference to those we work with. This book focuses strongly upon those important personal qualities and how we can enhance these and in doing so, contribute towards positive outcomes for the children, young people and families we work with.

The children, young people and families' (CYPF) workforce has changed and developed over the last few decades, and practitioners' roles are now much more diverse and wide-ranging than they were a generation ago.

Changes in expectations, cuts to funding and service reconfigurations have all resulted in professionals having to take on more responsibility within a wider remit. For example, many practitioners are finding themselves working within extended provision with children of a 0–19 age range whereas previously they may have worked solely in early years or youth provision. Family support work is on the increase and workers are in contact with more challenging family situations. Practitioners in schools are encountering young people with a wider range of needs and abilities than ever before. Moreover, there is now a growing recognition that the students of today will have to work longer and may well have a number of different professional roles during their working life (moving from early years to teaching to family support, for example) as their own circumstances, interests and aspirations change, and also to meet the changing needs of the workforce. It is also important to recognise that the UK has devolved governments in Scotland, Wales and Northern Ireland. Each of these nations will have their own legislation, policy agendas and priorities. Even within England, each local authority area is different and will have its own systems, approaches and working arrangements. This adds another layer of complexity to any conversation about the children, young people and families' workforce as this is by no means homogeneous. Therefore, students and practitioners are urged to contextualise the application of the themes of this book to their own local contexts.

However, whilst job roles and work tasks may change, there are a number of essential skills and qualities that are transferable across the workforce. This book, therefore, places the emphasis on the individual practitioner, examining qualities needed for success, regardless of the specific job role students or practitioners may be filling. This book explores the diverse and ever-changing CYPF landscape and the varied roles within that landscape. It considers the question of what the essential skills and qualities necessary are for working with children, young people and families today. It provides practitioners and students with opportunities to reflect upon what it means to be an effective practitioner, through the exploration of theoretical material and practice case studies from a range of professional disciplines. This book is not intended as a definitive list, nor as the last word on the qualities discussed in the chapters. Our purpose is to start a conversation about these qualities, to pique interest and to empower students and practitioners to find out more. This is why, at the end of each chapter, we have included a number of resources to support students and practitioners to go deeper into the themes introduced.

The children and families workforce

What do we mean when we talk about the children, young people and families workforce? It is tempting to start listing professions and job roles, or to think about the organisations that make up the wider sector. In the widest definition, the CYPF workforce includes those individuals and organisations that can play a role in delivering positive outcomes for children and families. This will, of course, involve those organisations and professionals with statutory responsibility for children's outcomes (for example, social workers, teachers, health visitors), but, equally, this broad definition will also encompass a much wider group of organisations and individuals who provide much-needed early intervention, community support and provision, often with low status and little formal recognition, and indeed with much of the work undertaken by volunteers. Furthermore, there will also be those organisations and job roles for whom working with children and families is an important aspect of their remit, but not their primary focus. Police, paramedics and leisure staff, for example, may play a significant role in securing outcomes for children and families. Moreover, we cannot underestimate the importance of those who undertake specific roles in society (e.g. planning public spaces) to ensure that they understand and champion the needs of CYPF.

Moreover, the CYPF workforce is made up not only of different areas of interest (e.g. health, sport) but also of a multiplicity of different professional disciplines, roles and job titles. The workforce is made up of individuals at different stages in their career, some of whom may be newly qualified and others very experienced. Moreover, practitioners may work in the statutory sector (e.g. local authorities, schools, hospitals), the private sector (e.g. childcare settings, schools) or the third sector (e.g. voluntary organisations, community projects). The CYPF workforce, therefore, is incredibly wide-ranging and diverse, embodying a whole range of knowledge skills and disciplines, cultures and practices.

Whilst this book is written primarily for those working in roles concerned primarily with the well-being of children, young people and families (e.g. teacher, family support worker, youth worker, social worker, children's nurse) it will also be of relevance to those who support CYPF as part of their role or indeed those who work in other contexts altogether, such as retail and hospitality. Indeed, I went dining out with colleagues in a restaurant recently we were served by a former student, now working there as a manager. She explained how her degree in Early Childhood Studies had helped her both to get the job and to do it well. 'My focus is on making dining out a positive experience for parents and children', she said. 'We have introduced lots of little changes to improve how we do things. I do actually feel like I am using my degree and making a difference.'

A challenging context

In a recent position paper, the Association of Directors of Children's Services (ADCS, 2019) identifies that the CYPF workforce is often uncoordinated, lacks a unified voice and operates within silos. They advocate a coordinated workforce strategy, investment in leadership development and the creation of a shared common core of training, values and approaches across the sector. Of course, none of this is new, but what is perhaps different from previous attempts to unify and coordinate is the unprecedented challenges faced within the sector. These challenges include financial pressures on local authorities and other statutory and non-statutory organisations, an increase in levels of child poverty (including families affected by 'in work' challenges in recruiting and retaining staff poverty), and an increase in safeguarding pressures.

Undoubtedly, this challenging context demands policy change and policy coordination, which are beyond the remit of this book. Moreover, there is an important role for the development of skills, knowledge, systems and approaches across the sector. However, where this book seeks to make a contribution is by putting the emphasis not on policy or systems but on the individual practitioner and the difference they can make, both to the families they support and to the organisations, networks and communities within which they operate.

The need for this book and a word about the case studies

The foregoing sections have explored the diverse and challenging contexts which make up the CYPF landscape. In the conversation below, we reflect upon the need for the book and what motivated us to write it. This forms our first case study.

The case studies throughout the book showcase real practitioners from a variety of different roles, disciplines and professional backgrounds. They are very diverse, both in the way they are written and also in the content they explore. Some of the case studies are from students or early career practitioners; others are from more experienced practitioners or indeed those who may have changed career. Each one has been chosen to help us consider not just the immense diversity of the sector, but also some of the common experiences that we share, as well as transferable practitioner qualities that will stand us in good stead whatever role we find ourselves in. They also provide an all-too-rare opportunity for practitioner voices to be heard. The case studies are not intended to be a definitive guide to practice, but rather as a starting point for your own reflection. The case studies are accompanied by reflective questions designed to enable you to consider your own qualities and attributes. The case studies can be used by practitioners and students alike. Whilst they provide a useful vehicle for individual reflection, they can also be used for group work or within team meetings to help explore different perspectives and to develop shared understandings.

Case Study – Alison and Angela reflect upon the need for this book

This case study takes the form of a 'conversation with a purpose'. It was recorded and transcribed.

AP: So, where did our idea for the book originally come from, do you think?

AH: I was very conscious that all of the books written from this centre were early-childhood-based and that we needed something that catered for practitioners working with children of all ages, and families.

AP: Yes, you're right, because there are plenty of social work books, and health, and early childhood books but it's very rare that you find something that reflects that multi-agency context in which the services are so often operating now.

AH: And for the course I lead, Integrated working with Children and Families, age 0–19, we wanted something that would encompass all of the skills and dispositions that practitioners need for the workforce today.

AP: Because it is a challenging environment that they're facing at the moment, isn't it? With roles that are maybe not as clearly defined as they were in the past and people being asked to work outside their usual professional boundaries. I was with a group of people on Monday who were trained as nursery nurses and they are now working in family support and they're parents, and they were all saying that actually they've learned on the job because there wasn't any course that helped them at that stage of their profession. I think, for me, it's about how we support those practitioners in what they need in order to be effective in those roles, recognising that those roles are changing all the time.

AH: Yes, and also, I think that these days people are more likely to change career, not stay in one job for their whole working lives. For example, from early years into family support or teaching assistants going into other roles, so people are more likely to go off in different directions. So, we wanted a book that would be useful wherever you work.

AP: Yes, and we wanted to draw on different examples from different disciplines. On Monday I was visiting a family support team and it was very multidisciplinary so there are people from health there, people from youth work backgrounds, early years, and so on. They also have social work and psychology input. It was really interesting seeing how their experiences, working in those areas, helped people to really understand things like attachment theory, and the reasons behind behaviour and also the wider determinants of health. It was great to observe them all learning from one another. That is what we want from the case studies – each case study will come from within a specific discipline, but will have something to say to people who are outside of that discipline.

AH: Yes, so on the Integrated Working course, for example, I have students who have trained in early years, students working with older children in secondary schools, childminders, family support workers, a youth worker, someone working with babies in hospital … The conversations between them in class are fantastic, they learn such a lot from each other's experiences, and so by using case studies in the book, we're encouraging more practitioners to learn from each other's sectors.

AP: Yes, and I suppose that is really important as well because it is helping to develop that shared understanding and also that shared vocabulary of how we support families. Because, I've found in the past, for example, just we use terms and phrases that mean different things to different disciplines. 'Early intervention', for example, means something very different if you're in education or in social work.

AH: Yes, and a lot of my students just understand the education aspect and they talk about observation and assessment, but what they hadn't considered was early intervention in parenting programmes, in youth work to help prevent crime, so learning about all of these different aspects would really broaden their horizons and their understanding of the bigger picture.

AP: So, it was part of our vision, wasn't it, to bring together those experiences and unpack them in terms of what it is that makes an effective practitioner working with children and families. And thinking of it in terms of not just their professional background, in terms of their discipline, but their personal attributes as well; what they bring individually into that agenda. So often, you'll have two support workers, one will be really good at working with families, and the other less so. So often it's not so much what is done, but the way in which that is communicated to families that determines how easy it is for families to become engaged.

AH: Yes and moving away from skills that can be taught to personal attributes and competencies, and dispositions that can be developed.

AP: That's interesting because I think we do believe, don't we, that they **can** be developed. In part, those qualities may be inherent, but there is so much that can be learned, practised and developed. Being part of a community of practice can help you with that. For me, a really good example of that is working in a strength-based way. So many of our former training programmes come from a deficit model which considers what the problem is and how it can be addressed, whereas now, we're thinking more of strengths and resilience. Actually, working in a strengths-based way takes a lot of practice and a lot of work.

AH: So does active listening. Or empathy.

Reflection on case study

- What were the key motivating factors that led to the writing of this book?
- Alison talks about the ways in which some of the important qualities explored in this book can be nurtured and developed. Do you agree? Can you think of any ways in which your own practitioner qualities have been developed and enhanced?
- In what ways has the workforce changed over the last few decades? What qualities do you think it will be important for practitioners to have as we move forward?

A focus on the practitioner

As we have already identified, the CYPF workforce is made up of diverse roles, specialties, interests and individuals. Within this milieu, some would argue that professional hierarchies are inevitable. Hugman (2003) attributes these hierarchies to notions of power (Bourdieu, 1985), holding that individuals make claims to exclusive bodies of professional knowledge and skills. Whilst differences in professional knowledge and specialism are important in preserving the complex web of skills and knowledge needed for supporting children and families, they can also result in what Beattie (1995) terms 'tribalism', which may adversely affect integrated working. Messenger (2010), writing in the context of family support, identifies how workers are affected by perceptions of status and hierarchy. However, she also makes the point that for staff, not being equal but 'being equally valued' was the most important thing. Such valuing taps into an intrinsic desire amongst many practitioners to undertake work that is meaningful and of worth, in other words 'to make a difference'. For many, if not most, of the practitioners within the CYPF field, that intrinsic motivation or 'public passion' (UNDP, 2016) is what draws people into the sector and retains them there, often despite pay freezes and growing work demands.

In other words, practitioners are often motivated less by extrinsic factors such as pay or rewards, and more by the perceived value of their work (endowed by themselves and others), their passion for that work and the pride they take in it (Burst and Lako, 2017).

If this is the case, then it makes sense to invest in supporting practitioners' professional development and enabling them to become the best practitioners they can be. Part of this will require the acquisition of skills, knowledge and where appropriate qualifications to support their chosen specialism within the sector. However, it is equally important to enable them to reflect upon their own personal qualities and attributes and how these contribute towards enabling them to develop as effective practitioners.

Practitioner qualities

As a conversation starter we asked a random sample of practitioners from various professional backgrounds to articulate what they see as the most important qualities for a practitioner. Here are their responses (Figure 0.1).

Empathy, kindness, authenticity and a non-judgemental approach all featured highly. Many practitioners also talked about valuing the individual. As Karen, a Principal Lecturer and former teacher, put it:

> For me it is about having total commitment to understanding the interests and needs of individuals.

Pat, a nurse working with children with profound disabilities, said,

> You need to gain trust and build trusting relations by listening to them with empathy. Find out what they want out of a given experience and work with them to always make a positive experience.

Other practitioners talked about the importance of being positive, resilient and ambitious for the families you work with. This led to Martha, a health

Figure 0.1 Important qualities for a practitioner as identified by practitioners

visitor, suggesting that in her opinion, one of the most important qualities for the practitioner is the ability to impart and inspire hope, even when situations look bleak. It is important for students to recognise that whilst this diagram prioritises the voices of practitioners it represents individual perspectives rather than robust research findings, and therefore should not be seen as definitive. Nonetheless, it does provide a useful insight into the qualities which practitioners believe are important when working with children, young people and families.

In developing this book, we have identified a number of qualities that contribute towards being an effective practitioner, and these are shown in the diagram below. This is not intended as an exhaustive list but rather as a starting point for reflection on the qualities that you bring as a practitioner, and, perhaps, where there is scope for development (Figure 0.2).

Evidently, each practice situation we find ourselves in will demand a unique approach, bringing different qualities to the fore. Also, by tuning in to the individuals that we work with, we will be able to recognise how best to provide support. We also need to recognise that practitioners with different strengths will be effective in different situations, and part of what makes an effective practitioner relates to effective matching of the practitioner to the situation and family. With restraints on budget and staffing levels, this may not always be practical, but where it is practised it certainly yields

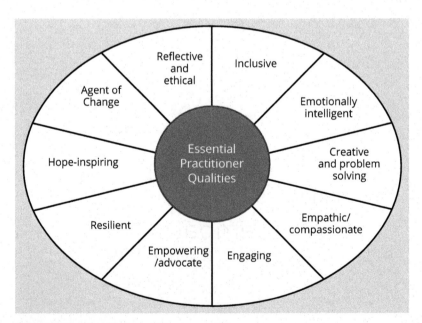

Figure 0.2 Essential practitioner qualities

positive results. As a manager of a preventative family support project shared with one of the authors recently,

> I spend time reflecting on the family and their needs. I know the individual strengths of the support workers well, and this enables me to think about who the family would be best able to relate to. It is about who will be in the best position to help them to make those positive changes. Sometimes they need a support worker with a gentle, quiet approach, sometimes it is best to have someone who brings fun and can energise and motivate.

What this also demonstrates is the importance of flexibility, adaptivity and attuned responsiveness when working with CYPF.

Careers within the CYPF workforce

The premise of this book is also that, whilst skills and knowledge may vary according to the specific role you are fulfilling within the CYPF workforce, the qualities of a practitioner are generic and therefore transferable.

There is a recognition that whilst in the past, people may have aspired to 'a job for life', now, with greater opportunities and longer working lives, many practitioners will fulfil a number of roles during their career. Whilst some individuals may have very clear career goals and aspirations, for others it is more about adding value to themselves and making the most of opportunities when they arise.

As authors of this book, with approximately 50 years of experience between us, we have reflected upon our own career journeys. We have thought about the core values and personal/professional qualities we bring to our work and how these have supported us in the various roles we have undertaken. In the case study below, we reflect upon our own professional journeys.

Case Study – Angela and Alison discuss their professional journeys

Angela's story

I did the NNEB training in 1982–84, and in those days, it was all about caring for children aged from birth to 7 years 11 months, a very specific age range. The training was very much care-based. I can't remember learning much about education at all, I remember learning about bottle feeding and changing nappies. We also had to learn to knit, and we had to knit a layette for a baby. We made wooden toys in woodwork and we had singing lessons and we had to learn how to play the recorder, so we could teach children to play. I know it sounds really old-fashioned; we did lots of work on storytelling and planning creative activities, so it was very much play-based and care-based, and we were being trained for one specific role, in a nursery, where I have spent very little of my career. And, of course, we were called 'nursery nurses', a title which is rarely used now, even though many of us went to work in schools as classroom/teaching assistants.

So that was the first formal training I had. My first job was as a nanny and from there, I went on to work in a special school with children aged up to 18. The training I'd had didn't prepare me at all for that job, so I learned from my colleagues. Since then, I've been in all sorts of roles. I worked in a primary school for many years and I set up an after-school club, so I had to learn all those management skills, managing staff, managing finances, setting up a business. I've done all sorts; I went to work for a Sure Start local programme, one of the first local programmes, so we were setting up services and starting to explore multiagency working for the first time, which was a challenge. I'd never worked with midwives, health visitors, social workers or benefits advisors before.

Since then I've worked as a Special Needs and Disability Advisor for a Local Authority Early Years team, and then studied for a degree and a masters' degree, then came into lecturing, first in an FE college and now at a university. I've always been drawn to the pastoral side of working with children and families, so I trained as a counsellor, and had various roles, working in a GP surgery, at Victim Support and at Childline, and those skills have changed the way I work in all areas of my life and career. But that original training I had was just the basic first step. The rest of it, you learn as you go along, don't you?

I think my original training prepared me for a career in one particular role in the 1980s, and the sector is so much more diverse today. Little of the training I had has been relevant to the roles I have undertaken, but I do feel that I developed a range of underpinning principles that have been with me since; things like equality of opportunity, safeguarding and appreciation of the individual child.

We do a really good job, don't we, of preparing people to understand child development, but then when it goes beyond that, sometimes those transferable skills that they're going to need as they move into other areas we don't cover as well. Jobs today have got a much wider remit, and I think that something else that we need to consider as well is that we don't know what the world is going to be like in 20 or 30 years' time, so the way I was trained doesn't suit what the world is like now, and we need to build on people's own qualities and things like problem solving and creativity and flexibility to be able to cope with the changes that are likely to happen in the future.

That adaptability is probably one of the key things, isn't it? And, you know, it takes confidence, professional confidence, and it also takes a bit of professional bravery as well, because you're stepping outside into the unknown and I just wonder how we can, through the book, equip people to be able to more seriously step outside their traditional boundaries and work with families in different ways.

It is about looking at people holistically, isn't it, rather than just looking through an education lens, or a social care lens. It is about looking at children and families holistically.

The following diagram maps out Angela's career to date.

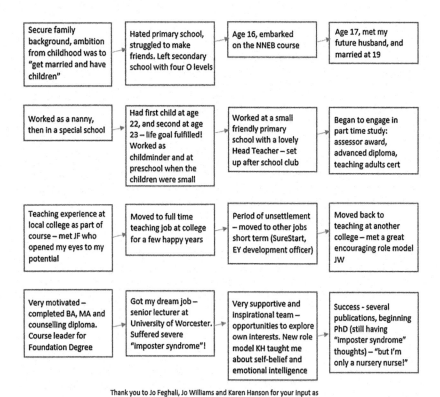

Thank you to Jo Feghali, Jo Williams and Karen Hanson for your input as
significant role models at important stages of my career

Figure 0.3 Angela's journey

Alison's story

*My story is a bit different. I grew up in the South Wales Valleys in the 70s and
80s. It is what we now call an area of multiple deprivation. I wouldn't say my
family were particularly poor; we were on a par with the rest of the community, but there was a lot of need in the community. And I think that was quite
seminal in thinking about what I wanted to do with my life. I saw so many of
my friends 'fall through the net'; people who had fantastic, creative, wonderful
things to offer and yet didn't achieve their potential for one reason or another.*

*So, I became really passionate about education and about how it did not
always provide what young people need. I know that sounds negative, but I was
aware how awful school was for kids who perhaps didn't fit into the traditional
mould, or who were a bit more challenging. At 18, I went to the other side of the
UK to university where I did a theology and philosophy degree, and then much
to everyone's surprise, I did a PGCE at Homerton College Cambridge and trained
as a middle school teacher, which in those days was ages 9–14. I was very keen
right from the outset to work in areas of multiple deprivation. So, I was working
in North London, for my first year of teaching in an interesting school, quite*

challenging. It was a very mixed community actually, in many ways, both economically and socially and in terms of some of the needs that presented there. I loved it, I loved my job and I loved the idea of using education to give people opportunities that they may not otherwise have.

Then I moved to Wales, to a secondary school context, again I was working quite close to my home community and even though I liked teaching A level and GCSE, my passion was teaching bottom sets as I loved the idea of building people's confidence and helping them to understand their brilliance that is sometimes not recognised within the school system. I worked in that role in schools in Wales and England for many years and ended up being Head of Department. I had pastoral responsibilities as well and I was in charge of PSHE, which also brought me into contact with parents and with other agencies.

But I was getting a little bit disillusioned and thinking, 'Here I am teaching RE and some of these children and young people actually haven't had breakfast this morning'. I got the sense that there was there was so much going on in their lives. So, I started thinking that I could only tinker around the edges of their experience and that actually a lot of the important work was done earlier and with parents. I was so fortunate to be offered a job in Sure Start, so I went from teaching A levels and GCSEs down to early years, working with parents with adverse life circumstances. We had target areas working with communities, and it brought me into contact with a wide range of people. Then, I worked in the community sector for a long time, just developing interventions for families who were struggling for one reason or another. I realised that, most of all, I needed to be open-minded, non-judgemental and to really listen to what the families wanted from their lives, and then find ways to empower them to make those positive changes.

Eventually, I went to work for the local authority as the Children and Young People partnership coordinator, so it was a more strategic role really, but within that then I was managing children's services broadly, which included working with health visitors, educational welfare officers, and so on. I loved that job, because we were really in a fortunate position because it was a mixture of strategic planning and more operational management. So not only were we responsible for developing the children and young people's plan, which was the priority for the multi-agency network moving forward, but we also delivered a lot of the services. So, I did a master's in the management of public services, and I got more and more involved in things like family support services and family support programmes, parenting programmes in particular, before coming to the University of Worcester. And again, I found myself immediately drawn into those issues around inequalities and adverse childhood experiences. That is where my passion lies and now my teaching and research reflects those interests. It is also about developing practitioners' confidence to empower them to see the difference they can make, even when they are working in very challenging circumstances.

The following diagram maps out Alison's career to date, highlighting some of the external factors and internal motivations that influenced her choices.

As authors of this book both Alison and Angela recognise the importance not just of formal learning and qualifications, but of learning from others.

Both identify role models as important to their professional and personal development. Moreover, whilst neither of their careers has been particularly linear, they recognise how much they have gleaned from each experience and how each different role adds to their professional identity.

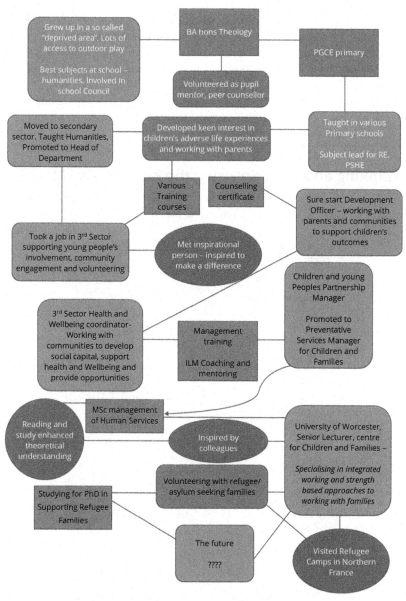

Figure 0.4 Alison's story

Case study reflection

- What practitioner qualities do Angela and Alison display in this case study?
- How have these qualities assisted them within the varied jobs they have undertaken in the children and families workforce?
- One thing Angela and Alison share is the desire to 'make a difference'. To what extent do you share this motivational drive? Can you think of one example where you feel you have made a difference to someone you were working with? What qualities enabled you to make that difference?
- Can you map out your career journey to date, perhaps using the Kawa River Model below (Iwama, 2006) to reflect upon your journey so far and your hopes for the future?

Thinking about career using the Kawa (River) Model

Michael Iwama, working within an occupational therapy context, developed a model using a metaphor of a river to depict one's life (Iwama, 2006). The

- Where did your river start?
  - o What is the landscape like?
  - o What driftwood helped you at this stage?
  - o Were there any boulders?
- Where did your river go next?
  - o Were there any meanders?
  - o Any rapids, or waterfalls?
  - o What was the landscape like?
  - o How was the flow?
  - o What driftwood helped you at this stage?
  - o Were there any rocks or boulders?
  - o How were these overcome?
- Where is your river now?
  - o How well is it flowing?
  - o What driftwood is helping you?
  - o Are there any boulders?
- Where would you like your river to go next?
  - o What will help you achieve flow?
  - o What rocks may you encounter?
- Where would you like your river to end?

Figure 0.5 Using a river model to reflect on career

model is very powerful as it considers the interplay between social and physical environments. Moreover, it examines where you have been, where you are now and where you wish to be. Within the river are rocks (barriers and challenges) and driftwood (assets that enable you to float); the aim is to break down the rocks to increase flow. Whilst the model is useful in client-facing, therapeutic contexts, it has equal relevance as a collaboration tool between professionals, or indeed as a means of reflecting on your own professional journey. We often ask our students to picture their life as a river. This provides a powerful tool for reflecting upon their journey. Below are some questions to help you use this tool. There are many other ways that you can use this model, which can be found on the website (details below) (Figure 0.5).

An overview of the chapters in this book

The next section summarises the remaining chapters in the book. Many of the themes overlap, and this is signposted within the chapters. Each chapter is supported by case studies and reflective questions.

Chapter 1 – The empathic and compassionate practitioner

Empathy and compassion are the cornerstones of working with children and families. For many practitioners, working with people is a vocation, and they have a desire to 'make a difference'. This involves being a person that children and their families can build a relationship with, someone who cares and who wants to help and support. This chapter will discuss the role and importance of these skills, along with ways of developing advanced empathy skills. The impact of this emotional labour on practitioners will also be explored.

Chapter 2 – The engaging and empowering practitioner

Autonomy and self-determination in individuals and communities is necessary in order to enable them to represent their own interests in a self-determined way. Empowering others enables them to overcome their sense of powerlessness and lack of influence, and to recognise and use their strengths and resources. This chapter explores how practitioners can move beyond the provision of support and employ strength-based perspectives to enable others to find their voice and proactively take control of their own futures. This may involve finding practical ways to overcome barriers such as poverty, language, education, cultural differences and mistrust of authority. It will almost certainly mean establishing rapport and building trust. The chapter argues that there is no single method for engaging all individuals and families, but rather that this requires a flexible, multi-modal ongoing strategy in which active listening and tuning in to parents and children's concerns, fears and aspirations is a central requirement.

Chapter 3 – The resilient and self-efficacious practitioner

Professor Angie Hart defines residence as: 'Beating the odds whilst also changing the odds' (Hart, Aumann and Heaver, 2010). Helping children and families to develop resilience is a crucial part of the practitioner role, but what about our own resilience as practitioners? In the increasingly complex, changing and turbulent context of today's working environment, developing the resilience of individual practitioners becomes essential in order to enable them to both survive and thrive. This chapter considers what resilience is and how we can develop it.

Chapter 4 – The practitioner as advocate

Advocacy means speaking up on someone else's behalf; there are different forms of advocacy, both formal and informal. However, many practitioners working with children and families employ advocacy skills on a regular basis. Although it is important to speak on behalf of someone who cannot speak for themselves, it is even more important that we enable children, young people and families' voices to be heard. Children's rights and participation and child agency will be explored in this chapter.

Chapter 5 – The practitioner as a leader and agent of change

This chapter considers the concepts of leadership and management in services with children, young people and families in the twenty-first century. Role modelling, empowerment and encouragement will all be considered as aspects of positive leadership in this field, as well as working within a policy framework. Leaders today need to possess a range of professional and personal qualities such as empathy, emotional intelligence and communication skills, which will be covered in more depth in later chapters. However, they also need resilience and the ability to take difficult decisions. Recognising the need for innovation and continuous improvement, we will consider the potential of catalytic leadership. Change is inevitable in services for children, young people and families. Whilst some of that change derives from external factors such as government directives, some necessity for change is identified by those working within a service as a means of better responding to need, improving quality or working more effectively. This chapter considers issues related to driving forward and managing change, including the change curve, resistance to change, overcoming resistance and making change stick.

Chapter 6 – The emotionally intelligent practitioner

The term 'emotional intelligence' includes four distinct elements – how we perceive emotion, how we use our emotions, how we understand the emotions of others and how we manage emotions. This chapter will examine models of emotional intelligence and ways of developing these valuable skills. Emotional intelligence can be increased and improved. Being emotionally intelligent is important in any work with people, but particularly so when working with vulnerable people or families under stress.

Chapter 7 – The communicating and collaborating practitioner

This chapter considers the vital role of communication and collaboration in working with children and families. The chapter explores the importance of working in partnership with parents/carers. It also considers the value of integrated working across professional and agency boundaries to help children and families to achieve positive outcomes.

Chapter 8 – The creative and problem-solving practitioner

Creative problem-solving skills are becoming more and more important in children and families' practice. Changes within the sector can create real challenges for services and so problem solving becomes necessary in order to provide the best possible support. In this chapter, we will explore types of creative thinking and how transferable skills are fundamental to today's professionals.

Chapter 9 – The reflective and ethical practitioner

Reflection is widely accepted as an essential aspect of professional practice for those working with children, young people and families. This chapter outlines the importance of reflective practice and the deeper dispositions of reflexivity and reflective activism. Reflecting on our own values and principles is essential in understanding ourselves and our personal philosophy. The role of personal values and principles are examined and analysed, in relation to professional ethics.

Chapter 10 – The inclusive, hope-inspiring practitioner

Working in services for children, young people and families brings the practitioner into contact with people from many different cultural, social, economic and religious backgrounds. Being aware of our own prejudices is essential. Children and families will present with different needs, strengths and abilities and all must be appropriately included, valued and supported. Developing inclusive practice requires practitioners to accept the responsibility for creating environments and practices in which all children can flourish and feel they belong. Moreover, this chapter considers the importance of inspiring hope in individuals or families who may have lost it.

Chapter 11 – The importance of practitioner self-care and self-management

Working with children, young people and families can be emotionally draining and physically tiring. Therefore, it is important that we, as practitioners, learn to take care of ourselves. In this chapter, we examine practitioner stress and burnout and possible ways of preventing or lessening the effects of this. We will explore a range of self-help strategies and support services available to practitioners. The link between self-care and supervision is also expounded and methods of appropriate supervision investigated.

Chapter 12 – The continually developing practitioner

Continual professional development is fundamental to practitioners working with children, young people and families, in order for us to improve our skills and to remain up to date with current practices. This chapter explores ways of developing professionally and what motivates individuals to do so. It also explores the links between professional and personal advancement in developing a professional identity. The changing world of careers and employment in the twenty-first century is examined.

 Further reading and resources

The Association of Directors of Children's Services (2019). *Building a Workforce That Works for All Children* [online], Manchester. Available at: https://adcs. org.uk/assets/documentation/ADCS_Building_a_workforce_that_works_for_ all_children_FINAL_11_March_2019.pdf [Accessed 8 August 2019].

- This position paper explores the current service landscape and calls for further investment in the CYPF workforce. It recognises the diverse contexts in which practitioners operate and makes reference to the challenges faced by children young people and families and the services that support them.

The Kawa River Model – http://www.kawamodel.com/

- This website gives further information about the Kawa model, which can be used and adapted in several ways, for therapeutic and for career purposes. It provides a helpful way of visualising our journeys and thinking about our strengths and resources, as well as the challenges we face.

Walker, G. (2018). *Working Together for Children: A Critical Introduction to Multi-Agency Working*. Bloomsbury.

- An up-to-the minute textbook, which provides useful background and context on a range of critical issues for those working with children and families.

References

Beattie, A. (1995). War and peace among the health tribes. In Soothill, K., MacKay, L. and Webb, C. (eds) *Interprofessional Relations in Health Care*. London: Arnold.

Borst, R. T. and Lako, C. J. (2017). Proud to be a public servant? An analysis of the work-related determinants of professional pride among Dutch public servants. *International Journal of Public Administration*, 40(10), 875–887. https://doi.org/10.1080/01900692.2017.1289.

Department for Children, Schools and Families (DCFS) (2008). *2020 Children and Young People's Workforce Strategy: Evidence and Knowledge Management* [online]. Leeds: DCFS. Available at: https://dera.ioe. ac.uk/10601/1/2020%20Children%20and%20Young%20People%27s%20 Workforce%20Strategy%20-%20Evidence%26Knowledge%20 Management.pdf [Accessed 8 August 2019].

Eisley, L. (1969). *The Unexpected Universe*. San Diego: Harcourt, Brace and World.

Global Centre for Public Service Excellence and United Nations Development Programme (2016). *New Public Passion. Reflections from New Zealand on Public Service Reform* [online]. Available at: http://hdr.undp.org/en/content/human-development-report-2016 [Accessed 8 August 2019].

Hart, A., Aumann, K. and Heaver, B. (2010). *Boingboing Resilience Research and Practice*. Available at www.boingboing.org.uk.

Hugman, R. (2003). Going round in circles? Identifying interprofessional dynamics in Australian Health and Social Care. In Leathard, A. (ed.) *Interprofessional Collaboration: From Policy to Practice in Health and Social Care*. Hove: Brunner-Routledge.

Iwama, M. (2006). *The Kawa Model: Culturally Relevant Occupational Therapy*. Philadelphia: Elsevier.

The Association of Directors of Children's Services (ADCS) (2019). *Building a Workforce that Works for All Children* [online]. Manchester. Available at: https://adcs.org.uk/assets/documentation/ADCS_Building_a_workforce_that_works_for_all_children_FINAL_11_March_2019.pdf [Accessed 8 August 2019].

LIST OF CONTRIBUTORS/CASE STUDIES

Name	Contribution chapter	Biography
James Boddey	1	James is the proud owner of a kindergarten in Ludlow, Shropshire. He is passionate about the work of Carl Rogers and the person-centred approach, which is a major influence on his practice and on how he and his staff interact with others.
Sophie Reid	2	Sophie was born and raised in Cardiff and has always been interested in learning about different religions, traditions and cultures, being keen to learn from others and recognising the benefits of inclusion. She has a strong work ethic and loves to throw herself into everything she does with enthusiasm and an open mind. Sophie worked as an inclusion family support worker with Barnardo's.
Sophie Fry	3	Sophie is a social worker in a Children's Safeguarding Team. She started her career working in children's centres before progressing into Child Protection. She is passionate about ensuring that professionals don't lose the value of human connection when working with vulnerable children and their families. She is reminded every day in her practice of the importance of relationships in this professional field.

Name	Contribution chapter	Biography
Claire Hiscocks	3	Claire is a specialist community practice health nurse (school nurse) at Aneurin Bevan University Health Board, working with children and young people. Prior to this role, she worked for a specialist child, adolescent and mental health day unit, working with a number of children with complex mental health difficulties. Claire has always been passionate about working with children and trained as a psychiatric nurse in 2010, gaining a first-class honours degree in 2013.
Enza Smith MBE	4	Enza is a devoted Christian, mother, grandmother and kinship carer. She is the founder of Kinship Carers UK and works tirelessly helping other carers in order to support them over the hurdles of kinship care. Her wish is that all kinship carers and the children they care for have the right to services they are entitled to.
Natasha Headley	4	Natasha works as a mentor for individuals that are either in prison and due for release, or who have been released on probation and are looking to turn their lives around by getting back into employment and education. She believes that family links are extremely important in this difficult situation.
Emma Davies	5	Emma is the manager of a thriving preschool setting in a rural market town. In late 2011, she took over the role of manager following an 'inadequate' Ofsted inspection. The setting is now rated 'outstanding'. Emma is a strong proponent of lifelong learning and is currently studying for her master's degree.

Name	Contribution chapter	Biography
Alison Ramshaw	5	Alison began her social work career as a volunteer working with young people on 'alternative to custody programmes', befriending these young people and working towards supporting them to build self-worth in order to lead them away from a life of crime. From here she secured a full-time post working in a small residential establishment which was home to three young people with severe physical and learning difficulties. She qualified as a social worker in 2002 and has held a number of positions, including working in child protection teams, as a Team Manager in an Intake and Assessment team, a Safeguarding Team Manager, the Regional Adoption Service Manager and finally her current post of Service Manager in Children's Services.
Rachel Price	5	Rachel has worked in children's social care since 2002, beginning her career as a trainee social worker in Blaenau Gwent. She was fortunate enough to be seconded to the Social Work Diploma, which she studied through the Open University, whilst working full time in Children's Social Services. She has been an assistant team manager and manager since 2007 and is now manager of preventative services in Blaenau Gwent. She says that the past two and a half years she has spent being part of the changes in the prevention agenda have been an amazing and rewarding experience.

Name	Contribution chapter	Biography
Lilly Faulkner	6	Lilly qualified as a mental health nurse in September 2019. She works on an inpatient assessment mental health ward, which is both challenging and rewarding. She sees patients when they are first admitted and in crisis. This requires her to have good assessment and risk-management skills. The environment is fast-paced and there is a high turnover of patients. As a result, she has developed resilience skills to enable her to provide the best possible nursing care. She enjoys meeting lots of different patients and building therapeutic relationships. She sees it as a privilege to listen to their stories and help people stay positive at a time which is often the lowest point in their lives.
Jade Maynard	6	Jade is currently a senior targeted family support worker in a Local Authority. She has worked with children, young people and families for 15 years, in a variety of settings. Jade sees working with children, young people and families as rewarding and challenging, as there is never a right answer. She sees her role as a career in which she and the families continually learn together.
Ruth Akbas	6	Ruth qualified as an NNEB Nursery Nurse in 1993 and worked in a development unit for preschool children with special needs. She then became a family support worker for her Local Authority. She has been in her current role for 11 years, supporting young people who have complex or emerging needs, and their families.

Name	Contribution chapter	Biography
Rebecca Thomas	7	Rebecca is a programme manager for Save the Children in Wales. Her role is to develop relationships and build capacity in order to transform the way children are supported in early years. She has extensive experience in the third sector in a variety of roles.
Dr Hazel Richards	7	Hazel is a Speech and Language Therapist who worked for 23 years in the NHS and then in further education with young adults with acquired brain injury. She is passionate about communication and interaction, social justice and support, and her career has always involved joint working. Indeed, she has learnt and grown significantly from listening to and learning from others throughout her career. She is currently a lecturer, teaching in the Department of Education Studies and the Department of Children and Families, and has recently completed her doctoral studies, which investigate the realities of Education and Health Care Plan implementation from the perspective of Special Educational Needs Co-ordinators.
Adam Taylor	8	Adam has worked in children's services for various local authorities in the West Midlands for the past 20 years. He has supported children of all ages, both in care and within the community. He specialised in attachment difficulties for looked-after children and helped them and their carers to overcome this unseen dilemma. He has recently chosen to leave this field due to his disillusionment with the bureaucracy that has overtaken the sector; but he still has lots of dealings with young people in his community through his involvement with local voluntary groups.

Name	Contribution chapter	Biography
Chloe Jones	9	Chloe is a newly qualified social worker, having recently graduated from the University of Bath. Her practice experience covers a range of settings involving children's services, homelessness, substance misuse and working with adults with disabilities. Her voluntary experience is focused on working with children with disabilities, those experiencing bereavement, children with mental health difficulties and young carers. Chloe is passionate about promoting inclusion, equal opportunities and advocacy for children. Volunteering was inspirational in terms of her decision to pursue a career as a qualified social worker.
Dr Karen Hanson	9	Karen is a principal university lecturer. She completed her doctoral research in supporting students in developing a reflective disposition. This action research study enabled Karen to understand the significance of previous experiences and environmental influences for undergraduate students. Her expertise in working with young children and families in a variety of settings has enabled her to understand the complexities of education and care and creating appropriate pedagogical approaches to suit individual and contextual needs.

Name	Contribution chapter	Biography
Karen Appleby	9	Karen is a principal university lecturer. Karen's teaching interests have focused on children's learning, including their development as communicators, language users, readers and writers. Her professional interest in reflective practice continues to inform her teaching, research and publications. Karen has worked independently and collaboratively with colleagues on a range of publications related to reflective practice. Karen has had a range of leadership roles and for many years she was actively involved as a primary school governor with specific responsibility for early years and literacy.
Martha Sercombe	10	Martha has worked in the NHS for the last 24 years. She trained as a children's nurse and a health visitor. She has worked as a health visitor for the last 12 years, mostly in a Specialist Health Visitor role. She has worked within several projects in partnership with Rhondda Cynon Taf Community Borough Council: Sure Start, Flying Start and the Resilient Family Service. She supports families who request additional support with a wide range of difficulties, including domestic abuse, relationship and attachment difficulties, and infant and perinatal mental health. She also provides training on the Solihull Approach, attachment and domestic abuse. Additionally, she is a peripatetic tutor for Warwick Infant and Family Wellbeing Unit in Parent Infant Interactions (PIIOS).

Name	Contribution chapter	Biography
Lauren Evans	10	Lauren qualified as a physiotherapist three years ago, and now specialises in musculoskeletal conditions. She strongly believes in treating the person, rather than the condition, and is passionate about maintaining an inclusive and non-judgemental practice.
Wendy Neale	11	Wendy qualified as a counsellor in 2005. She then also did a post-16 teaching qualification and took up a part-time teaching post alongside working as a counsellor part time at Halesowen College. In 2008, she left the college to work for West Midlands Police (WMP), and she is currently still in post there. Her training focus at WMP was to specialise in trauma therapy. Wendy works as part of the occupational health team, where officers and staff are referred in for therapy. She really enjoys her job and is very glad she chose counselling and psychotherapy when she decided to change career.
Erica Brown	11	Erica is a Senior Research Fellow, Vice President of Acorns Children's Hospices and a Trustee of the Myriad Centre, caring for adults with complex needs. She has long-standing experience as a senior manager and headteacher in schools and worked as Head of Special Education at Oxford Brookes University. Erica has lectured and published nationally and internationally. She is a visiting Fellow at Harris Manchester College Oxford and Fellow of the Royal Society of Arts.

Name	Contribution chapter	Biography
Annie Pendrey	12	Annie started her career as an NNEB. She has taught from early years to HE, having taught for many years in a behavioural unit and supporting children with SEN. She is now a professional development manager, managing the pastoral curriculum in an FE college, and is lead trainer for Autism Awareness in addition to training the teachers of the future.
Annabel Collins	12	Annabel is an Outreach and Participation Co-ordinator at Worcester University. During her 18 years in the role, she has been involved in many projects within the Communication and Participation department. She currently manages Worcestershire Children's University for children aged 5–14, she coordinates, develops and delivers the Beeline Storytelling Festival every October to schools and families across the West Midlands and she assists with the organisation and management of a team of 11 Graduate Ambassadors promoting the benefits of higher education to schools and colleges nationwide.
Mandy Ajmal	12	Mandy is an experienced early years practitioner who studied the Foundation Degree in Early Years and the BA top-up as a mature student. She is passionate about learning and has utilised what she has learned in order to change and improve her practice in many ways following her studies. Mandy has enjoyed learning so much that she is now studying as a part-time student for an MA, whilst working with children and families.

Name	Contribution chapter	Biography
Claire Ashforth	12	Claire is currently employed within a three-form-entry primary school. Having started as a Newly Qualified Teacher in Key Stage Two in 2016, she now leads in Year 2. After working with children for over 20 years, first as a paediatric nurse and now as a primary teacher, she is always looking for ways to improve her practice in order to achieve the highest possible standards. Providing a safe, secure learning environment in which children can achieve their full potential is her overriding priority.
Abigail Broome	12	Abigail is a BA student. She studied the Foundation Degree in Early Years as a part-time student and has recently begun a BA top-up programme. In her final year of the Early Years course, in a module focused on reflective practice, Abi created a diagram showing the influences on her reflective journey. This was such an effective description that her tutor (Angela) wanted to include it in this book.

1 THE EMPATHIC AND COMPASSIONATE PRACTITIONER

Chapter outcomes

This chapter will enable practitioners to engage with the following:
- The role and importance of empathy and compassion skills in working with children, young people and families
- Types and levels of empathy
- The development of empathic understanding
- Applying advanced levels of empathy and compassion when working with children, young people and families
- The risks of 'empathic distress' and 'compassion fatigue'

Introduction

Compassion and empathy have long been accepted as valuable aptitudes, particularly for those working with people. In the words of the Dalai Lama, 'In the first step toward a compassionate heart, we must develop our empathy or closeness to others' (The Dalai Lama, 2001). In response to those in need, it is essential to have a workforce who care and who understand. Whilst compassion is defined as concern for the misfortunes of others, empathy is the ability to understand and share the feelings of others, so they are similar qualities with slightly different perspectives. These qualities are often described as 'soft skills' and there has been a cultural shift in recent years that has led to these 'soft skills' being more appreciated within the workplace (Kamin, 2013, p. xv). The role of compassion and empathy in working with children is complex, due to concern about professional boundaries. Page (2011) writes about the concept of 'professional love' within the early years sector, her belief being that parents want practitioners to 'love' their children to provide the best possible care. Other academics express concern about these traditional 'mothering' skills being at odds with 'professionalism' (Osgood, 2006, p. 191). In her research 'Passion, Paradox and Professionalism', Moyles (2001) explores the tensions between being a passionate and caring person and being a professional teacher. However, all of these writers stress the need for compassion and empathy skills in any work with children.

Compassion is one of the six fundamental values outlined by the NHS; 'the 6 Cs – care, compassion, competence, communication, courage and commitment' (DoH, 2012, p. 5). This was an outcome of the Francis Report (RCGP, 2013) in response to failings in care in the Mid Staffordshire NHS Foundation Trust, which prompted a culture change. The NHS define compassion as 'care given through relationships based on empathy, respect and dignity' or 'intelligent kindness' (DoH, 2012, p. 13). Compassion is feeling *for*, rather than feeling *with* another person. Kamin (2013, p. 208) asserts that compassion is powerful; that demonstrating compassion gives us power and empowers others and that compassion is essential within communities.

Empathy is one of the 'core conditions' illustrated by the father of person-centred counselling, Carl Rogers (1902–1987), along with 'congruence' and 'unconditional positive regard'. Rogers (1980, p. 85) described empathy as the 'sensitive ability and willingness to understand the client's thoughts, feelings and struggles from the client's point of view'. Being able to understand how another person may be feeling, to 'see the world through his/her eyes', or to 'walk a mile in his/her shoes' is acknowledged as contributing to successful relationships. This ability to recognise how people feel is important in all aspects of personal and professional life (Akers and Porter, 2003) and there is much literature about the use of empathy in nursing, medicine, social work and education (Pierce and Pierce, 1982; Irving and Dickson, 2004; Morse et al., 2006; Cameron and Maginn, 2007; etc.). The UK National Occupational Standards for Youth Work now includes the principle 'Show empathy for other people's feelings, needs and motivations' (Lifelong Learning, 2008, p. 118). Empathy, then, is widely seen as an essential skill within the children, young people and families (CYPF) workforce.

Types and levels of empathy

Various types of empathy have been described, ranging from primitive empathy to advanced empathy (Table 1.1). There are others described in counselling literature, including instinctive empathy, relational empathy, experiential empathy, primary empathy and compassionate empathy (Hoffman, 1990; Rogers, 1951), but there are three basic levels of empathy: primitive, cognitive and advanced empathy.

Advanced empathy

Advanced empathy is the most powerful and valuable skill to use when working with children, young people and families. Advanced empathy, according to Egan (2002, pp. 199–205), is 'a composite skill which is very elegant and satisfying to use. The intention is to read between the lines … an interpretive skill.' In work with adults, advanced empathy is about becoming aware of feelings that are deeply buried in the other person's subconscious;

Table 1.1 Types of empathy

Type of Empathy	Features	Example	Key Ideas
Primitive Empathy	This level of empathy is not conscious, and so is unlike imitation. It involves primitive 'automatic' reactions to emotion.	A person yawns and others in the group also yawn. A baby in a nursery cries, and others begin to cry.	Belzung (2014)
Cognitive Empathy	This type of empathy requires 'theory of mind' and enables us to act without emotional contagion. The person can understand the feelings of others and has a desire to help. It is based on our ability to understand how another person may be feeling, by imagining how the situation would feel to us.	If we see another person fall and hurt themselves, we can imagine how the pain must feel to the person and so we want to help. When seeing a child upset and crying, we understand how she is feeling and we want to do something to stop her being upset.	Belzung (2014)
Advanced Empathy	Picking up and offering back unstated feelings picked up from body language or voice tone. Becoming aware of feelings that are deeply buried in the other person's subconscious. Being aware of feelings that children are not yet able to understand or articulate.	When talking to others, we can pick up on subtle signs that people show which give away their emotional state (e.g. wringing of hands expressing anxiety). In a keyworker–child relationship, the worker 'tunes into' the world (the lived experience) of the child.	Egan (2002) Claxton (2003) Bright (2015)

feelings that may not be perceived by them or which may have been forgotten (Egan, 1994). With children and young people, it is concerned with being aware of feelings that the child is not yet able to understand or articulate. It concerns picking up on unspoken signals and reflecting back; Egan

(1994) talks about having 'a conscious awareness of subtle primitive signs that serve as a way of communicating emotional states'.

Wong (2004) calls this listening with a 'sixth sense'. This sixth sense is very closely connected to intuition, as described by Claxton (2003), who explains the use of implicit learning and sensitivity as unconscious 'ways of knowing'. Advanced empathy is certainly beyond our consciousness and is often concerned with 'just knowing'. However, advanced empathy can allow us to develop a conscious awareness of the subtle primitive signs that serve as a way of communicating emotional states (Egan, 2002). Dr Wong (2004) describes this rather poetically: 'Advanced empathy requires the listener to go beyond verbal and non-verbal expressions, to develop an insightful aware-ness and understanding of another person's intentions, desires and unspoken concerns. It requires the skill to listen with the sixth sense, to feel the pulse of the innermost being, and to make explicit what is hidden beneath consciousness.'

This sort of advanced empathy is present in attached parent–child rela-tionships, and the keyworker–child/young person relationship mirrors this in many aspects; empathy being associated with attachment and good-quality care. McCarthy Veach et al. (2007) suggest that in a counselling situation, advanced empathy is best used tentatively and only in a well-established rela-tionship; in a keyworker–child relationship, the relationship is a well-established close one and it needs to be so, and so using the skill is appropriate. In our relationships with the children and young people we work with, we can 'enter the world of' the child and 'move around in that world and [...] feel at home in the ebb and flow of the client's lived experience' (Bright, in Pattison et al., 2015, p. 26).

Benefits of empathy

The benefits of using advanced empathy in working with children and young people are apparent. Practitioners know that children need emotional secu-rity and a good attachment to a key person in the setting. Since the early work of celebrated author John Bowlby (1969, 1988), we have agreed that attachment security stems from a child understanding and trusting that the caregiver will be available and responsive in times of distress. A figure who consistently, sensitively and appropriately responds to a distressed child will promote a secure attachment (Ainsworth and Bowlby, 1991). Sir Richard Bowlby (2003), continuing his father's work and writing about the early years practitioners of today, affirms that between practitioner and child a 'special relationship ... affectionate and sensitive to a child's needs' is crucial in providing comfort and security. This special relationship will embrace empathy and compassion. Taggart (2013) identifies today's practitioners as 'agents of compassion'; a key component of feeling compassion for others is empathy. One of the instances where advanced empathy can be crucial is when managing children's transitions. Change can have a major impact on children and young people and transitions which include stress and separation anxiety can affect emotional health and cognitive and intellectual development (O'Connor, 2012). Transition is potentially traumatic for young children, but in an emotionally supportive climate, where children experience a sense of being deeply understood, there should be 'a diminishment of psychological threat' (Clark, 1998, in Clark, 2010). Secure attachments in the early years of life also promote positive dispositions in children, including the development of empathy. Fonagy (2003, in Gerhardt, 2004, p. 25) emphasises the importance of modelling empathy and demonstrating to children that it is possible to interpret the feelings of others. Research carried out by both O'Connor (2012, p. 77) and Panfile and Laible (2012) give examples of children demonstrating empathy towards other children, after being shown empathy by an attachment figure at school. O'Connor (2012) stresses the importance of empathy when supporting children through transitions, and the importance of showing empathy to parents who may be finding the separation from their child just as difficult. Advanced empathy may allow a practitioner to identify emotions in parents who appear to be handling the situation well but are feeling unease on the inside.

Development of empathy

Although some individuals appear to be more able to feel and show empathy, it is a skill that can be developed. There are things we can do that will help to develop empathy; McNaughton (2016) identifies three prerequisite elements which, when developed, result in increased empathic understanding. These are:

- self-awareness

- bodily awareness

- taking others' perspectives

Hoisington's 'developmental model of empathy' illustrates stages of empathy that practitioners may progress through in their career, from having a predisposition and desire to be empathetic, through competence and proficiency, to 'empathy expertise'. On reaching 'empathy expertise', the practitioner will be proficient at using empathy and will experience oneness with the client (in this case the child/young person), which is advanced empathy. Hoisington identifies another phrase; 'halopathy', an ultimate form of advanced empathy, which he describes as 'a holistic form of advanced empathy … a wholeness of the empathic experience, "being one with the other"' (2003, p. 20). In Hoisington's model, stages of a practitioner's career development include; pre-practitioner, conventional professional training, conditional autonomy, exploration and integration, individuation and finally, integrity, being oneself. It is in this latter stage, according to Hoisington, when a person is really able to understand and empathise with the client.

Luhrmann (2000, in Hoisington, 2003) proposes that constantly being put in the position of hearing others' emotions might help practitioners to develop their empathic senses more accurately. Amongst experienced practitioners, there is often an understanding of a 'sixth sense', a 'gut feeling' and a need to trust this, when working with children and young people; this may effectively describe advanced empathy. Claxton (2003) might call this intuition, or a 'way of knowing', whereas Egan (2002, p. 199) would call it a subskill of advanced empathy: 'sharing hunches based on empathic understanding'. Advanced empathy is more than intuition because it involves emotions. Egan's advice for skilled helpers (a term that could easily be applied to CYPF practitioners as well as counsellors and therapists) includes provocations to consider when working with others, such as 'so what are they trying to say here, what is between the lines, what is hinted at but not spelled out?' (Egan, 2002, p. 205). Practitioners are accustomed to reflective practice being a critical feature of the profession and 'emotionally attuned forms of professional reflection' (Elfer, 2012) include features of advanced empathy. Although empathy may be a part of who we are, it can also involve effort and risk taking (Mearns and Thorne, 2000). Picking up on unspoken signals and reflecting back what you have understood can involve risk, especially when using it with adults (e.g. parents/carers).

Many people are seen as naturally empathic; others less so. However, the latest neuroscience research shows us that 98 per cent of people have the ability to empathise wired into their brains (Krznaric, 2015). However, for those who have not tapped into their full empathic potential, empathy can, to a certain extent, be learned and increased. Empathy can be increased by:

- Practising non-verbal observation
- Active listening
- Learning about the importance of empathy
- Listening without judgement
- Learning about voice tone
- Being curious about strangers
- Being vulnerable
- Expanding your circle of empathy
- Listening out for people's feelings
- Looking for the human behind everything

Barriers to empathy are stress, lack of time and self-absorption. As discussed later, in Chapter 11, there are ways of decreasing stress and this is important for everyone. Mindfulness, exercise and rest are just some of the positive ways that we can fight stress. Just like in an aircraft safety talk, where we are told to put on our own oxygen mask before helping others with theirs, caring for yourself is crucial before you can care for others. Self-absorption is often seen as a synonym for self-obsessed or self-centred, but this is not always the case. Self-absorption can be a symptom of anxiety or depression. When we are anxious, we can feel powerless and unworthy, feelings that can affect our everyday functioning. Depression can lead to overwhelming feelings of worthlessness, and so the sufferer may appear to be self-absorbed. Both conditions can make empathy very difficult, as it is difficult to appreciate the world around us when our focus is directed inward (Seltzer, 2016)

Emotional impact on practitioners

Working with CYPF can be a very rewarding and fulfilling profession, but it is also hard work and can be emotionally draining. 'The call to vocation … is also a double-edged sword, often synonymous with self-sacrifice or burn-out rather than job satisfaction' (Taggart, 2016, p. 86). The emotional demands of using empathy and compassion in our work can lead to exhaustion and burnout, which Taggart (2013) refers to as 'compassion fatigue', asserting that 'the daily experience of alleviating the suffering and dependency of others' is evident in those working with children just as much as in other health and care professions. There is an emotional cost to practitioners and many practitioners are struggling to find a work–life balance (Hodgkins, 2019, p. 45). Tone and Tully (2014) warn that empathy is a 'risky strength', with the internalising of others' pain causing stress and depression in some vulnerable practitioners. Singer and Klimecki (2015) suggest that practitioners should be empathic but they warn of 'empathic distress', leading to 'burnout' and poor health.

There is a need for a supervision model within all professionals dealing with CYPF, as is common practice in other professional disciplines working with families who have complex needs (Richards, 2011). In nursing, medicine and social work, there are areas of excellent practice in supervising staff, but this is not always the case in other areas (e.g. early years, family support), where supervision is less consistent. Practitioners who are working closely with vulnerable children and families, and who are using advanced empathy skills need to be able to talk through their feelings and the impact on themselves to a trusted and experienced adult in a confidential environment (more about self-care in Chapter 15).

James Boddey is a manager of a nursery in Ludlow, Shropshire who has written several articles for *Nursery World* and *Teach Nursery* on the importance of empathy in building relationships with children, families and professionals. Here, he gives his views on empathy and outlines positive experiences he has had in using his own personal empathy approach with children and families in his role as a manager.

Case Study: James Boddey – A compassionate philosophy

I have been working in childcare and education since leaving school myself in 2004. Over the years I have had the joy of working in a range of settings with a variety of passionate team members, fascinating children and inspirational parents/carers. My key philosophies have always been working closely with parents/carers, building relationships and respectful consideration of individual differences. On the break between Early Years Foundation Degree and Early Years Teacher Status I came across the work of Carl Rogers which complemented my thoughts and feelings and has been the theory that underpins a lot of what we do in my setting.

After reading the work of Carl Rogers and explaining it to the staff team we shifted the dynamic of the setting away from de-humanistic, EYFS goal-based, 'we are the experts' and more to a philosophy based on compassion, relationships, considering each child as a unique and special individual with unique targets who live within a family unit that is totally unique with their own strengths, challenges and beliefs (a good example of this is I ask a member of staff and I to look out of the window together. Do we see the same things? No because we have our own perception of the world). When we moved away from considering ourselves as the experts it enabled us to fully empathise with the children and others. We were not just considering and judging them against the EYFS, we were opening ourselves up to truly getting to know them and developing the best setting for them. The child and their family are experts in their own life and we are just guides, signposting the possible best ways forward, being consistently there for them and unconditionally recognising them as special and fantastic human beings. To do this takes empathy and compassion and also we need to be confident in our abilities but also confident in ourselves. When you are asking others to be allowed into their lives in order to build this empathic relationship we as staff need to be self-confident, self-aware, genuine and real. Trust and relationships cannot be built with someone who is being false. The other advantage to being genuine and real is that it removes conditions of worth as it puts you at the same level as others who like us make mistakes, feels emotions and strive for the best.

Before letting others into our lives we need to consider and look at ourselves. At the setting we spend lots of time considering our emotional intelligence and learning to be self-aware and controlling/understanding our own emotions. 'He who knows others is wise; he who knows himself is enlightened.' — Lao Tzu

When asked to describe empathy I use the analogy of a bridge. Empathy bridges the gap between differences and between people without removing or ignoring the gap and differences. With empathy, we can reach out to people, connect with others and all support and help each other. As well as being a key component of relationship building empathy is also important for nurturing and strengthening relationships over time. Every day new situations arrive, which lead to different emotions and changes and therefore we need to be flexible and adapt to these changes and developments.

At my setting we promote unconditional positive regard which means that whatever mood a child is in, whatever behaviour they are demonstrating ('good' or 'bad') we still care and show them positive regard. What this means in practice is that we do not judge or treat anybody differently but care for them unconditionally. A key part of this is empathy and 'putting ourselves in their shoes'. When we do this we are able to consider why they are acting or behaving as they are, which helps us to understand them better and offer better support whilst still caring for them unconditionally.

Whether a child is having an angry outburst or telling you about a tough situation at home, it is only natural that you are going to have your own reaction. Responding with empathy and compassion means putting that aside and letting your child's reaction come first. That doesn't mean you have to bury your own feelings or mean you have to agree with her or accept her behaviour. It just means you're hearing her and trying to see things through her eyes.

Recognising our own feelings At the setting we have a 'feelings' display board at the children's eye level. The display shows photographs of children showing different emotions e.g. crying, smiling as well as situations that may lead to certain emotions e.g. a birthday party, ice cream being dropped on the floor. On the display there are three mirrors so children can practise making the faces and reacting to the different situations on the photographs. This is a popular display with the children and a fantastic way of developing empathy by asking questions such as 'How does that child feel?' 'What could you do if your friend was crying?' This helps them to distinguish their feelings from others. The other main reason I like the display is that I read that just by pulling a certain face your brain feels the emotions e.g. by pulling a sad face you begin to feel sad. Decety and Jackson (2004) detected changes in brain activity and changes in heart rate, skin and body temperature when people made certain facial expressions.

Recognising the feelings of others We support children in being able to recognise the feelings of others throughout the day via our interactions with the children. We would ask questions like, 'How do you think that makes Tommy feel?' etc. The other way that we teach recognising the feelings of others is through role play. The role-play corner is changed on a fortnightly basis depending on the children's interests, story of the week, etc. This year the role-play corner has been a dentist, opticians, superhero house, two houses so that children could practise moving to a new house, and many, many more. The children enjoy being superheroes and 'flying' around the room helping people. This is a great opportunity to support empathic understanding and rewarding empathic behaviour. The other key aspect of our practice we constantly work on is our mindfulness. Empathy and compassion rely on us being fully engaged in the moment – to our own thoughts and feelings and to the world around us. When we do this well we can be fully engaged in a child's activity and therefore offer the best support or next steps for their development. As well as that though we can give them that extra special feeling that we understand what they are doing and want to play too. This works for adults too, and when we are fully in the moment and actively listening to an adult they will feel it, and that is brilliant for building relationships and a key component of empathy.

Case study reflections

- In which ways does James relate theory to practice?
- How do you think the children in James' nursery are influenced by his views? What about the parents/carers? The staff?
- Consider what James has to say about empathy. What lessons can you take from this for your own practice?

Conclusion

This chapter began with highlighting the importance of, and the benefits of empathy and compassion in work with children, young people and families. These are two of the foundations of practitioners' work and, although the skills come naturally to many, they can be developed over the span of a career. By using empathy and compassion, practitioners can make a real difference to those they work with. We have seen how James' views on empathy and compassion affect the whole philosophy of his setting and it is easy to see how positively this impacts on his staff and the children and their families. Whilst acknowledging the emotional impact on practitioners, and being aware of the need to protect ourselves from overwhelming stress (see Chapter 11), an empathic and compassionate environment is positive for all.

 Further reading

Cameron, R. J. and Maginn, C. (2007). The authentic warmth dimension of professional childcare. *British Journal of Social Work*, 38, 1151–1172.
  - This journal article discusses an approach to empowering social care workers and foster carers providing sensitive, emotional support.
Rogers, C. (2004). *On Becoming a Person* (new edition). Edinburgh: Constable.
  - The original ideas of Carl Rogers, the father of the person-centred approach.
Singer, T. and Klimecki, O. (2015). Empathy and compassion. *Current Biology*, 24(18).
  - An interesting article describing neuro-scientific and psychological perspectives on empathy and compassion.

References

Ainsworth, M. D. S. and Bowlby, J. (1991). An ethological approach to personality development. *American Psychological Association*, 46, 333–341.
Akers, M. D. and Porter, G. L. (2003). Your EQ skills: Got what it takes? *Journal of Accountancy*, 195(3), 65–69. New York: American Institute of Certified Public Accountants.

Belzung, C. (2014). Empathy. *Journal for Perspectives of Economic, Political, and Social Integration*, 19(1–2), 177–191.

Bowlby, J. (1969). *Attachment and Loss*, Vol. 1. New York: Basic Books.

Bowlby, J. (1988). Lecture 7: The role of attachment in personality development. In *A Secure Base: Parent–Child Attachment and Healthy Human Development*. New York: Basic Books, pp. 119–136.

Bowlby, R. (2003). *Stress in Day Care*. Available at: http://socialbaby.blogspot.co.uk/2007/04/richard-bowlby-stress-in-daycare.html [Accessed 18 March 2016].

Clark, A. (2010). Empathy: An integral model in the counselling process. *Journal of Counselling Development*, 88(3), 348–356.

Claxton, G. (2003). The anatomy of intuition. In Atkinson, T. and Claxton, G. (eds.) *The Intuitive Practitioner*. Maidenhead: Open University Press.

Decety, J. and Jackson, P. (2004). The functional architecture of human empathy. *Behavioral and Cognitive Neuroscience Reviews*, 3(2). https://doi.org/10.1177/1534582304267187

Department of Health (2012). *Compassion in Practice: Nursing, Midwifery and Care Staff – Our Vision and Strategy*. Department of Health. Available at: https://www.england.nhs.uk/wp-content/uploads/2012/12/compassion-in-practice.pdf [Accessed 9 August 2019].

Egan, G. (1994). *The Skilled Helper*, 3rd ed. Pacific Grove, CA: Brooks Cole.

Egan, G. (2002). *The Skilled Helper*, 4th ed. Pacific Grove, CA: Brooks Cole.

Elfer, P. (2012). Emotion in nursery work: Work discussion as a model of critical professional reflection. *Early Years*, 32(2), 129–141.

Gerhardt, S. (2004). *Why Love Matters: How Affection Shapes a Baby's Brain*. London: Routledge.

Hodgkins, A. (2019). Advanced empathy in the early years: A risky strength? *NZ International Research in Early Childhood Education Journal*, 22(1), 46–58.

Hoffman, M. L. (1990). Empathy and justice motivation. *Motivation and Emotion*, 14, 151–172.

Hoisington, D. (2003). *An Initial Investigation into the Possibility of Advanced Empathy*. Syracuse University, ProQuest Dissertations Publishing.

Irving, P. and Dickson, D. (2004). Empathy: Towards a conceptual framework for healthcare professionals. *International Journal of Health Care Quality Assurance*, 17(4), 212–220.

Kamin, M. (2013). *Soft Skills Revolution: A Guide to Connecting with Compassion for Trainers, Teams, and Leaders*. San Francisco, CA: Centre for Creative Leadership, Wiley.

Krznaric, R. (2015, 29 June). Can you teach people to have empathy? *BBC News Magazine*. Available at: http://www.bbc.co.uk/news/magazine-33287727 [Accessed 9 August 2019].

Lifelong Learning (2008). *National Occupational Standards for Youth Work*. Available at: www.LifelongLearningUK.org [Accessed 9 August 2019].

McCarthy Veach, P., Leroy, B. and Bartels, D. (2007). *Facilitating the Genetic Counselling Process: A Practice Manual*. New York: Springer

McNaughton, S. M. (2016). Developing pre-requisites for empathy: Increasing awareness of self, the body and the perspectives of others. *Teaching in Higher Education*, 21(5), 501–515.

Mearns, B. and Thorne, B. (2000). *Person-Centred Therapy Today: New Frontiers in Theory and Practice*. London: Sage.

Morse, J., Bottorff, J., Anderson, G., O'Brien, B. and Solberg, S. (2006). Beyond empathy: Expanding expressions of caring. *Journal of Advanced Nursing*, 17, 809–821.

Moyles, J. (2001). Passion, paradox and professionalism in early years education. *Early Years: Journal of International Research and Development*, 21(2), 81–95.

O'Connor, A. (2012). *Understanding Transitions in the Early Years*. London: Routledge.

Osgood, J. (2006). Deconstructing professionalism in early childhood education: Resisting the regulatory gaze. *Contemporary Issues in Early Childhood*, 7(1).

Page, J. (2011) Do mothers want professional carers to love their babies? *Journal of Early Childhood Research*, 9(3), 310–323.

Panfile, T. and Laible, D. (2012). Attachment security and child's empathy: The mediating role of emotion regulation. *Merrill Palmer Quarterly*, 58(1), 1–21.

Pattison, S., Robson, M., and Beynon, A. (2015). *The Handbook of Counselling Children and Young People*. London: Sage.

Pierce, L. and Pierce, R. (1982) The use of warmth, empathy and genuineness in child care work. *Child Care Quarterly*, 11(4), Winter 1982, Human Sciences Press.

Richards, C. (2011). Quality matters because quality protects. In Reed, M. and Canning, N. (eds.) *Implementing Quality Improvement and Change in the Early Years*. London: Sage.

Rogers, C. (1951). *Client-Centred Therapy*. Boston, MA: Houghton Mifflin.

Rogers, C. (1980). *A Way of Being*. Boston, MA: Houghton Mifflin.

Rogers, C. (2004). *On Becoming a Person* (new edition). Edinburgh: Constable.

Royal College of General Practitioner (RCGP) (2013). *The Francis Report*. Available at: http://www.rcgp.org.uk/policy/rcgp-policy-areas/francis-report.aspx [Accessed 9 August 2019].

Seltzer, L. (2016). *Self-Absorption: the Root of All (Psychological) Evil?* Available at: https://www.psychologytoday.com/blog/evolution-the-self/201608/self-absorption-the-root-all-psychological-evil [Accessed 9 August 2019].

Singer, T. and Klimecki, O. (2015). Empathy and compassion. *Current Biology*, 24(18).

Taggart, G. (2013). The importance of empathy. *Nursery World*. Available at: https://www.nurseryworld.co.uk/nursery-world/opinion/1106788/impor-tance-empathy [Accessed 9 August 2019].

Taggart, G. (2016). Compassionate pedagogy: The ethics of care in early childhood professionalism. *European Early Childhood Education Research Journal*, 24(2), 173–185.

The Dalai Lama (2001). *An Open Heart: Practicing Compassion in Everyday Life* (Edited by Nicholas Vreeland). Boston: Little, Brown and Company.

Tone, E. and Tully, E. (2014) Empathy as a 'risky strength': A multilevel examination of empathy and risk for internalizing disorders. *Development and Psychopathology, suppl. Multilevel Developmental Perspectives Toward Understanding*, 26(4), 1547–1565.

Wong, P. (2004). Creating a kinder and gentler world: The positive psychology of empathy. *International Network on Personal Meaning*. Available at: http://www.meaning.ca/archives/presidents_columns/pres_col_mar_2004_empathy.htm [Accessed 9 August 2019].

2 THE ENGAGING AND EMPOWERING PRACTITIONER

Chapter outcomes

This chapter will enable readers to explore the following concepts:
- Multiple adversity and its impact on families
- How engaging with opportunities and services helps support families
- Some common barriers to engagement and how they can be overcome
- Strength-based approaches to working with individuals
- How fostering resilience supports a model of empowerment
- The implications for practitioners arising from this chapter

---

Introduction

This chapter explores the important themes of engagement and empowerment. The former is crucial if we are going to be able to work proactively with individuals within a relationship of trust. The latter determines not only the sustainability of our interventions, but also the progress that the individual can make independent of our involvement.

In other words, your goal as a practitioner in providing family support is to make your role redundant, by supporting individuals as they develop the tools and confidence to be able to move forward without you. When fully grasped and embraced, this paradox has the potential to completely transform our practice and the experience of those we work with. When we ignore it, we are perhaps unwittingly contributing to confining individuals within a cycle of dependency and powerlessness.

Of course, many families will find it easy to source and engage with opportunities (and, where needed, services) that enable their families to develop social capital, build skills and thrive. However, for other families, particularly those who are challenged by multiple adversity, it may be much more difficult for them to identify, access and engage with such opportunities. Such families are often described as 'hard to reach' or 'hard to engage'. This chapter argues that we need to reframe our thinking about such families and consider the ways in which it is the services themselves that may be difficult to access (Crozier and Davies, 2007), and to explore the ways in which the individual practitioner can support engagement within an ethos of empowerment.

What is multiple adversity and how does it impact on families?

All families can face difficulties from time to time and navigating one's way through them can be challenging. At such times families may need extra support. Such support can often come from within families' own social circles but there may also be a need for specialist input from support services.

Some families may experience multiple difficulties and challenges. Vinson (2007, p. 1) describes this as: 'a range of difficulties that block life opportunities and which prevent people from participating fully in society'. A report by the now-defunct *Social Exclusion Taskforce* (UK Cabinet Office, 2007) estimated that approximately 2 per cent of families are challenged by five or more adversities. However, worsening economic circumstances for many families would suggest that in 2020 that figure may be considerably higher. The links between disadvantage and later outcomes is well rehearsed (Levitas et al., 2007; Allen, 2011; Magnuson, 2013; Shonkoff and Garner, 2012). The ways in which families experience these difficulties will vary tremendously, and we must avoid being too prescriptive in our definitions of multiple adversity, because in categorising we risk missing out key factors that impact on the family. However, the adversities that families may face can be broadly categorised as follows:

- poverty, debt, financial pressures
- child abuse/child protection concerns
- family violence/domestic violence
- parental illness/disability
- parental substance abuse
- parental mental ill-health
- family separation/bereavement/imprisonment
- parental offending, anti-social behaviour

Many studies highlight the compounding effect over time of multiple adversities, arguing that 'multiples matter' (Spratt, 2011). Sabates and Dex (2012), for example, stress that whilst single adversities can impact negatively on families' experiences and ultimately outcomes, it is an accumulated number of risks that appears to be most damaging and also most predictive of longer-term detrimental outcomes. Rankin et al. (2004) identify the essence of multiple adversity as implying both breadth of need (i.e. a number of needs which may be complex and interrelated) and depth of need (profound, severe, serious or intense needs). Another key factor that impacts on families can be how long the period of adversity lasts, which requires us to recognise that for some families, life is an ongoing series of struggles with little or no respite.

In recent dialogues, the concept of multiple adversity is often connected to the idea of *intersectionality*. This term is often used to describe the ways in which the effects of multiple forms of discrimination (for example, racism, sexism, and classism) combine or *intersect*. Intersectional discrimination is typically experienced by marginalised individuals or groups: for example, in the UK, a report by the Resolution Foundation highlighted that black women graduates experience the largest gender pay gap, earning an average of £3,000 per annum less than their white counterparts (Henehan and Rose, 2018), thus demonstrating the intersectionality between gender and race/ethnicity. Crenshaw (1991), who first coined the term intersectionality, urges us to think of injustices and inequalities derived from gender, race and class, not as isolated experiences, but rather as overlapping and interconnected.

How can engaging with opportunities and services support families?

Given the difficulties that many families face, and the compelling evidence that these difficulties can continue to impact on the family members well into the future, the question arises as to what can be done to support families who find themselves in situations where they are facing multiple adversity? There is much evidence from research that involvement with high-quality early childhood opportunities and family support services can mitigate the effects of disadvantage caused by multiple adversity (Felitti et al., 1998; Dube et al., 2003; Allen, 2011). Such opportunities can help families to develop social networks, support the development of skills and promote confidence and self-efficacy.

However, families who are challenged by multiple disadvantages can often find such opportunities difficult to identify, access and engage with. They may not be aware of services available, may find it physically hard to attend or there may be psychological barriers that need to be overcome in order to enable the family to engage.

In this context, we are talking about engagement as something that goes beyond a superficial level of engagement or simply 'showing up'. True engagement will involve more than physical involvement in services and opportunities. It will entail families (and the individuals within them) being motivated to understand and identify not only their own needs, but also the strengths and resources they have to address these needs. Engagement, therefore, is about being empowered to make positive changes to enhance family life and well-being or, as Professor Angie Hart describes it, to make their own 'resilient moves' (Aumann and Hart, 2009).

What are some common barriers to engagement and how can they be overcome?

The barriers to families engaging with services and opportunities may be complex and numerous. These may include practical or physical challenges, such as location and timing of sessions. Such barriers may be easy for the practitioner to address through listening to families' needs, careful planning and creative problem solving. However, some of the barriers that families face may be profound and psychological. In order to address these barriers, the practitioner will need to tune in to the family and build rapport. Such engagement may take time, commitment, consistency and development of trust. Below are just some of the barriers that families may face when considering engaging with opportunities and services (Table 2.1).

Such barriers, if not addressed, can make it difficult for families to access services and receive the support they need. Engaging with families should be viewed as a process and not a one-off activity for practitioners. It requires intentionality, ongoing commitment and an openness to new ways of working. Cortis et al. (2009) discusses the importance of meeting families where they are. This could be seen as physically meeting where the families live and congregate (e.g. home visiting, local community centres, parks, schools, etc.) or it could be viewed more metaphorically as recognising the perspectives of families and the emotional barriers they face when accessing services, and working purposefully to break down those barriers.

Table 2.1 Barriers to engagement

Practical Barriers	Emotional Barriers
Venue and timing of sessions	Prior negative experiences of services
Not knowing what opportunities are available	Low self-esteem
Physical access issues (such as disability or other health needs)	Concerns about being accepted/fitting in/feeling comfortable/being judged
Language barriers	Gendered issues
Literacy issues	Fear of professionals becoming involved in family life
Cost and availability of transport and/or childcare	Uncertainty about the benefits of engaging and any consequences of not engaging

Addressing the practical barriers to engagement may require joint working with other services such as local schools and community groups in order to provide timings, venues and models of working that families find easier to engage with. Whilst there may be resource implications for addressing some of these barriers, more often it is about identifying different, more responsive ways of working. Such changes may require the practitioner to be very flexible and adaptive, and the organisations they work for to develop policies that embrace more agile service delivery. This in itself will require leadership and effective change management.

Recognising the psychological barriers families face when engaging with services is equally important and perhaps even more challenging. It requires the practitioner to look beyond what is visible on the surface of a person's behaviour and to engage with the more nebulous concepts of beliefs, values, aspirations, fears and perceptions. In his celebrated Iceberg Model, Goodman (2002) provides a useful way of thinking about this. The practitioner must recognise that what they are able to observe and what they are told may only be a small part of what is going on for a family/individual in relation to the challenges they experience when accessing services. Hence, it is important to find ways to develop relationships that allow some of those invisible aspects to be shared and addressed.

It is important to see engagement as a reciprocal process. Not only are we asking the individual/family to engage with our services but also we need to engage with them. Sometimes, this will take us outside our comfort zone as we engage with cultures, beliefs, values and attitudes that may be very different from our own. As explored in other chapters within this book, the development of authentic, respectful and trustful relationships is essential in order to enable those we are working with to open up and to feel comfortable working with us. Integral to such positive relationships is a non-judgemental approach. Not only does the practitioner need to keep an open mind, they may need to challenge their own assumptions if they are to responsively work with the family to break down barriers. Brookfield's lenses (Brookfield, 2005) and the Johari window (Luft and Ingham, 1955) provide helpful approaches to support practitioners in their efforts to better understand their own biographies and perspectives.

The importance of the personal attributes and professional qualities of the individual practitioner in their work of engaging with families cannot be overstated. Time and time again, in undertaking service evaluations, I have been told by families of the difference an individual practitioner made. I have come to the conclusion that whilst **what** we do is very important (i.e. the evidence base of our interventions and the quality of their delivery), the **way** that we do it is at least as important. Below are some of the qualities that families have told me that they value in a practitioner (Figure 2.1).

Hence, the individual practitioner can and often does make a real difference in helping families to engage with services and opportunities. It is often the relational aspects that families value. We owe it to those we work with to welcoming * trustworthy * *keeps their word* * turns up on time * sense of humour * **available** * kind * *non-judgemental* * supportive * good listener *helps me to problem solve *goes the extra mile * friendly * positive * involves me * knowledgeable * experienced * *easy to contact* * does not over-promise * **recognises my difficulties** * no jargon * tells me what I am doing well * warm * not easily shocked * remembers things I said last time* *approachable* * interested in me

Figure 2.1 Practitioner qualities valued by those they work with

make the process of engaging as comfortable as possible and to remove any unnecessary barriers that could prevent the family from getting involved.

In this case study, Sophie Reid, a Family Support Worker within a third-sector organisation, talks about her experience of engaging with parents and young people, whom some may describe as 'hard to reach'. Here Sophie applies her own autobiographical lens, reflecting upon what works in practice.

Case Study: Sophie Reid – Engaging families (Part 1)

I was drawn into the area of work of supporting others, as I feel a strong connection with other people, I am intrigued by others and since a very young age have felt there was a huge injustice towards people that needed support and I felt I wanted to make a difference. I am passionate about equality. Everyone has a story and there is always a reason or choice made resulting in a particular behaviour.

So how did I end up in this line of work? I studied child development in college full time for two years and then went on to a large range of full time employment which gave me a wealth of life experiences that have helped me in my work with vulnerable individuals, even though the roles may not seem as though they were relevant. For example: – criminal legal secretary, this supported my computer skills and office work and working through case files highlighted the need for my support to be accurately recorded. Assistant manager in retail, allowed me to understand there may be times when you work beyond your hours for the best interests of the business. Nursery nurse, gave me first-hand experience of the benefit of recognising each child's abilities and strengths rather than comparing them. Bar work, enabled me to see how having a positive attitude and friendly face let people feel enjoyment from the conversation with you even if very brief. Travelling, now this one may sound a bit of a cliché but this allowed me to go on my own personal journey of growth. I then went on to work for a large children's charity where I have remained for many years and specialise in support with asylum seeker and refugee children, young people and families.

When considering what works well, never underestimate the power of your personality. This makes you a real person and more than just the role you are playing for your job. This makes it easier for people to relate to you and then want to engage with you more. To work well with others and engage people I start with the approach of interest and what I can do for them, rather than what I think they need. This sets a tempo for mutual respect. People I have supported over the years have all been involved in any support plan that is put in place and this has been communicated with them clearly in a way that is easy to understand. Having high-quality levels of participation are key to doing this well from the offset.

That initial meeting is so important. I dress casually so that I am not intimidating but at the same time I give thought to any cultural sensitivities in the way that I dress. I make sure that my notebook is floral or patterned so it doesn't look too official. I always try to meet the family in their own home where they are comfortable, and I accept any foods and drink that I am offered as this is often really important to the families I work with.

I have had to adapt to different situations, rather than expecting people to adapt to me. For example when supporting asylum seekers and refugees from various countries around the world, I am aware that the professional role I have may not be one that they have ever heard of or can comprehend as it simply doesn't exist in some countries other than in western societies, therefore I have to be aware of fitting a mould that allows the family to understand I am there to support, which could include being called a family friend, aunt, or teacher, however while doing this you have to be mindful of your working role and maintain the professional boundaries.

To empower others I have learnt to have a good work–life balance which allows me to detach myself from the support I am giving when I need to. What I mean by this is that whoever I am supporting is made aware right at the start that there will be a point when the support ends, and that is a positive thing. I also reflect any comments the person makes about how the changes or differences that they have made were because of me; I reflect them back to give them ownership of the changes and progress and thank them for letting me be a part of it. The good work–life balance means that when I leave a support session I can reflect on it when appropriate to do so, and then continue with my life without this impacting me.

Leading to an ending of support can be difficult for some people so within my current way of working I keep an open door when possible and make the offer that they can send a letter, or text with updates of how they are getting on if they want. This offers reassurance to that person that the time and effort they invested in the support sessions is not totally forgotten when it ends and puts them in a position of control over what they share with me in the future and when. I found this allows them to continue recognising and sharing positive progress for themselves.

From working with asylum seekers and refugees for a number of years I have learnt that I always have something to learn, and each family I meet humbles me more every time. People see certain groups of people as 'hard to reach', whereas I feel if people remain 'hard to reach' then as professionals we are reaching in the wrong way so there is a need to try a different approach.

I have learned that you have to keep an open mind all the time, as well as honesty being the best policy. Being open minded allows someone to not feel judged, and being honest from the off sets a precedent for being able to discuss concerns or questions, things that you are not sure about, which of course is crucial in safeguarding terms.

I personally feel it would be easier to work with and support vulnerable people if all professionals regularly undertook equality, diversity and inclusion training to enable them to reflect on their own practice and perspectives. Participation training would also help to keep in the forefront of people's minds the value of ensuring that families have their voices heard and their opinions valued.

I feel you have to have a passion for a role so that it continues to interest and excite you. I am driven by what challenges me and the adrenaline and pride I get from doing what others may feel reluctant or fearful of due to differences and the unknown.

Case study reflections

- How does Sophie's own autobiography impact on the work she does and the values she brings to it?
- Sophie talks about the importance of questioning your own perceptions and stereotypes when working with individuals. She says that, 'Everyone has a story and there is always a reason or choice made resulting in a particular behaviour.' In recognising this, Sophie is demonstrating emotional intelligence. Why is this so important in working with individuals, particularly those from different backgrounds to yourself?
- Sophie discusses the importance of the first meeting with a family. What does she consider when planning this visit? How does she use this meeting to lay foundations for future engagement?
- What can you learn from Sophie's experience in relation to engaging and empowering individuals?
- How does Sophie's offer of the 'open door' support families in move on?

What are strength-based approaches to working with individuals and how can these serve to empower those individuals?

The case study above highlights the importance of working with families within an ethos of unconditional positive regard (Rogers, 1951). This creates an environment where a trustful and productive working relationship can be established and where the family can explore the issues they face within a non-judgemental and supportive setting. This is further explored in Chapter 11. Some authors suggest that many of the policy and policy and practice responses designed to counter inequality and address needs have been based on 'deficit models' of parenting and family life. These can serve to highlight the family's perceived failings and to perpetuate a sense of hopelessness. Walsh (2006) emphasises that in order to help families make progress practitioners need to focus not on what makes them fail, but rather how they can succeed. In other words, practitioners are ideally placed to help families identify their own strengths, talents and assets (along with positive resources in the wider family and community) and thereby to build resilience (Prowle and Musgrave, 2018). We read much about 'toxic trios' of issues faced by families (i.e. mental health difficulties, substance misuse and domestic abuse) (Department of Education, 2012). Such combinations of issues create toxic stress for families, resulting in situations which are hard for families to change or move beyond. However, through using strength-based approaches, practitioners can support the development of a virtuous triangle of positive approaches which enable families to take ownership and create positive futures. This is illustrated in Figure 2.2.

As Whalley (2007) identifies, practitioners can support families in making decisions, in their efforts to be self-directing and to encourage families' belief that they **can** change things. This is not, as some would argue, about absolving the State of its responsibilities but rather redressing power balances and providing families with the tools and strategies they need in order to move forward. It is an exemplification of the ancient proverb, 'Give a man a fish and he will eat for a day; teach him to fish and he will eat for a lifetime.'

Below are just some of the ways that practitioners can help to support families to become empowered:

- Support approaches to build confidence and self-esteem

- Provide opportunities to develop basic and enhanced skills

- Help families to identify things that are going well and can be built upon. Also help them realise the strengths and assets that they have around them.

Figure 2.2 Virtuous trio of strength-based approaches

- Encourage self-care
- Provide opportunities for choice and dignity
- Value the individual and their contribution
- Support the development of flexible and responsive routines
- Enable peer support and community involvement
- Provide information
- Support the family in attending community events and programmes
- Meaningfully involve the individuals in decision making

A key aspect of empowerment is giving people a voice. This entails recognising some of the power balances that are present in any practitioner/individual relationship and working hard to build trust and to show that the individual's perspective is both valued and valuable. This demands going beyond tokenistic telling or consultation into a meaningful dialogue that genuinely seeks to understand the individual's perspectives and help them to identify their own solutions, resulting in a co-constructed plan to move forward. Working in this way is not a quick fix to the issues the family are facing; it is time-consuming and demands commitment from both the practitioner and the family. However, the outcomes from this more empowering approach are likely to be better and more sustainable in the long term. In the following sections we will explore two theoretical models that help us to conceptualise what it might mean to work with families to support their empowerment.

Social capital and empowerment

Social capital can be defined as the scope of non-monetary resources that the individual or family can draw upon through their community and social networks. This would include local infrastructure and services but also the connections between individuals that can support well-being. Below are just some of the elements that could be considered social capital (Table 2.2).

Clearly, this diagram just shows some aspects that could be considered as contributing towards social capital. These are not presented in any particular hierarchy, and further work would need to be undertaken in order to explore how, and to what extent, they impact positively on the individual/community.

The Think Family Literature Review (Cabinet Office, 2011) considers ways in which social capital can be passed on inter-generationally, whereby families with high levels of social capital will strive to 'conserve' that capital and potentially to exclude others from accessing its benefits (Bourdieu, 1979). Similarly, families with lower social capital may find it difficult to access the opportunities and develop the social networks that will support their development and well-being. There has long been a recognition that some communities have low levels of social capital, particularly in relation to infrastructures

Table 2.2 Social capital

Element of Social Capital	Examples								
Infrastructure	Schools and workplaces	Libraries	Parks	Community centres	Transport links	Heath centres	Leisure facilities
Physical/Natural Resources	Mountains	Forests	Lakes	Beaches	Open spaces	Rivers and canals	Hedgerows
Community Groups and Projects	Faith community	Community allotments	Sports and arts groups	Clothes/book exchange	Community food Boxes	Playgroups and after-school clubs	Landscaping projects
Support Services	Local exchange trading Systems	Credit unions	Food banks	Debt counselling	Basic skills support	Benefits advice	Employment support
Social Links	Social groups	Befriending services	Community festivals	Coffee mornings	Support groups	Volunteering opportunity	Home visiting projects
Access to Sources of Power/Decision Making	One stop shops	Councillor/ MP surgeries	Patient health forum	Youth council	Residents committee	Advocacy projects	Community consultation

23

and opportunity, and successive initiatives have sought to address this. Community development in these areas may have supported the creation of community-led, user-friendly services and networks such as community groups, local exchange services networks, credit unions and health and education projects. Halpern (2005) discusses the relational aspects of developing social capital, identifying three main types of interaction:

- **Bonding** – the strong ties created by people with much in common. This can create opportunities for mutual support and sharing of experience which can, in itself be very empowering.

- **Bridging** – the connections between diverse groups of people but with some shared interest or concern.

- **Linking** – the connections with external groups and agencies which may have power to influence a change.

Hence, social capital is generated collectively but can be accessed by the individual, although this process may need to be scaffolded and supported.

Some theorists have criticised Social Capital Theory as a way of avoiding difficult discussions about neoliberalism and the role of the State in supporting marginalised groups. Others have argued that that social capital is difficult to measure. Recent studies are focusing on the role of social media in developing social capital.

However, for practitioners, social capital remains a useful concept. Practitioners can make themselves aware of the opportunities that exist locally and support the individual in the first instance in accessing them. There may well also be a role for practitioners in identifying gaps in provision and working in partnership with communities and other agencies to develop opportunities that address these needs. Such work will also draw upon the social capital of the worker, who may need to galvanise their own contacts. This is one of the reasons why networking is so important. Also crucial to this agenda is up-to-date information relating to what services, opportunities and resources are available to support individuals and families. One-stop shops, family information services and community newsletters can be invaluable in supporting practitioners and those they work with by letting them know what opportunities exist.

How does fostering resilience support a model of empowerment?

Resilience has been variously described as the ability to bounce back from difficulties or to overcome challenges. A useful definition is found within the BoingBoing resilience project (www.boingboing.org.uk) which describes resilience as, 'Overcoming adversity, whilst also potentially changing, or even dramatically transforming, (aspects of) that adversity' (Hart et al., 2016, p. 3).

This embodies the idea that not only can individuals bounce back from adversity, they can make 'resilient moves' (Aumann and Hart, 2009, p. 11) which assist in reframing or improving the adverse situations in which they find themselves.

In what she describes as 'ordinary magic', Masten (2014) argues that fostering resilience does not have to be a major event; rather it is in the proactive approaches of the attuned practitioner continuing to do things that help build confidence, self-awareness and coping mechanisms. This approach sees resilience not as a character trait which an individual either has or doesn't have, but as something which can be fostered and developed and where the practitioner can play an active role in supporting this development.

The use of a resilience framework can help practitioners work with families to identify risk and protective factors. Walsh (2002) is quick to point out that ALL families have the potential for resilience. In other words, something has kept them functioning for this long, so the task is to identify both current and potential strengths, moving away from a focus on problems and risks. Aumann and Hart (Boingboing, undated) have created an interactive resilience framework which can be used with children and young people but can also be adapted for other individuals or families. This framework identifies broad themes of well-being such as basic self-care, learning, coping, belonging and sense of self along with specific strategies to support the individual in making resilient moves. Underpinning all of this is a set of core values which Aumann and Hart describe as 'noble truths'. These include acceptance and commitment, but also the conserving of trust and relationships and the enlisting of self and others to help the individual make resilient moves.

Within such a framework the ownership lies with the individual/family. The role of the practitioner is to support and enable. In the case study below, Sophie describes a specific piece of work that she has undertaken to empower a family and support their resilience.

Case Study: Sophie Reid – Engaging families (Part 2)

In 2016 I began work with a family. The family unit composed of mum, a brother and sister aged 12 and 14 years. Key concerns with this family on referral included fear of deportation, risk of vulnerability to re-trafficking and emotional difficulties resulting from Adverse Childhood Experiences in their home country.

After introductions, the initial sessions focused on developing trust and building rapport with the family through playing games and informal conversations whilst visiting local facilities.

After 1 month a family review took place for them to consider if they wanted to continue with support. Once agreed, further sessions were planned with the family's full involvement. They chose to focus on managing difficult feelings, coping with nightmares and building self-esteem. Sessions commenced using creative activities allowing them to consider their sense of self using a Dutch resilience model – I am, I have, I can (Grotberg, 1995). This naturally transitioned to safely exploring their identified topics and became the start of introducing coping strategies to try over the weeks and then feedback on these.

Each session comprised of two elements; the first being focused activity planned by myself, second being an activity they had planned and would lead. Sessions were planned to allow a gentle transition from one to the other. Over time it developed that the part led by the children became a rolling activity whereby they started to teach me a traditional dance from their country, then build in music, included costumes and built up to a performance to their mum.

After 10 sessions, another family review took place. Together we agreed sessions would now focus on goal setting, with the children setting short- and long-term goals for themselves and together as a family. The sessions moved to fortnightly allowing them to carry out steps towards their goals one week and report back on this the next. Activities at this time included opportunities to identify how they could help each other achieve these goals. This support fell over the Halloween period so an activity was planned for them to move out of their comfort zone by taking part in a trick-or-treat game Although this was fun for them, it also demonstrated how they were able to embrace a huge element of trust in someone and have confidence in themselves to try new things.

Often during support the family thanked me for what I had done for them, and I would rephrase this, giving the thanks back to them by sharing, if it was not for the effort they had put into sessions such successful outcomes would not have been achieved.

I also held sessions on a one-to-one basis with mum. This made mum aware of the coping strategies the children were trialling, to allow similar approaches within the home. The meetings provided an opportunity for her to share her thoughts about the children's well-being and development, and also identify any support needs of her own, now that she felt comfortable that the children were accessing support – which had been her main priority. I introduced her to support groups which she then attended whilst the children were in their sessions.

A final review took place which included reflective time to consider all they had engaged with, and plan an ending to the support. The ending sessions allowed for activities around recognising change, growth and progress. Both children planned the ending independently and presented the ending plan to me. The final session included the whole family and myself, and had music and games. I presented them with scrapbooks each of which documented the activities and sessions to remind them of the effort they put in and what they had achieved, as well as a reminder of strategies for them to refer back to if needed in future. The scrapbook had empty pages at the back and I explained the purpose of this was for them to continue to add to it when they wanted as the years went on. There was a certificate of achievement presented to all of them for giving their time and effort in participating in the support.

Case study reflections

- How does Sophie work with the family to identify strengths and assets?
- In what ways is Sophie empowering the family?
- How does Sophie help the family to make resilient moves?
- How does Sophie prepare the family for when she is no longer involved?
- What knowledge, skills and personal and professional qualities does Sophie demonstrate within this case study?

Conclusion: What are the implications for practitioners arising from this chapter?

This chapter has considered the importance of engaging and empowering families. If family support work is to be effective and sustainable, it is vital that we conceptualise the family positively not as weak and failing, but as strong, capable and with the potential for resilience and self-determination. Whilst there may be initial needs that will need to be supported, our emphasis must be on empowering the family to make resilient moves and to make best use of the resources available to them, both internal resources and the assets available within their wider family and community. Ultimately, engaging and empowering others is about believing that individuals have the ability to make positive changes in their lives, whilst also tackling the structural inequalities they face in meeting their potential.

 Further reading and resources

Carnegie Trust (undated) www.participatorymethods.org/sites/participatory-methods.org/files/empowering%20young%20people.pdf
- This online report provides an excellent theoretical overview of engaging young people, as well as providing ideas for practice.

Laura, W. (2016). Engaging hard to reach families: Learning from five 'outstanding' schools, *Education* 3–13, 44(1), 32–43. https://doi.org/10.1080/03004279.2015.1122321.
- This article questions the idea of hard-to-reach families, arguing that services (in this case schools) can be hard to reach. The article then looks at examples of good practice.

Prowle, A. and Musgrave, J. (2018). *Utilising Strengths in Families and Communities to Support Children's Learning and Wellbeing* in *Pedagogies for Leading Practice. Thinking about Pedagogy in Early Childhood Education.* London: Routledge.
- This chapter provides an overview of strength-based practice within early years. It is supported by case study materials.

References

Allen, G. (2011). *Early Intervention: The Next Steps*, 1 January 2011, Cabinet Office and Department for Work and Pensions. Available at: https://assets.publishing.service.gov.uk/government/uploads/system/uploads/attachment_data/file/284086/early-intervention-next-steps2.pdf [Accessed 9 August 2019].

Aumann, K. and Hart, A. (2009). *Helping Children with Complex Needs Bounce Back: Resilient Therapy for Parents and Professionals.* London: Jessica Kingsley.

Bourdieu, P. (1979). *Distinction: A Social Critique of the Judgement of Taste*, 1st ed. London: Routledge, p. 6.

Brookfield, S. (2005) *Becoming a Critically Reflective Teacher.* Michigan: Wiley.

Cortis, N., Katz, I. and Patulny, R. (2009). *Occasional Paper No. 26 – Engaging Hard-to-Reach Families and Children.* Available at: https://www.dss.gov.au/sites/default/files/documents/op26.pdf [Accessed 9 August 2019].

Crenshaw, K. (1991). Mapping the margins: Intersectionality, identity politics, and violence against women of color. *Stanford Law Review*, 43(6) (July, 1991), 1241–1299.

Crozier, G. and Davies, J. (2007). Hard to reach parents or hard to reach schools? A discussion of home–school relations, with particular reference to Bangladeshi and Pakistani parents. *British Educational Research Journal*, 33(3), 295–313.

Department of Education (2012). *New Learning from Serious Case Reviews: A Two Year Report for 2009–2011.* Available at: https://assets.publishing.service.gov.uk/government/uploads/system/uploads/attachment_data/file/184053/DFE-RR226_Report.pdf [Accessed 9 August 2019].

Dube, S. R., Felitti, V. J., Giles, W. H. and Andra, R. F. (2003). The impact of adverse childhood experiences on health problems: Evidence from four birth cohorts dating back to 1900. *Preventative Medicine*, 37(3), 268–277.

Felitti, V. J., Andra, R. F., Nordenberg, D., Williamson, D. F., Spitz, A. M., Edwards, V., Koss, M. P. and Marks, J. S. (1998). Relationship of childhood abuse and household dysfunction to many of the leading causes of death in adults: The Adverse Childhood Experiences (ACE) Study. *American Journal of Preventative Medicine*, 14, 245–258. https://doi.org/10.1016/S0749-3797(98)00017-8.

Goodman, M. (2002). *The Iceberg Model.* Hopkinton, MA: Innovation Associates Organizational Learning.

Grotberg, E. H. (1995). *A guide to promoting resilience in children: Strengthening the human spirit.* The Hague: Bernard van Leer Foundation.

Halpern, D. (2005) *Social Capital.* Cambridge: Polity Press.

Hart, A., Gagnon, E., Eryigit-Madzwamuse, S., Cameron, J., Aranda, K., Rathbone, A. and Heaver, B. (2016). Uniting resilience research and practice with an inequalities approach. *Sage Open*, 1–13.

Henehan, K. and Rose, H. (2018). *Opportunities Knocked? Exploring Pay Penalties Among the UK's Ethnic Minorities.* London: Resolution Foundation.

Luft, J. and Ingham, H. (1955). The Johari window, a graphic model of interpersonal awareness. *Proceedings of the Western Training Laboratory in Group Development*, Los Angeles.

Levitas, R., Pantazis, C., Fahmy, E., Gordon, D., Lloyd, E. and Patsios, D. (2007). *The Multi-dimensional Analysis of Social Exclusion*. Available at: https://dera.ioe.ac.uk/6853/1/multidimensional.pdf [Accessed 9 August 2019].

Magnuson, K. (2013). Reducing the effects of poverty through early childhood interventions. *Institute for Research on Poverty*, 17.

Masten, A. S. (2014). *Ordinary Magic: Resilience in Development*. New York: The Guilford Press.

Prowle, A. and Musgrave, J. (2018). Utilising strengths in families and communities to support children's learning and wellbeing. In Cheeseman, S. and Walker, R. (eds) *Pedagogies for Leading Practice – Thinking about Pedagogy in Early Childhood Education*. New York: Routledge.

Rankin, J., Regan, S. and IPPR (2004). *Meeting Complex Needs: The Future of Social Care*. Available at: https://www.ippr.org/files/images/media/files/publication/2011/05/Meeting_Complex_Needs_full_1301.pdf [Accessed 9 August 2019].

Rogers, C. (1951). *Client-Centered Therapy: Its Current Practice, Implications and Theory*. London: Constable. ISBN 1-84119-840-4.

Sabates, R. and Dex, S. (2012). The impact of multiple risk factors on young children's cognitive and behavioural development. *Children & Society*, 29(2). https://doi.org/10.1111/chso.12024.

Shonkoff, J. P. and Garner, A. S. (2012). The lifelong effects of early childhood adversity and toxic stress. *American Academy of Paediatrics*. Available at: http://ohioaap.org/wp-content/uploads/2016/08/peds.2011-2663.full_.pdf [Accessed 9 August 2019].

Spratt, T. (2011) Why multiples matter: Reconceptualising the population referred to child and family social workers. *The British Journal of Social Work*, 42(8), December 2012, 1574–1591. https://doi.org/10.1093/bjsw/bcr165

UK Cabinet Office (2011). *Think Family: A Literature Review of Whole Family Approaches*.

UK Cabinet Office Social Exclusion Task Force (2007). *Families at Risk Background on Families with Multiple Disadvantages*.

Vinson, T. (2007). *Dropping Off the Edge: The Distribution of Disadvantage in Australia*. Melbourne: Jesuit Social Services.

Walsh, F. (2002). A family resilience framework: Innovative practice applications. *Family Relations*, 51(2), 130–137.

Walsh, F. (2006). *Strengthening Family Resilience,* 2nd ed. New York: Guilford Press, 384 pp. ISBN 1593851866.

Whalley, M. (2007). *Involving Parents in Their Children's Learning*. London: Sage.

3 THE RESILIENT AND SELF-EFFICACIOUS PRACTITIONER

Chapter outcomes

This chapter will enable readers to explore the following concepts:
- The importance of practitioner resilience
- How practitioners can develop their own resilient approaches
- How practitioners can maximise their contribution and impact
- The implications for practitioners arising from this chapter

---

Introduction

Angie Hart defines resilience as 'Beating the odds whilst also changing the odds'. Helping children and families to develop resilience is a crucial part of the practitioner role (as we will explore in Chapter 7), but what about our own resilience as practitioners? In the increasingly complex, changing and turbulent context of today's working environment, developing the resilience of individual practitioners becomes essential in order to enable them to both survive and thrive. This chapter considers what resilience is and how we can develop it.

What is resilience and why is it important?

Resilience has been variously defined as the ability to bounce back, to recover from setbacks, to overcome challenges or to keep going when circumstances are difficult. As we saw in Chapter 2, Ann Masten (2014) helpfully describes resilience as 'ordinary magic'. She presents a positive and hopeful perspective on resilience as a natural resource that we all possess to some extent, but which, importantly, is not only adaptive to new circumstances and challenges but can also be nurtured and supported.

Luthans et al. (2006) view resilience as a form of 'psychological capital' or in other words, a strength or psychological capability that 'can be measured, developed and … managed' (Luthans, 2002). Drawing upon positive psychology to inform human resource development, they argue that resilience,

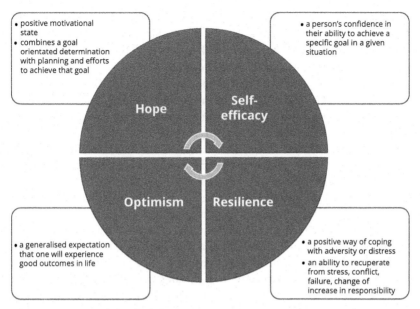

Figure 3.1 Elements of resilience

hope, optimism and self-efficacy operating together create a 'core construct' which is strongly related to employee satisfaction and also work-related performance. These four elements are seen as distinct, but interrelated, as shown in the diagram below (Figure 3.1).

Whilst the other three elements can exist without a negative 'trigger' event, resilience operates specifically in how we frame adversity and how well we bounce back from it.

Practitioners in the CYPF workforce labour in increasingly complex and often stressful situations. For example, service cuts coupled with rising demands on the service may result in staff feeling under pressure. Similarly, technologies such as email may intrude on life outside work. Moreover, the human nature of the contexts that we work in means that we are often confronted with others' challenging stories and difficult emotions, and this too, can be stressful for the practitioner, as Sophie highlights in the case study below.

Skovholt and Trotter-Mathison (2011) identify a number of 'professional hazards' associated with what they call 'high touch' occupations, defined as 'highly skilled professional attachment, involvement, and separation over and over again with one person after another' (Skovholt and Trotter-Mathison, 2011, p. 106). These hazards include: constant empathy, a difficulty in saying no, dealing with others' emotions. Bimrose and Hearne (2012) adds to this the difficulty of managing client expectations and dealing with multiple and complex client issues as well as measuring outcomes. In the context of this complex and demanding work, she defines resilient behaviour as 'having the capacity to deal with challenges, unpredictability, being psychologically armed to contend with the unknown of what "comes through the door"' (2012, p. 10). Resilience in this context is crucial, if the practitioner is to avoid toxic stress or burnout.

So how can we develop resilience in ourselves and also promote it in our colleagues? Maben et al. (2012) make the point that having resilient staff with positive well-being is not only important for the staff themselves, but is also an antecedent to providing high-quality support for those using the service.

There is much debate about the extent to which resilience is heritable and how much depends on environment and experiences. Most theorists agree that it is a combination of both aspects. Hence, whilst there may be some innate ability to be resilient, it is also something that can be nurtured and developed.

Elias et al. (2005) argue strongly that resilience can be learned, and that techniques that help a person keep things in perspective and stay present in the moment can be practised and mastered. This could include approaches such as mindfulness or meditation. Indeed, a study by Pereira et al. (2016) found that more effective practitioners demonstrated higher levels of mindfulness, which in turn had a positive impact on resilience. However, Hearne suggests two additional important conditions for maintaining resilience: firstly having effective support in the workplace, and secondly having a life that is separate from work. Moreover, the practitioners in her study (guidance counsellors) highlighted the importance of being part of a team, and the fact that resilience develops with experience.

Aumann and Hart (2009) talk about the importance of making 'resilient moves', which help to reframe adversities or to improve conditions around them. Such moves may be within the workplace or outside it. In fact, within their resilience framework, Hart and Blincow (2007) identify five domains with which to support resilience for young people. These are, basic needs, a sense of belonging, opportunities for learning, strategies for coping and an understanding of our core self. In the diagram to the right, we have adapted these domains of support to apply to practitioners (Table 3.1).

Using the blank resilience framework template on the Boing Boing website (https://www.boingboing.org.uk), practitioners could populate this framework with the specific approaches that work for them. Just making small changes could result in resilient moves that add up to a more resilient way of being.

It is important, however that the practitioner does not wait for adversity to strike before trying out the resilient moves. Such approaches work far better when applied proactively as part of a drive to maintain high levels of personal well-being. This proactive approach also models resilience to others around us.

The following case study, by Sophie Fry, describes some of the things that she has had to deal with at the beginning of her social work career and she talks about how to build emotional resilience. Social work is a profession that is known for its stressful work and high turnover of staff. Some of the reasons for this high turnover could be 'defensive organisational structure, poor social support and unmanageable caseloads' (McFadden et al., 2015, p. 1558).

Table 3.1 Domains of resilience

Basics	Belonging	Learning	Coping	Core Self
It is difficult to be resilient when you are not having your basic needs met. For practitioners this could mean they need to address physiological needs such as getting enough sleep, making time for exercise or taking lunch breaks. It could also involve focusing on their own physical and emotional safety.	This aspect involves relationships. For the practitioner this could include in-work relationships and networks, as well as family and friendship connections.	This aspect emphasises learning and development. In the workplace, this could involve mentoring, CPD or taking on new experiences. It could also involve out-of-work opportunities such as learning a new skill or starting a course.	This involves finding ways to cope when adversity strikes. This could mean setting and maintaining boundaries, reframing and reappraising, gaining support from others and problem solving.	This domain refers to our beliefs, values and perception of self and others.

Case Study: Sophie Fry – Bearing the unbearable in children's social work

My role in a Locality Children's Safeguarding Team is vibrant, rewarding, exciting, draining, exasperating but all-round extraordinary, and I feel privileged to be working with vulnerable children and their families. I develop Child Protection and Child in Need Plans, working in line with the Children Act 1989, developing safer family lives for those that need it most. Of course, there are children for whom it will be simply too unsafe to remain at home and therefore I can sometimes find myself moving children to other family members or maybe even foster carers. I listen as parents bravely share their traumatic childhood experiences, I play alongside children who have never been played with before, and I battle with partner agencies to get the right services for my families.

I am 'bearing the unbearable'. These were the words used by Professor Harry Ferguson, who came to deliver a lecture to our Local Authority a few months ago, and they have echoed in my mind ever since. Social workers need to immerse themselves in the 'unbearable' to make proper assessments and tune into the lives of the children they are caring for.

Having only been a qualified social worker for just over a year, you would have thought that concepts such as 'compassion fatigue' and 'burnout' would have not yet entered my mind; being relevant only to those having practised for years. This however is simply not the case. After all, 'bearing the unbearable' is sure to manifest itself to my emotional detriment somehow; or is it? I think not. This is because, so I have learnt, 'bearing the unbearable' builds emotional resilience and emotional resilience protects from burnout.

There is lots to read about building emotional resilience as a way of preventing burnout. We read practical advice about time management, self-care, striking a work–life balance. Of course, we are all human beings and particularly in my line of work, where the use of self is central, you need to make sure that you nurture enough of yourself to give to others. I am of the opinion however, that the key to building emotional resilience on this job, lies within the work itself.

I have learnt that emotional resilience builds itself over time and this is partly because it takes time to see the positive changes take effect for the children. For example, about six months ago, I was involved in the removal of three children from their dangerous home environment. They were not children allocated to me; I was assisting a colleague. The police were required, and the children were naturally very frightened and unwilling to leave their home. This impacted upon me emotionally in a way that I suppose was to be expected, but left me questioning my emotional resilience. That was, until I saw these children four months later, settled and safe within their foster placement, and I realised the necessity of their removal and the positive changes we had been able to make. It was absolutely heart-warming to see these children and I think it increased my emotional resilience significantly. Since then, when dealing with emotive and challenging situations, I can project my thinking forward to the safety of the children and I feel much more emotionally resilient within that moment. The more experience I have, the more examples like this I can draw upon, creating a snowball effect when thinking about the development of emotional resilience.

This then prompted my thinking about the transient nature of this job and the subsequent fluidity of emotional resilience; everything is temporary. This is another way of thinking that has aided the development of my resilience, but equally is something I could have only learnt over time. Keeping this in mind has enabled me to 'hold things lightly' safe in the knowledge that what might consume me at this time, will be a memory at some point and is mostly likely to have impacted positively upon the life of a child.

I suppose the key message here, regarding emotional resilience, is trust the process and hang on in there. The more you practise, the better your perspective becomes and the more you can protect yourself emotionally.

> **Case study reflections**
>
> - Sophie talks about 'bearing the unbearable' within her role. How does this impact on her own well-being?
> - What strategies does Sophie use to safeguard her own well-being?
> - What does Sophie mean by 'holding things lightly', and how does this support her resilience?
> - Sophie views gaining experience as essential to developing a resilient approach. Do you agree? Can you reflect on your own practitioner journey and think about how situations may have challenged you, but simultaneously helped you to develop a resilient approach?

Practitioners are people too

It is important to recognise that practitioners have lives outside of the workplace. Moreover, within those lives they may be facing difficult situations that challenge their own resilience. Bereavement, family breakdown, financial hardship or caring responsibilities are just some of the challenges practitioners may be coping with in their lives outside work. There is a growing recognition that balancing demanding work roles with the priorities of their own busy and challenging lives can impact negatively on the well-being of practitioners. In extreme circumstances, this can lead to stress, burnout and mental ill health. These issues are covered more fully in Chapter 12. A wide-ranging report on mental health within the workplace across all functions and sectors, commissioned by the Prime Minister (Farmer and Stevenson, 2017), identified that whilst a majority of employees report being generally happy at work, mental health fluctuated according to other things that were going on in their lives. There is also a recognition that not everyone deals with situations in the same way, and, for example, whilst some individuals find a little pressure motivating, for others it can cause them to feel overwhelmed.

The Kawa River Model (Iwama, 2006) discussed in Chapter 1 can be a useful tool for enabling staff to reflect on the challenges they are facing (their rocks) and the 'driftwood' that is keeping them floating, as well as those activities, rituals and relationships that help enable 'flow' (Csikszentmihalyi, 1990). For each practitioner the tools that work to support their resilience in the face of different life pressures will be unique. For all, though, having time to invest in activities that they enjoy and that allow them to be fully engaged and present in the moment can be helpful in enabling them to achieve flow, which, in turn, will have benefits for both their work life and their lives more generally.

How can organisations help support practitioner resilience?

The following considerations will help managers and their teams to support practitioner resilience.

- Provide and prioritise regular high-quality supervision

- Find opportunities to discuss and encourage self-care (for example, taking work breaks)

- Provide opportunities for critical reflection on practice, both individually and as a team. Action-learning sets or a reflective practice forum can be useful ways of enabling this. It is important that this approach considers not just situations that have not turned out well (such as critical incidents and near misses) but also explores what *has* worked well (such as successful approaches and interventions)

- Source and secure a wider range of opportunities for professional development

- Provide debriefing, mentoring and peer support for workers

- Acknowledge and celebrate good work and positive outcomes

- Encourage staff to access the organisational supports that are available.

- Foster a collaborative culture and encourage sharing of practice

- Consider different ways of supporting practitioners to create a positive work–life balance (for example flexible working arrangements)

Self-efficacy

Self-efficacy is the confidence we have in our own abilities, in particular, our belief that we can overcome barriers and challenges and be successful. It is, therefore, our belief that we can succeed. In this sense, self-efficacy is more than the nebulous notion of self-esteem; it is less about how we define our self-worth and more about the belief in the possibility of success that we bring to the task in hand. Henry Ford famously suggested 'whether you believe you can, or you can't, you're right'. In other words, it is our belief that determines the outcome. Whilst talent and tenacity play an important role in delivering positive outcomes, some theorists would suggest that it is self-belief that plays the most important role.

Bandura developed a theory of self-efficacy, arguing that there are two types of self-belief systems which deliver very different outcomes. He defined these as 'those with high assurance in their capabilities' and those who 'doubt their capabilities' (Bandura, 1994, p. 2). The following table shows the characteristics of these categories of self- belief (Table 3.2):

Table 3.2 Self-belief vs. self-doubt

Level of Self-Belief	How This Manifests Itself in Attitude and/or Behaviour
High levels of self-belief	• Views difficult tasks as challenges to be overcome or skills to be mastered • Sets challenging goals and remains committed to them • When faced with setbacks, they redouble their efforts • When faced with failure, sees this as due to insufficient effort. Alternatively perceives that they have a deficit of skills or knowledge that can be acquired • When faced with difficult situations, approaches these with a belief that they can exercise control over aspects of them
High levels of self-doubt	• Avoids tasks they view as difficult • Sets low aspirations and often gives up on goals if they seem difficult to achieve • Concentrates on the barriers or challenges and obstacles rather than the skills needed to overcome them • Gives up in the face of difficulties • Allows setbacks to prevent trying again • Experiences stress and depression • Perceives that they are either good at something or not

In response to the question of where self-efficacy comes from and what enables it to flourish, Bandura proposes that there are four sources of self-efficacy. These are shown in the following diagram (Figure 3.2).

Bandura suggests that the most important source of self-efficacy is that of experiencing mastery. Firstly, success breeds success, particularly when part of that success takes the form of overcoming obstacles. Secondly, we can experience that mastery vicariously, through observing the successes of those around us, particularly when we perceive that the people experiencing success are like us. Moreover, verbal persuasion can contribute to enabling us to believe in our own ability to achieve a given goal, and this is where others like coaches or teachers can play a role. Finally, our emotional (or indeed physical) state can influence our self-efficacy, with stress often negatively affecting our confidence, and positive emotions sometimes serving to boost our self-belief (Bandura, 1994). Maddux (2005) adds to these

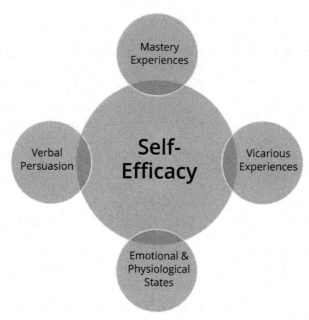

Figure 3.2 Sources of self-efficacy

sources of self-efficacy the possibility of visualising or imagining success. Conjuring up an image of yourself being successful can, suggests Maddux, be effective in boosting self-belief. Bandura is at pains to argue, however, that self-belief cannot substitute for skills or competencies, but if these are already in place, then self-belief can contribute to enabling people to achieve their potential.

Amongst our students, it is easy to discern those who have high self-belief and those who are plagued by self-doubt. However, this, in itself, is not always a predictor of outcomes. Many students who experience high levels of uncertainty and who continually question themselves, their abilities and their actions, often achieve very high standards, as they are highly reflective and always striving for improvement. Similarly, over-confidence can lead to complacency and lack of effort. Hence, self-efficacy as defined by Bandura does need to be balanced with other practitioner qualities such as tenacity and reflection (Bandura, 1997).

Mindset theory and self-efficacy

Carol Dweck's mindset theory provides another way of thinking about self-efficacy. Dweck identifies that there are two possible mindsets. The first of these is a 'fixed' mindset which sees abilities as being set and therefore unable to be developed. So, for example, one is either good at maths or one is not; this is seen as immutable and there is nothing the individual can do to change the situation. A 'growth' mindset, conversely, enables an individual to believe that abilities and talents can be developed. Whether through hard work, skills acquisition or input from others, individuals with a growth mindset are not deterministic about their abilities and are open to the possibility of growth and positive change. Dweck points out, however, that our mindset itself is malleable and that all individuals have a mixture of growth and fixed mindsets. Our mindset can fluctuate as circumstances and environments change. Whilst some individuals may have a dominant mindset, this can shift over time or as conditions change. Although mindset is usually applied within a learning context, it is equally relatable to ideas of self-efficacy. In an inspiring TED talk, Dweck (2006) explores what she describes as 'the power of yet' in which she describes the difference between those with a fixed mindset, who run from difficulties and challenge, and those who embrace the challenge and work through the difficulties, recognising that grappling with a challenge now does not mean one will never master it, but rather that one is just not there yet. In other words, the idea of 'not yet' opens up possibilities of future success. She argues that praising process rather than outcome helps develop resilience, perseverance and creative engagement. What are the implications of this theory for practitioners? Well firstly, knowing about mindsets enables one to recognise when one's mindset is fixed and how this may be impacting on one's ability to achieve positive outcomes. Secondly, finding ways to step outside the constraints of a fixed mindset, whilst often uncomfortable, can enable us to open ourselves to the possibility of growth and development. Thirdly, mindset theory can provide a useful tool for supporting the children, young people and parents we work with in understanding their own self-limiting thought patterns and help them to find ways to overcome them. Finally, within our teams or networks we can model and promote a growth mindset, recognising that, for example, how we use praise or how we talk about failure can impact greatly on both the working culture and on individuals' performances. Scarlett (2016) points out that even by discussing the concept of mindsets and the difference they make, individuals can increase their self-knowledge and ultimately performance.

The following diagram explores some of the ways in which you can help develop growth mindsets for yourself and others (Figure 3.3).

In the following case study, Claire, a children's nurse reflects on how some of the adversities faced in her own life have prepared her for practice. She sees overcoming obstacles and making brave choices as key to developing a resilient approach. Here, she looks back on her career to date and thinks about what has helped shape her philosophy and approach. She also focuses on the importance of not giving up in the face of adversity and how, in the long term, challenges faced can be used as powerful tools for understanding and motivating others.

Figure 3.3 Developing a growth mindset

Case Study: Claire Hiscocks – Overcoming adversity and building resilience in others

My journey into nursing wasn't always straightforward. After school and a short stint at college, I got a job working at the County Council, specifically in school support. I'd always loved working with people, and had been involved in community activism growing up, fundraising for a new community centre and helping out at the local youth club. Life hadn't always been easy though. Like so many mothers, I faced real difficulty going back to work after giving birth. Looking back, I was probably suffering from postnatal depression, but hadn't been able to put a label on it. But going back to work was probably one of the best things I ever did, and I wish I'd done it sooner. I learned early on, before my nursing journey even began, that exposure is often the way forward. I see the same behaviours in some of the young people I've worked with, they want to hide from their problems and pretend they don't exist. Avoiding the issue is never the best way to go, and facing it head-on is scary but also freeing.

Despite loving my job at the council, I made the big decision to take a risk and apply to university. I'd had an incredibly tough few years. My marriage had broken down when both children were very young, and I'd also lost my mother to a really difficult illness. I knew I wanted to give my children a better life and a brighter future, but I also knew I wanted to better myself. Hardship and adversity had made me stronger and more resilient, so I knew it was time to really challenge myself. My daughter had been ill as a baby and seeing the change that nurses could make in a child's life completely inspired and motivated me – I knew I wanted to be like them. So I decided to apply for paediatric nursing, a course notorious for being incredibly competitive. But I got in!

After graduating, I was drawn to school nursing for a few reasons. My mother's illness had a huge impact on both my life and practice, and I'd often wondered how different her life could have been if she'd had effective preventative health education. I truly believe it could have saved her life. In a society facing such complex health needs, promotion and prevention have never been more important, and schools are the best and most effective places to start. School nursing is about planting seeds. You're given the unique opportunity to work with children from aged four and follow them throughout their school career. Compare this to something like health visiting which, while completely vital, only allows for a short, concentrated period of care. In school nursing, we can build a bigger picture and slowly move towards changing whole communities. This is especially pertinent in more working-class areas like mine, where children are already more likely to face health difficulties later in life. In these cases, effective and sustained health education can be a powerful tool of social mobility. Early intervention is vital, and the power and impact of education at this young age can be life-changing.

I did a master's degree in order to help me to qualify as a health visitor and school nurse. After spending hours searching for jobs, I came across a position in Child and Adolescent Mental Health Service (CAMHS). I'd worked in the service on a placement whilst training and had loved it. Despite this, my confidence was low, having been rejected for a previous job, and I felt like a kind of imposter – did I really have the experience to bring something to this team? Could I actually do it? Well, I got the job, working at a day hospital with young people suffering from a whole range of different mental illnesses. It was here that I really came to understand the power of team support. When someone tells you that you're good enough again and again, you really do start to believe it. I learned the vital importance of validation, something I now try and bring forward to my patients. CAMHS is an endlessly challenging but massively rewarding place to work, and I feel so lucky to have been able to hopefully make a difference in the young peoples' lives.

Now, I'm going back to school nursing, taking all the experience and the lessons I've learned in CAMHS with me. The way we think about health and healthcare is becoming increasingly connected anyway. The priorities for school health are starting to change, with the mental health and well-being of our children and young people topping the agenda. Being a teenager can be really tough, and it's so important for young people to have someone they can talk to and trust, and that's what I hope I can bring to this new role.

I probably could have happily stayed in my first job forever. Change is scary, but I chose to take a risk, step away from a job I loved and reach for something more. Every position I've held, every person I've worked with, every difficult experience that I've been through have made me the person and practitioner I am today. For me, this is what it means to be resilient, and it is this resilience I want to model to the young people I work with.

Case study reflections

- How has facing adversity helped shape Claire's philosophy and practice?
- In what ways can a resilience-promoting approach help support children and young people's emotional well-being?
- Claire talks about self-doubt and sometimes feeling like an imposter. She shares this with many of the other practitioners in this book (see, for example, Rachel in Chapter 2). Is self-doubt always a negative thing or can it sometimes have positive benefits? Can you think of an example from practice where you have experienced self-doubt? What did you learn from this situation?
- In what ways does Claire demonstrate self-efficacy?
- Claire talks about the importance of modelling resilience for young people. How can you model resilience within your own role?
- How can you apply mindset theory to this case study?

Conclusion: The implications for practitioners arising from this chapter

This chapter has considered the importance of developing resilience and self-efficacy. Moreover, these are seen as highly desirable qualities which can also be modelled to others. As with other qualities explored in this book, resilience and self-efficacy are seen, not simply as innate qualities, which one either has or does not have, but rather as mutable and capable of development. We have considered ways in which we can support the development of our resilience and also maximise our potential to self-determine and demonstrate our efficacy. These qualities can play a major role, not only in how we approach difficulties and challenges, but also the example we set to colleagues and to the children and families we work with.

 Further reading and resources

https://www.boingboing.org.uk
- This is an extensive online resource that includes research findings, publications, blogs and video clips.

Jenson, J. M. and Fraser, M. W. (eds) (2016). *Social Policy for Children and Families: A Risk and Resilience Perspective.* Los Angeles: Sage.
- This is a great text, focusing on resilience. Whilst it is written from an American perspective, it has much to offer students in the UK.

Masten, A. S. (2018). Resilience theory and research on children and families: Past, present, and promise. *Journal of Family Theory & Review*, 10, 12–31.
  – This article offers an overview of resilience theory as well as an exploration of models and approaches.
TED Talk by Carol Dweck, *The Power of Yet* – https://www.youtube.com/watch?v=J-swZaKN2Ic&vl=en-
  – This is a thought-provoking video that introduces growth mindset theory.

References

Aumann, K. and Hart, A. (2009). *Helping Children with Complex Needs Bounce Back: Resilient Therapy for Parents and Professionals*. London: Jessica Kingsley.

Bandura, A. (1994). Self-efficacy. In Ramachandran, V. S. (ed.) *Encyclopedia of Human Behavior*, Vol. 4. New York: Academic Press, pp. 71–81. (Reprinted in H. Friedman [Ed.], *Encyclopedia of Mental Health*. San Diego: Academic Press, 1998.)

Bandura, A. (1997). *Self-Efficacy. The Exercise of Control*. London: Worth.

Bimrose J. and Hearne L. (2012). Resilience and career adaptability: Qualitative studies of adult career counseling. *Journal of Vocational Behavior*, 81(3), 338–344. https://doi.org/10.1016/j.jvb.2012.08.002

Csikszentmihalyi, M. (1990). *Flow: The Psychology of Optimal Experience*. New York: Harper Collins.

Dweck, C. S. (2006). *Mindset: The New Psychology of Success*. New York: Random House.

Elias, M. J., Parker, S. R. and Rosenblatt, J. L. (2005). Building educational opportunity. In Brooks, R. B. and Goldstein, S. (eds.) *Handbook of Resilience in Children*. New York: Kluwer Academic/Plenum.

Farmer, P. and Stevenson, D. (2017). *Thriving at Work: The Stevenson/Farmer Review of Mental Health and Employers*. Published October 2017 for HM Government. Available at: https://assets.publishing.service.gov.uk/government/uploads/system/uploads/attachment_data/file/658145/thriving-at-work-stevenson-farmer-review.pdf [Accessed 11 August 2019].

Hart, A. and Blincow, D., with Thomas, H. (2007). *Resilient Therapy: Working with Children and Families*. London: Brunner Routledge.

Iwama, M. K. (2006). *The Kawa Model: Culturally Relevant Occupational Therapy*. Philadelphia: Elsevier.

Luthans, F. (2002). Positive organizational behavior: Developing and managing psychological strengths. *Academy of Management Perspectives*, 16(1), 57–72. https://doi.org/10.5465/AME.2002.6640181.

Luthans, F., et al. (2006). *Developing the Psychological Capital of Resiliency*. University of Nebraska- Lincoln. Online at: https://digitalcommons.unl.edu/cgi/viewcontent.cgi?article=1161 [Accessed 12 February 2020].

Maben, et al. (2012). *Exploring the Relationship Between Patients' Experiences of Care and the Influence of Staff Motivation, Affect and Wellbeing*. National Institute for Health Research, 1 November 2012.

Maddux, J. E. (2005). Self-efficacy: The power of believing you can. In Lopez, S. J. and Snyder, C. R. (eds.) (2009). *The Oxford Handbook of Positive Psychology*. Oxford: Oxford University Press.

Masten, A. S. (2014). *Ordinary Magic: Resilience in Development*. New York: Gilford.

McFadden, P., Campbell, A. and Taylor, B. (2015). Resilience and burnout tin child protection social work: Individual and organisational themes from a systematic literature review. *The British Journal of Social Work*, 45(5), 1546–1563.

Pereira, J., Barkham, M., Kellett, S. and Saxon, D. (2016). The role of practitioner resilience and mindfulness in effective practice: A practice-based feasibility study. *Administration and Policy in Mental Health and Mental Health Services Research*, 44(5), 691–704.

Scarlett, H. (2016). *Neuroscience for Organizational Change: An Evidence-Based Practical Guide to Managing Change*, London: Kogan Page Limited.

Skovholt, T. M. and Trotter-Mathison, M. (2011). *The Resilient Practitioner: Burnout Prevention and Self-Care Strategies for Counsellors, Therapists, Teachers and Health Professionals*. New York: Routledge/Taylor & Francis Group.

4 THE PRACTITIONER AS ADVOCATE

Chapter outcomes

This chapter will enable practitioners to engage with the following:
- Types of advocacy – self, peer, independent, and being an 'agent of change'
- Children's rights and participation
- Child agency and activism – children and young people's voices
- Developing our skills in creating a culture of advocacy

Introduction

Advocacy, the process of supporting and enabling vulnerable people, is a competence that is fundamental to practitioners. This competence is required not only the provision of formal advocacy services for families, but in the informal context of enabling children, young people and families to assert their rights and have their voices heard. Children's rights and the value of children's participation will be explored in this chapter, as well as some of the tensions arising between rights and protection. As advocacy is so important, ways of developing skills to enable us to advocate, and to enable others to advocate, will also be examined (Table 4.1).

Children's rights and participation

Since the ratification of the United Convention on the Rights of the Child (1989) and the publication of The Children Act (1989) and the later Children & Families Act (2014), there has been a requirement for those working with children and young people to ensure that the voice of the child is heard and that children are actively included in decision making which concerns them. The idea of children being included in decisions made about them is not a new one, but guidance now supports the rights of children to have their voices heard and acted upon. Many schools have adopted the 'Rights Respecting School' (UNICEF, 2019a) agenda and have achieved the Rights Respecting School award, which demonstrates their commitment to

Table 4.1 Types of advocacy

	Definition	Example
Advocacy	Advocacy means speaking up for people, particularly those who are vulnerable or unable to speak for themselves. With children and young people, it involves making sure that their views and rights are respected. It is also concerned with helping them to have a voice, and to make sure that their voice, views and wishes are heard and acted upon, thereby helping children to be involved in decisions made about their lives.	✓ a Learning Support Assistant attending a school meeting and stating a young child's wishes ✓ an early years worker identifying the needs of babies through observation, and planning accordingly
Self-Advocacy	Self-advocacy is the ability to stand up for yourself and have your views heard, so it is closely related to assertiveness. Part of an advocate's role can be to encourage others to speak for themselves and make themselves heard, so teaching children and young people the skills they need to be able to do this can be very empowering. It is about encouraging people to be independent and to make their own choices. The goal of self-advocacy is for the child to decide what they want and to be responsible for making it happen.	✓ a child speaking up as a school council representative ✓ coaching families to advocate for themselves (see Case Study 1 – Enza)
Peer Advocacy	Peer advocacy is about helping someone in a similar situation, or with a similar difficulty to the person offering help, to have their voices heard. Peer advocates are people who understand the issue and so can offer personalised support to others. An example of peer advocacy is someone with a mental health disorder helping others with the same disorder to have their voice heard in their treatment. Having the ability to empathise with someone's situation can be very helpful and can empower others to make their own decisions.	✓ a transgender person helping others with gender identity issues to have a voice ✓ a child who was bullied volunteering to be an anti-bullying mentor

Agents of Change	An agent of change is someone who makes a change for others or acts as the catalyst for a change. It can be a major change or a very small one, within the organisation the person works in or for the people within the organisation. The change is a way of advocating for others by making a change to enable this to happen. *(more about this in Chapter 5)*	✓ a hospital play worker reorganising a bed space so that a child can take part in messy painting activities ✓ a new Youth Work Manager transforming youth services within a community
Independent Advocacy	Organisations such as charities supply trained advocates for particularly vulnerable groups, such as looked-after children and disabled children. These advocates are independent and are there to speak on behalf of children and young people in meetings, case conferences and in court. The role of the advocate is not only to speak on behalf of the child/young person, but to build a relationship with the child and to empower them to have a voice. However, as a formal advocate is independent, the relationship is likely to be unique, and respect and relationship building are important (Pona and Hounsell, 2012)	✓ a formal advocate representing a child's views in court ✓ a teenager with learning difficulties whose family are unhappy with decisions being made by their local council about housing provision for her, so they enlist the help of an independent advocate

upholding the rights of children and young people. The current government expresses its commitment to the promotion and protection of children's rights (DfE, 2014), citing the benefits of this approach as follows:

- Children encouraged to become active participants in a democratic society
- Improved achievement and attainment, through increased confidence and motivation.

Even in the child protection field, where the imbalance of power is very apparent, children should be able to participate and voice their wishes. There is much evidence to suggest that, in this arena, children feel powerless in their dealings with social workers, police and the court system (Duncan, 2019), so there is still room for improvement (Figure 4.1).

At times, there can be tension between children's rights and child protection, which can be challenging for practitioners. For example, imagine that a girl of 12 at a youth group wants to use social media to chat to friends she has met online. As practitioners, we acknowledge that she has the right to choose what she wants to do, and she has the right to privacy, but we also have the responsibility to protect her from potential danger. There is a conflict which needs to be managed responsibly and respectfully. A more sombre example is that of young people making decisions about their own medical care. Research by Coyne et al. (2014) suggests that children are not always involved in such decisions, especially if the illness is serious, when treatment is seen as something that has 'got to be done'. The study pointed out that adolescents were allowed to make some choices but that these did not relate to anything serious.

Useful guidance on children and young people's ability to make their own decisions is given in the Fraser guidelines, which were produced following the Gillick case in 1982 (NSPCC, 2018). This was a landmark case in which a mother (Victoria Gillick) attempted to stop doctors from giving contraceptive advice to children under the age of 16. In 1985, the High

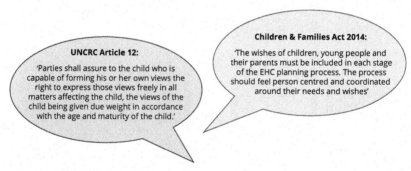

Figure 4.1 Children's rights

Court dismissed the case, but guidelines were subsequently drawn up by Lord Fraser, in which he made an important point about children's rights:

> parental right yields to the child's right to make his own decisions when he reaches a sufficient understanding and intelligence to be capable of making up his own mind on the matter requiring decision. (NSPCC, 2018, p. 2)

A test of 'Gillick competency' means that, if the child understands the advice given, and is mature enough to understand what is involved, then the child has the right to confidentiality.

Invisible groups

When considering the voices of children and young people, we should acknowledge those groups who are 'invisible' to many. The latest Children's Commissioner's report (Longfield, 2018, pp. 14–15) identified 67 vulnerable groups of children and young people in England. These are listed in seven categories within the report. The groups include children, young people and families who are:

- receiving statutory care/support
- known to have experienced specific personal harm
- disabled, or experiencing ill health or developmental difficulties
- in a household with a family which has a higher likelihood of current or future harm
- vulnerable or of concern by virtue of their identity
- at risk in relation to activity outside the home
- caring for others.

The report claims that 1,570,000 children with complex family needs are not currently known to be receiving support (Figure 4.2).

If we look at the diagram above, it is apparent that there are children and young people who may be invisible to the adults working closely with them. How many of us would know which of the children or young people we work with are living in insecure housing, or have a parent in prison? This makes the need to get to know children and to build relationships crucial, so that we can learn about the children in our care and speak on their behalf, taking action to ensure that their needs are met and that they are able to access the support they require. It is vital that we engage with children individually, rather than just managing their care, which often happens, particularly within social work (Barnes, 2012, p. 1275).

looked after	victim of FGM	young carers	living in poverty
refugee	informal kinship care	mentally ill parent	abused or exploited
parent in prison	LGBTQ+	radicalised	gang member

Figure 4.2 Just a few of the vulnerable groups of children/young people in England

∗ For advocacy relating to the children of prisoners, see Natasha's case study (page 57)

∗ For advocacy relating to the children of kinship carers, see Enza's case study (page 54)

Child agency and activism

Over the past decade, there has been a move towards seeing children as being competent and capable (Ruscoe et al., 2018) rather than innocent and power-less. The agentic child (Sorin, 2005) is a child who is an expert in his/her own life and should be an active participant in all aspects of that life, including co-constructing the curriculum. This view has led to changes in early years set-tings, with child-centred and 'in the moment' planning (Ephgrave, 2017) based around the child's interests, and observed 'sparks of fascination' for the very youngest children. A study by Ruscoe et al. (2018) demonstrated that children as young as 5 are able to decide for themselves what is important for them to learn and how they can learn best. Learning is no longer seen as a one-way process of transmission from teacher to child; we learn from the children and young people we work with. It is equally important to feed back to chil-dren and young people. Morgan (2005 in James, 2007) claims that many organisations now consult with children, but there is often a lack of feedback to them. Consulting with children and young people about things that con-cern them, and then not feeding back on how their views have been responded to, can leave them feeling unimportant, not truly valued.

> 'You need to listen and learn from kids and trust us and expect more from us. You must lend an ear today, because we are the leaders of tomorrow' from Adora Svitak, age 12's TED Talk, 2010

The rise of child activism in recent years has highlighted inspirational examples of children and young people fighting for what they believe in. Malala Yousafzai, human rights advocate and the youngest winner of the Nobel Peace Prize, and Greta Thunberg, climate activist, are examples of the incredible things that young people can achieve. There are many more examples of children and young people making a difference, but often there are adults in the background supporting them, encouraging them to think deeply and to question. In the past, children were seen as passive beings, needing to be protected from the world by adults, but there has been a shift in thinking. At an early age, many children are encouraged to be independent and to make their own choices. Children are then able to be active participants in their own learning and development (Munn, 2010).

Dear friends, on 9 October 2012, the Taliban shot me on the left side of my forehead. They shot my friends, too. They thought that the bullets would silence us, but they failed. And out of that silence came thousands of voices. The terrorists thought they would change my aims and stop my ambitions. But nothing changed in my life except this: weakness, fear and hopelessness died. Strength, power and courage was born.

Malala Yousafzai

Developing a culture of advocacy

A culture of advocacy can be defined as one in which children have a voice, their voices are acknowledged and valued, and opportunities are created to make sure that those voices are heard (Frankel, 2018). Advocacy should not be something that we 'add on' to our work with children and young people: it should be integral to our services/provision. Rather than a tokenistic occasional gathering of children's views, in a culture of advocacy, children and young people are seen as partners whose participation is welcomed within a shared community. Children are not seen as passive recipients of services, but as people who have the power to shape the context itself (Frankel, 2018, p. 18). Many services for children and young people have made efforts to listen to their voices: for example, schools usually have some sort of school council or 'pupil parliament'. The UK Youth Parliament, founded in 1998, provides opportunities for 11–18-year-olds to represent their views on a wide range of issues which affect them, including tackling knife crime, gang culture and homelessness, welcoming refugees and promoting interfaith tolerance (UK Youth Parliament, 2019). This is an example of young people taking the initiative of directing strategies which are important to them.

Hart's ladder of participation (1997) describes a model of children's participation, ranging from non-participation (manipulation, decoration, tokenism), to degrees of participation. There are many examples of children being consulted and informed about decisions, for example the Children in Hospital Improvement Partner Service (CHIPS) project in Herefordshire. Twelve young patients were asked to share their views about children's hospital services in order to make improvements (Wye Valley NHS Trust, 2019). However, true participation is much more than this. Imagine that a secondary school is considering creating a conservation area in the grounds. This is how the levels of participation might look (Figure 4.3).

Creating a culture in which children and young people feel competent and confident enough to approach adults with their ideas is the key to a culture of advocacy. Opportunities should be provided for children and young people to work closely with adults without adults making assumptions about what they want and think. The adult's role with younger children or those with special needs/communication difficulties can be to interpret children's voices, as long as care is taken to hear the child's authentic voice, without conjecture. Treating children and young people as partners in a shared community enables them to feel ownership and builds confidence.

Too often, in our society, children (particularly teenagers) are perceived in a negative way, as 'threatening' or 'troublemakers'. Shopkeepers put up signs that say 'no more than two children at a time', the assumption being that children steal. Police dispersal orders send groups of young people home, the belief being that they must be up to no good. The media help to foster this negative view of children and this only encourages an 'us and

Assigned but informed
- The school informs the children about the plans for the conservation area

Consulted and informed
- The school carries out a survey, asking children for their views on the conservation area

• Adult-initiated, shared decisions with children
- Children are involved at every stage of planning and construction of the area

• Child-initiated and directed
- Adults notice children becoming interested in conservation, so they suggest that the children set up a conservation area

• Child-initiated, shared decisions with adult
- Children come up with the idea of a conservation area and approach adults for their support

Figure 4.3 Levels of participation

them' attitude and stereotypical assumptions about this group. It is up to all of us to challenge these assumptions and to help everyone to see children as people in their own right and a valued part of society. Challenging people in public can be daunting, but getting adults to consider their actions can change things for children in small but significant ways.

Advocacy skills

Speaking up for the children and young people we work with is an important responsibility that we all share. We can do this by taking the time to listen, making eye contact, putting away our mobile phones and listening without judgement. When speaking on a child's behalf, it is important to use their words, even if we feel that they do not make sense or are inappropriate or unrealistic. It is the child's voice that needs to be heard, not our interpretation of what we think they want or need, or what we think is appropriate for them. The diagram below outlines some of the skills that we need in order to act as informal advocates in our dealings with children and young people (Figure 4.4).

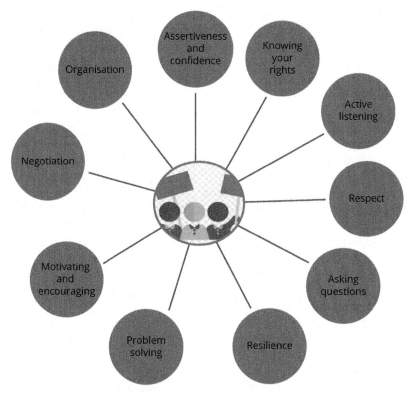

Figure 4.4 Advocacy skills

Case Study: Enza Smith MBE – Advocating for kinship carers

I became a kinship carer for my grandson, 20 years ago when he was 2 years old, and then later for my granddaughter when she was 6. As a family, we had voiced our opinions to Social Services saying, 'You need to do something because we can't, we're trying to keep her safe', but it wasn't until the school raised a concern that Social Services became involved. It went to court, and we were awarded an SGO (Special Guardianship Order). I contacted Social Services, and when I asked them what support was available, they said 'nothing'; support for kinship carers was non-existent, it was all private and nobody wanted to talk about it. I then contacted the Family Rights group, who told me all about the order and what it meant legally. They said 'have you thought about starting a support group up? You'll find that people will turn up', so I did, and they did. The following month, through word of mouth rather than advertising, I started the group, and within 6 months we had about 10 families.

Every month, people came and discussed their situations and why they had their grandchildren (they were all grandchildren at that particular point) and the stories were getting deeper and deeper. I came across one awful story that I can't repeat, it was terrible, and I thought 'how on earth are these people going to cope?' and they said that if it wasn't for the group, they didn't know what they'd do. They said they had been praying for somebody to help, because they didn't know anyone else in their situation. I hadn't when it happened to me either, and so they were able to just let it all out at this group and they didn't hold back. It was so sad, and I wondered where the support was and for these children? The couple had been handed these two children, who were little more than babies, one who had been sexually abused, and they had no support; no plan, no social workers, no nothing. I thought this was very wrong and I wondered what I could do, who I could talk to. I looked online and I started signposting people to services, and that's where it started. These families have all been through some sort of trauma, but kinship carers are a hidden group. People don't want to talk about their children who have gone off the rails as adults and made their choices and left you with their children. They don't want to publicise that; what they want is to get these children the support that they need to get over the trauma. I started hearing their stories and thinking 'I know, I'm a teacher, my husband was a special needs teacher, so we know what sort of support the carers should be getting.' I was better equipped to do that, and I was a lot younger than many of these grandparents, I was quite a young grandparent, and it just progressed from there.

It started as a way of giving carers a voice, and signposting, and then people started saying things like, 'I'm too frightened to go to the school, I don't know what to say' and I'd said 'I'll come with you, what is it you want to say?' As a former teacher, I knew what support the children were supposed to have, so it started off with me going to meetings and supporting people, which then turned into 'advocacy', being the voice for the carer. Some of the carers were so intimidated after going through trauma; some people had to fight for these children to keep them out of care. The trauma of dealing with professionals was too much, so I took it on and said, 'I'll do it'. Then I started getting calls from people that were going through the court process and they were all alone. There were lots of single parent carers and grandmothers on their own and they were frightened about the court process, not knowing where to go, who to talk to, so I ended up sitting outside the courts with them until they were called in, and then, in some cases, some judges allowed me to accompany them into court without saying anything. I was just in there to sit and hold their hand, so it was informal advocacy rather than legal advocacy.

We now have many carers in the support group who have got over the trauma of their own kinship assessment and the first few years of being a carer and working with other professionals confidently. Because I couldn't cope with the flow of people coming through, I would put them in touch with the person that I thought could help them. So, now other people go to court or go to schools with carers and offer peer support, so it has progressed from peer support into advocacy, from people having the confidence and the knowledge that they have already been through it.

The charity is called Kinship Carers UK. We started off as a very small charity, Kinship Carers Worcestershire, and we were just dealing with people in Worcestershire but then it spread as far as Scotland and Wales. Scotland have different laws, but we still provide the emotional support on the phone. All people want to do is just tell somebody 'I've had a really bad day, this is what I've gone through' and for someone to say 'yes, I know, I've been there' and that makes them breathe a sigh of relief because they no longer feel as if they're on their own. Advocacy is about providing the emotional support when people aren't strong enough to do it, when everything drags them down and they just need somebody to say, 'It's alright'. It's a full-time job, when I'm at home with my husband, I'm often sitting there on the phone, and of course I am not paid, but it helps so many people.

We have a few sibling carers and young carers as well and you want to put them under your wing because of what they're doing. They have often given up their lifestyle to take on their younger brother or sister. They could easily just walk away, but they do an amazing job and yet they're being manipulated, instead of supported by the system.

To be an advocate, I believe that you need to have lived the story yourself; anybody can show empathy, or sympathy, but experience speaks a lot and I think that to be an advocate for a kinship carer, you need to be one, you need to know the journey to be able to really understand it. It's very, very different from raising your own children, it's starting again at a different stage of life. Once you've grown your teenagers up, and they've turned into adults and left the nest, it's the last thing you want to do. What you're looking forward to is being a grandmother, having the grandchildren for visits and then handing them back. To be a suitable advocate, is to have walked in the shoes of that person and to be confident that you've managed it and have lived it and you've overcome the trauma of what your child has done to the family. And then, you *need to be confident in listening but not always giving advice, so it's about knowing your limitations as well. I don't think that I'm particularly strong or assertive, but what makes me speak up is the injustice that I see people suffering. My confidence can go up and down like anybody else's. I look at MPs and other professionals in high-paid positions, like Directors of Children's Services, and I think 'well, I've been to University, I've been a teacher. I can read, I can write, I can study. That's your field, and I know as much as in my field, so what makes me so different to you?' I think my educational standing gives me the confidence to do what I do. The volunteers who haven't been to university can do the job just as well, because they're confident in other ways and experiences. It's understanding that the people you're talking to are no better and no worse than you.*

If I see injustice, and I see people struggling, that's what gives me the strength to do it. You can advocate for anybody if you're passionate enough to do it. Just walking into a room with somebody, and them knowing that you're there is enough. I've gone into many situations where I've not said a word and wasn't allowed to. However, there's nothing stopping me from holding the carer's hand and giving them a squeeze when they're just getting a little bit emotional or, if they're starting to get angry, a little nudge under the table.

The Family Rights Group were the ones who put me forward for the MBE. I was part of their kinship panel, so I started off going to meetings with the group, meeting MPs and professionals with them and speaking on behalf of kinship carers. I do quite a bit of work with them all over the country. Then Kinship Carers UK started to grow, people were talking about how much we'd helped them as a charity. I don't like to blow my own trumpet, but Cathy Ashley CEO just said that you do wonderful work and you're not paid. I believe it's a Christian way of helping people, something very close to my heart. I just think the lack of support is so unfair and disproportionate; it's these kinship children that make me want to make a difference for them and their carers.

Case study reflections

- Enza describes a range of ways that she and the charity support families. Can you identify examples of different types of advocacy in her story?
- Enza believes that, to be an advocate for a specific group of people, like kinship carers, you need to have shared similar experiences yourself to be able to truly understand the issues. What are the benefits of experience over empathy and a willingness to learn?
- Many personal qualities have been identified in this case study; reflect on what Enza considers to be the qualities and skills that enable her to do the job she does.

The following case study is also about advocacy, but in a very different situation, in prison. Natasha gives her experience of working with prisoners' families and advocating for the rights of this often-forgotten group of vulnerable families.

Case Study: Natasha Headley – Advocating for the families of prisoners

Although it is one individual that is imprisoned, imprisonment inevitably has a massive impact on the families left on the outside, as they are left to continue living their lives without their loved one. Incarceration can cause a huge strain on relationships; it has been estimated that over one in five married prisoners become separated or divorced as a result of going to prison. Problems frequently experienced by prisoners' families are family relationships, financial hardship, stigmatisation and a negative impact on children.

Families of prisoners are marginalised because of their connection to incarceration, but also within the criminal justice system. Their friends or extended family may shun the existing family for supporting the prisoner, or a stigma may be formed against the lone parent simply for being a lone parent or a partner of a prisoner. Family members suffer harm as a consequence of their relative's imprisonment; their own individual rights may be breached, and they experience marginalisation and discrimination.

In addition to the effects on the family as a whole, children's lives need to be considered, as the majority of prisoners leave innocent children behind. As prison populations have grown across the world, so too have the numbers of children with a parent in custody. Unfortunately, children of prisoners are not identified in education or child protection policy, nor in wider criminal justice and court practice. Children affected by parental imprisonment can suffer trauma, strain, stigma and labelling. Having a parent in prison as a child has also been associated with significantly increased risks of mental illness, unemployment, substance misuse and anti-social behaviour in adulthood. This, however, is not the case for all children with incarcerated parents; in a lot of cases their parent's situation encourages children to aspire against living a criminal lifestyle and achieve their own goals in life.

Although there are seemingly many negative impacts on the family regarding incarceration, in some cases it can bring the family closer together and build resilience within the family. This can, for example, be the case in situations where a parent has abused family members and/or is heavily drug dependent. In these circumstances, particularly if they have become dependent on alcohol or drugs, the family may be partially relieved that their loved one has been imprisoned and has the opportunity of rehabilitation. In addition to this, once the family member is released from prison, if they are committed to their probation conditions and transform their lives in a positive way, this will automatically improve the families' connections.

Although in the majority of cases it is the father within the family who is incarcerated, there are also mothers in prison, which is even more complex, as mothers are more often the primary caregiver. Children who lose their relationship with their mothers to incarceration are more likely to suffer with behaviour issues, social isolation/withdrawal, social stigma and a range of strong emotions such as grief and loss, depression and shame.

Prisoners are entitled to a visit from their relatives or friends once they have been imprisoned for a certain period. Each prison has its own policies and procedures as to when they allow visits to commence. A number of claims have been made regarding the importance of prisoners staying in touch with their family through prison visits, firstly from a humanitarian perspective of enabling family members to see each other, but also regarding the impact of maintaining family ties for successful rehabilitation, reintegration into society and reduced reoffending. Whilst in prison, depending on the crime they have committed, offenders work closely with their probation officers to discuss their plans for release and how they intend to achieve their ambitions. Having this positive outlook helps motivate them for the future and encourages them to aspire to change their lives completely.

In advocating for the family, and in order to address the families' needs, family support programmes linked to prisons are doing some excellent work on behalf of the families. Family support programmes offer one-to-one support, advocacy and referral for prisoners and their families, with the goal of maintaining and strengthening family ties and promoting resettlement. They focus on the impact of incarceration on a child's life and identifying ways that parents can still contribute positively. Fathers are often concerned about having very few visits from their children and they worry about the lack of guidance and supervision available to them.

There is increasing support in place to support prisoners and their families. Barnardo's (2018) supported at least 1,300 children and their families affected by a parent in prison. There are also helplines, such as The Offenders' Families Helpline which is a free and confidential helpline provided for families of offenders. The more support provided to the prisoner whilst they are in prison, the lower the possibility of them reoffending, therefore it is beneficial for support to be provided whilst the individual is serving a custodial sentence, in addition to support once released.

Former prisoners face tremendous challenges on release from prison, particularly in their reintegration into family relationships. Research evidence indicates that family support is essential to avoid reincarceration. It is important to support the 'whole family', rather than focusing narrowly on rehabilitation of the father, as the rest of the family also require support, not just the prisoner.

The organisation that I work for provides support to prisoners' families indirectly, through supporting rehabilitation and the completion of a risk assessment that covers all aspects of an individual's life including their

*financial, physical and mental well-being. If they appear to be struggling men-
tally and have problems within their families, they are signposted to counselling that may include the family. We consider the family in everything we do
when working with offenders and ex-offenders.*

Case study reflections

- Children and young people who have a family member in prison are
  one of the 'invisible groups' discussed earlier in this chapter. Why do
  you think this is and what can we do to enable these children's voices
  to be heard?
- In what ways does Natasha's organisation advocate for the families
  of prisoners?
- Read the recommendations from the report 'Voice of a Child' (The
  Howard League for Penal Reform, 2011) – in what ways can the voice
  of the child be heard in this situation?

Conclusion

In this chapter, we have considered the importance of advocacy in work with
children, young people and families. Types of advocacy have been explored,
including peer advocacy, self-advocacy and both formal and informal forms
of advocacy. Advocacy is central to ensuring that children are afforded their
rights, as set out in the United Nations Convention on the Rights of the
Child (1989). However, there are some tensions around rights and responsibilities; the overriding principle is that the welfare of the child is paramount
(Children Act 1989).

When children are afforded their rights and given responsibility, wonderful things can happen, as seen in the amazing stories of Malala Yousafzai and
Greta Thunberg. These cases demonstrate the power that young people can
have and the impact that they can make on the world. Children and young
people are capable of really making a difference, standing up for what they
believe in and making adults listen. If we, as adults, encourage deep thinking
and questioning, rather than strict obedience, we are emboldening children
to take responsibility.

Everyone can be an advocate; whether it is for a particular group in need,
as seen in the case studies by Enza and Natasha, or, in general, by standing
up for children's rights and making a difference. In making a small change
for a child, we can impact on their learning, development and happiness
significantly and we can do this by tuning into the child with empathy and
understanding.

Further reading

Boylan, J. and Dalrymple, J. (2009). *Understanding Advocacy for Children and Young People*. Berkshire: Open University Press.
- A comprehensive guide to advocacy with children and young people, in all sorts of situations.

Duncan, M. (2019). *Participation in Child Protection: Theorizing Children's Perspectives*. Basingstoke: Palgrave Macmillan.
- This book prioritises the voices of children recounting their experiences within the child protection system.

Frankel, S. (2018). *Giving Children a Voice: A Step-By-Step Guide to Promoting Child-Centred Practice*. London: Jessica Kingsley Publishers.
- A very accessible book which gives practical advice about children's rights within settings.

UK Youth Parliament (2019). *Votes at 16 Campaign*. Available at: http://www.ukyouthparliament.org.uk/campaign/include-16-17-year-olds-public-elections/ [Accessed 8 August 2019].

References

Barnes, V. (2012). Social work and advocacy with young people: Rights and care in practice. *The British Journal of Social Work,* 42(7), 1275–1292.

Coyne, I., Amory, A., Kiernan, G. and Gibson, F. (2014). Children's participation in shared decision-making: Children, adolescents, parents and healthcare professionals' perspectives and experiences. *European Journal of Oncology Nursing*, 18(3), 273–280.

Department for Education (2014). *Listening to and Involving Children and Young People*. Available at: www.gov.uk/governmentpublications [Accessed 8 August 2019].

Duncan, M. (2019). *Participation in Child Protection: Theorizing Children's Perspectives*. Basingstoke: Palgrave Macmillan.

Ephgrave, A. (2017). *Planning Next Steps in the Moment: Early Years Foundation Stage Forum*. Available at: https://eyfs.info/articles.html/teaching-and-learning/planning-next-steps-in-the-moment-r217/ [Accessed 8 August 2019].

Frankel, S. (2018). *Giving Children a Voice: A Step-by-Step Guide to Promoting Child-Centred Practice*. London: Jessica Kingsley Publishers.

Hart, R. (1997). *Children's Participation: The Theory and Practice of Involving Young Citizens in Community Development and Environmental Care*. London: Earthscan.

Howard League for Penal Reform (2011). *Voice of a Child*. Available at: https://howardleague.org/publications/voice-of-a-child/ [Accessed 8 August 2019].

James, A. (2007). Giving voice to children's voices: Practices and problems, pitfalls and potentials, *American Anthropologist,* 109(2), 261–272.

Longfield, A. (2018). *Children's Commissioner Vulnerability Report Overview, July 2018*. Available at: https://www.childrenscommissioner.gov.uk/wp-content/uploads/2018/07/Childrens-Commissioner-Vulnerability-Report-2018-Overview-Document-1.pdf [Accessed 8 August 2019].

Munn, P. (2010). Children as active participants in their own development and ECE professionals as conscious actors. *International Journal of Early Years Education*, 18(4), 281–282.

NSPCC (2018). *Gillick Competency and Fraser Guidelines*. Available at: https://learning.nspcc.org.uk/research-resources/briefings/gillick-competency-and-fraser-guidelines/ [Accessed 8 August 2019].

Pona, I. and Hounsell, D. (2012). *The Value of Independent Advocacy for Looked After Children and Young People*. The Children's Society. Available at: www.childrenssociety.org.uk/research [Accessed 8 August 2019].

Ruscoe, A., Barblett, L. and Barratt-Pugh, C. (2018). Sharing power with children: Repositioning children as agentic learners. *Australasian Journal of Early Childhood*, 43(3), 63–71.

Sorin, R. (2005). Changing images of childhood – Reconceptualising early childhood practice. *International Journal of Transitions in Childhood*, 1, 12–21.

UK Youth Parliament (2019). *UK Youth Parliament Manifesto 2018/2019*. Available at: http://www.ukyouthparliament.org.uk/wp-content/uploads/UK-Youth-Parliament-Manifesto-2018-2019.pdf [Accessed 8 August 2019].

UNICEF (2019a) *Rights Respecting Schools*. Available at: https://www.unicef.org.uk/rights-respecting-schools [Accessed 8 August 2019].

Wye Valley NHS Trust (2019). *Voice of the Child*. Available at: https://www.wyevalley.nhs.uk/visitors-and-patients/county-hospital-(acute)/a-z-departments/paediatrics/voice-of-the-child.aspx [Accessed 8 August 2019].

5 THE PRACTITIONER AS A LEADER AND AGENT OF CHANGE

Chapter outcomes

This chapter will enable readers to explore the following concepts:
- Definitions, styles and importance of leadership
- Leadership in the context of working with children and families
- What it means to be an 'agent of change'
- The implications for practitioners arising from this chapter

---

Introduction

Much has been written about leadership, its importance in the modern world and what makes a good leader. Most experts would agree that good leadership is essential for all organisations, particularly in the context of high-paced technological and societal change. However, the same experts may well disagree about precisely what constitutes good leadership and how it can be achieved. This chapter recognises the complexity of the discourses surrounding leadership, but takes the stance that in the complex and ever-changing environments in which we work, leadership is about having a clear vision for the future and knowing how best to achieve it. Moreover, it is about working with others to create, implement and achieve that vision within an environment where innovation, risk-taking and continuous improvement can flourish. Whilst leadership is often discussed in relation to success and profits with in the commercial sectors, it is important to remember that leadership theory originated in a military context, where human lives were at stake. Within the children and families' workforce, similarly, leadership, is not about 'how much money you make; it's about the difference you make in people's lives' (Michelle Obama, former First Lady of the United States). The following sections explore definitions and models of leadership that are consonant with this conception of leadership as contributing towards positive, life-enhancing change, with ensuing benefits for self, for staff and most importantly for the children and families with whom we work.

What is leadership and why is it important?

The following section explores some of the traditional views of leadership, challenges them in light of contemporary leadership theory, and then seeks to present them within the context of working with children and families.

Leadership myth 1: You are born a leader

The term 'a born leader' is widely used in common parlance and suggests that leadership is an innate quality owned by an elite and, perhaps, elusive to lesser mortals. In line with other nature/nurture debates, contemporary research evidence suggests that the interplay between genetic and environmental factors is far more complex than this. In other words, whilst there may be some inborn characteristics that support leadership, it is also the case that leadership is something that can be nurtured and developed. Recent emphasis on leadership development suggests that good leadership requires a wide-ranging and complex set of skills, many of which are acquired through experience, learning from others, self-development and reflective practice.

Leadership myth 2: All leaders have the same traits or personal qualities

Traditional models of leadership often emphasise the traits (or personal qualities) of leaders, arguing that there are defined personal characteristics that are associated with leadership. Indeed, as Northouse (2010) points out, many organisations use psychometric testing to find out whether potential employees have these desirable qualities. Kirkpatrick and Locke (1991) suggest that research has identified particular qualities as important for leaders to display. These traits, they argue, include drive, a desire to lead others, ambition, integrity, self-confidence and a high degree of cognitive ability. Others have emphasised the importance of personal charisma for effective leadership. In a wide-ranging study of charisma, Tskhay et al. (2018) define charisma as embodying a high degree of affability (an ability to get along with others), coupled with influence (an ability to lead and guide others towards a specified goal).

However, 'trait theory' as described above is not without its critics. Some theorists (for example, Pervin, 1994) have suggested that trait theory places more emphasis on the reactions of followers than the effectiveness of the outcome. Moreover, it does not account for the fact that different situations require different types of leaders, or indeed that leadership can be developed and learned. Trait theory also presupposes that there is only one way of effectively being a leader, whereas evidence suggests that leaders with very different personality traits and demeanours can be equally effective in a given role, taking things forward in their own unique way. A commercial organisation recently undertook a study involving more than 2,000 people. It identified a list of 33 attributes in leaders that others find inspiring. From this, they identified that those with the potential to inspire others are very diverse, and, indeed, leaders only need one truly inspiring characteristic in order to be considered inspirational.

Leadership myth 3: Only extroverts can be leaders

Directly related to trait theory is the idea that only those who are gregarious and outgoing can make good leaders. In an inspiring TED talk, Susan Cain explores the previously unsung virtues of introverts, in particular, their ability to make meaningful connections with others, to be reflective and to make considered decisions. Whilst it may be true that introverts are less likely than their extroverted peers to seek out leadership positions, studies have shown that as leaders, introverts can be highly effective, particularly in relation to fostering a culture of collaboration, mobilising the capacities of others and creating 'win–win' solutions in difficult circumstances.

Leadership myth 4: Leadership is the same as management

Much has been written about the difference between leadership and management. Harvard professor John Kotter provides an extensive exploration of the distinction between leadership and management, which he perceives as two distinct but complementary skill sets. Leadership, he argues, involves dealing with change, and management is more about dealing with complexity (Kotter, 1988). So, within this model, leaders create a vision and inspire and empower others to help make that vision a reality. Managers, conversely, are more concerned with processes, such as budgeting, staffing and handling day-to-day situations.

Of course, this does not mean that managers cannot themselves demonstrate leadership, or indeed that management is inferior to leadership. Both are vital, and in many cases will be undertaken by the same person. Pound (2008) recognises this, arguing that within the children and family sector staff will often move seamlessly between leadership, management and teamwork roles as they fulfil their daily responsibilities.

Leadership myth 5: Good leaders can handle every situation

One of the problems with traits theory (explored above) is its assumption that there are desirable qualities for leaders to have. This in turn suggests that a leader owning those desirable qualities is likely to succeed in all circumstances or situations. Hersey and Blanchard (1969) developed the concept of situational leadership, arguing that different contexts and circumstances require different kinds of leaders. As Northouse (2010) points out, leaders will use a combination of directive and supportive behaviours designed to meet the needs of the situation and get the best out of their teams. Such leaders will need to know their teams well, to be reflective and adaptive (Walls, 2019) and to use participatory approaches in order to maximise team contributions.

Leadership myth 6: Leading from the top/leading from the front

The final myth we will explore involves the assumption that only the individuals at the top of the organisation can exercise leadership. In reality, leadership can occur throughout the organisation. In fact, one could argue that the primary role of the most senior person is to promote and enable leadership throughout the organisation. This is often referred to as distributed leadership. It embodies the notion that leadership can emerge from any team member, regardless of their position within the organisation, and this should be championed and empowered by those in senior positions.

Linked to this is the idea of leading from the front. This embodies the idea of the leader leading by example, going ahead and expecting others to follow. This can be very empowering to team members, who see that the leader is prepared to do themselves what they ask of the staff. However, more contemporary theories of leadership also allow leaders to 'stand back' and allow others to showcase their ideas and talents. This idea of 'leading from behind' is fully in line with the idea of distributed leadership and can result in staff empowerment and creative problem solving.

Leadership styles

Traditional leadership styles have often been characterised according to the level of control exerted by leaders. At one end of the spectrum is the authoritarian style, which exercises high levels of control, whereby leaders make the decisions with little or no input from staff. This approach can leave staff feeling resentful, uninvolved and fearful of making mistakes. At the other end of the spectrum is 'laissez-faire' leadership, a hands-off approach which often leaves staff feeling exposed and unsupported.

More contemporary theory suggests that just as different situations demand different kinds of leaders, so leaders themselves need to be highly adaptive, and whilst all leaders will have their own preferred style, they need to be highly flexible and respond to the needs of both the context and the team. A style that works well in one context may be completely unsuitable for another.

The figure below builds on the work of Daniel Goleman (2000) and describes some leadership styles that may be helpful to consider in the varied and challenging contexts within the children and families' sector (Figure 5.1).

These leadership styles rely heavily on emotional intelligence, and require the leader to demonstrate self-awareness, as well as to be cognisant of the needs of the team and the demands of the situation.

Leadership Style	Features	Apply this when...
Commanding	• Demands compliance • High control	In a crisis situation To start a process of change in a failing organisation
Pace Setting	• Setting performance standards	In a high-performing team To get quick results
Affiliative	• Creates harmony • Develops team relationships	To motivate staff in stressful situations To heal divisions
Democratic/Participative	• Builds consensus • Involves others • Creates shared ownership	To foster 'buy in' to decisions To allow staff to feel valued
Visionary	• Inspires others with a vision of how things could be	When a change in direction is needed
Coaching	• Developing others • Empathy	To help improve performance To develop future capacity
Authentic (not one of Goleman's styles)	• Integrity and emphasis on honesty • Transparency • Self-awareness	To encourage a change in culture To build trust and foster engagement

Figure 5.1 Contemporary leadership styles

Leadership in the context of working with children and families

The complex and ever-changing contexts of working with children and families demand leaders who can juggle the competing needs and aspirations of a range of different stakeholders (for example, parents, children, staff government agencies, regulatory bodies). Such challenging roles demand adaptability, resilience, tenacity and a high degree of emotional intelligence. Moreover, there needs to be clear communication and collaboration with service partners in order to achieve shared goals.

It is also important to point out that leadership is not just about leading teams. Equally important is the idea of leading practice. In general management theory, the word leading is used as an adjective which is coterminous with 'best' practice. However, within early years, the term has a more specific meaning. The word leading is used here as a verb, coterminous with guiding, directing or piloting practice.

Mary Whalley (2011), writing in the context of early years, emphasises the community development aspect of leading practice, recognising the connections between staff, children, parents/carers, partner agencies and the wider community. The leader, she argues, is able to support a wide range of objectives within this learning community, including pushing boundaries, enabling people to question and not accept the status quo, building individuals' confidence and self-determination, promoting learning, and enabling equality of opportunity.

The empowering aspect of leading practice is borne out of the fact that it is not just the person with the designation of leader who can lead practice, but that all practitioners have this opportunity. Such leadership of practice involves tuning into individuals, keeping up to date with evidence-based interventions, adapting practice where required and adopting a critically reflective approach. Clearly this kind of approach has resonance beyond early years with applications for youth work, family support and beyond.

Case Study: Emma Davies – The rise of the reluctant leader

My leadership journey began unexpectedly in December 2011. An Ofsted inspection at the preschool setting where I was employed had not gone well, resulting in an inadequate grade and the immediate resignation of the manager. Someone needed to take responsibility for driving the setting forwards. The position of manager was offered to me, but I refused initially, totally daunted by the responsibility, the sheer amount of work required and the coming re-inspection. However, following a period of reflection on what was best for the setting, I reluctantly accepted the challenge.

Having no management experience, I felt completely unprepared. Every morning, I woke with a lurching feeling in my stomach at the responsibility and amount of work involved. This affected my confidence and left me feeling very vulnerable. Could I really do this? Being a key person was what I was good at but management was a complete unknown, not to mention the embarrassment of being seen as 'inadequate'. One thing which proved to be an important factor in helping me collect my thoughts, evaluate what I needed to do and make necessary changes was being a student at the University of Worcester. I had begun my foundation degree studies just a couple of months previously and relished the learning opportunities and the chance to put theory into practice. Learning is what I love and being able to link this to my work situation was a blessing and driving factor in what I was later to achieve.

A period of 'learning on the job' followed, but thankfully I had a great team who worked with me and trusted my decisions. Together, we built a community of learning where we worked towards a common goal – to give the parents and children what they deserved, a 'good' setting. I felt the need to inspire and motivate the team and although there were times when I felt incredibly daunted, my anxiety reduced as I could see the hard work of the team pay off. Changes I had initiated were working, creating a space where children were happy and motivated to play and learn. Measures to engage parents were successful, new policies and procedures were efficiently implemented and my confidence grew.

Distributed leadership was a subject which particularly interested me during my foundation degree studies. The team of practitioners I was managing had specific skills and experience I could utilise, enabling them to feel a sense of ownership and value over aspects of the setting. I had reached the point where I had accepted that I couldn't do everything on my own and, as a perfectionist and someone who likes to be in control, this was a big step! Distributed leadership was successful in developing a team of experts who undertook certain roles including phonics teaching, Forest School training and subsequent leading of sessions, cookery groups and circle time sessions. This 'letting go' and allowing an element of autonomy required reflection and critical discussion as a team to ensure it was working and was enhancing the experiences of the children. It continues to be an element of our setting which works well.

The shared vision for the future saw us come together as a team, building resilience against the previous feelings of failure. Under my leadership, we were responding to the difficulties and challenges we faced as a result of a poor inspection and were empowered to succeed. I was learning to be a leader! The test was in July 2016 when we were re-inspected – my first inspection as a manager! Changes I had implemented, and the vision of the team was evident and we were recognised to be a 'good' setting.

Although I had achieved my goal of improving the quality of the setting and reflecting on my own practice along the way, I knew I still had a lot to learn. Leadership can be volatile, with many factors impacting on performance, quality and well-being. However, I was growing to feel proud and protective of what we had achieved at Busy Bees. Through the process of developing myself as a leader, in practice and through qualifications, I had begun to realise that I had an influence. My lecturers at university had developed the reflective practitioner in me, which I used to identify quality gaps in my setting. I felt a constant drive to improve my professional practice and the outcomes for children. It required me to be responsive to the needs of the children attending, ensure quality teaching and learning experiences, develop our position within the community and empower the team to achieve.

By the time we were inspected again in July 2016, the feeling of failure had been replaced with confidence and positivity. I knew we'd done a good job and had complete trust in my team. The inspector showed particular interest in my studies and how my foundation degree, BA Hons and EYTS had impacted on the quality of the setting. No one will ever understand the pride I felt when the inspector mentioned the word 'outstanding'. We had done it!

Even as an 'outstanding' setting, the drive to continuously improve was still evident. There followed a very uncertain period when we were potentially homeless but, as we'd proven before, we were resilient and protective of what we had achieved. We moved into our new setting in the summer term 2018 and felt like this was 'home'. I revelled in the opportunity to organise the space and resources, embracing the changes I was required to lead, from policies and procedures, managing the transition for children and ensuring requirements were met in the new premises.

My time as a leader has been eventful and challenging but this has shaped me into the confident and intuitive professional I am today. The qualifications I have gained along the way have empowered me to grow from a reluctant leader, fearful of failure and daunted by change. I am now completing my master's and look forward to the challenges the future holds now that I finally believe in myself.

Case study reflections

- Emma describes herself as a 'reluctant leader'. She explains that she had never really envisaged herself in a leadership role. What factors helped her make this transition? What were the factors that could potentially have held her back?
- One of the enduring debates in leadership theory explores whether leaders are 'born or made'. What does Emma's experience offer to this discussion?
- What values, skills, dispositions and qualities does Emma demonstrate in this example?
- How does Emma's experience relate to the leadership theory explored earlier in the chapter?
- Emma successfully led the setting through a period of change. What factors contributed towards enabling the setting to flourish?
- Now that the setting is thriving, are there any potential leadership challenges ahead? Is a different kind of leadership required from Emma now?

What does it mean to be an 'agent of change'?

In the example above, Emma successfully led an ambitious programme of change in order to turn around an inadequate setting. However, all practitioners have the potential to be agents of change within their settings.

McDowell Clark (2012) explores the potential and challenges for practitioners inherent in 'lead[ing] from within' arguing that despite a perceived lack of authority, and a tendency to experience 'imposter syndrome', practitioners have the potential to achieve incremental improvements in quality which, over time, can result in significant advances. Such change agency has the potential to impact the practice of others, creating small but valuable changes to a setting's practice. McDowell Clark describes this 'informal and emergent' leadership activity as 'catalytic leadership'. When combined with the catalytic leadership of others, this approach has the potential to be systematised and embedded within a culture of continual improvement. Clearly, in order for catalytic leadership to thrive, the environment needs to be conducive, empowering and democratic. This requires leaders who themselves are committed to quality improvement, willing to enable others to implement their ideas and able to create an environment in which staff can safely take risks and learn from mistakes.

The case study below features managers from Families First (a Welsh-government-funded preventative family support programme) in Blaenau Gwent County Borough Council in South Wales. The service was recently redesigned in order to provide better services for families and to meet the Welsh Government's new service guidance. Here, Alison and Rachel engage with me (Alison Prowle) in a candid discussion about leadership and being agents of change.

Case Study: Alison Ramshaw and Rachel Price – Improving family support services

AP – Alison Prowle
AR – Alison Ramshaw
RP – Rachel Price

AP: So, what led you both into this area of work?

AR: I started as a young girl by volunteering with the Phab Club (a sport and leisure club for people with disabilities). The chair of the club took me under her wing and got me some voluntary work in probation service. Several years later, after having my children, I wanted something for myself, so I worked in alternative provision for offenders. I was always curious to find out what had happened in people's backgrounds that led them to offend. And then after getting that experience I was in a position to do my social worker (SW) training.

RP: Like Alison I volunteered as a teenager. Then, on qualifying as a social worker, I worked in a number of roles in child protection. Always front-line stuff, intake and assessment, fostering and adoption; it felt very chaotic and pressured. This job was an opportunity to do something different. It took me 6 months to feel my feet and realise that there is a world outside child protection. I had to learn a whole new way of working and manage people from different professional backgrounds. Changing jobs was a bit like a bereavement; it shook me to the core. I lost confidence in myself, my identity and knowledge base, and my team. It was about learning a whole new way of engagement, but now, 2 years on, I can say it has been a wonderful opportunity.

AP: That is interesting. Do you think this experience helped you to understand the team when you are making big changes to the service, you know that sense of disequilibrium?

RP: I am more aware, and I realise the need to bring people with me, it pays dividends in terms of the service. And I realise too that there is a whole emotional aspect to change that staff need support with. That is why we make ourselves so available to staff and have an open-door policy. We want to involve them as much as possible.

AP: So, what was it that made you begin to see yourself as leaders?

AR: I am resilient and have a good sense of self-awareness which can be self-critical at times, always questioning. You and Rachel were talking about being collaborative, but I've always done well under leaders who, as well as being supportive, offer a clear direction. I feel safe with that type of manager. I agree that you need to bring people along with you but I also think that a part of keeping staff safe, you need to make difficult decisions, in a manner that encourages staff to feel safe.

AP: That is interesting because it strikes me that while you and Rachel have a lot of commonality, you are also different, personality-wise. Is that dynamic part of what a makes the team so successful? That balance?

AR: Rachel's style is very different. Sometimes she can help me see things differently, as sometimes I am a bit removed from the frontline. You tend to lose sight, not intentionally but I have budget issues, strategic priorities, but Rachel is driving the vision forward and sees the opportunities not the barriers. She is in the moment, whereas I like an action plan. It takes me out of my comfort zone working with Rachel, in a good way!

AP: And I have observed, Rachel, that you are always looking at what needs to change and continually looking for those enhancements and developments. You almost seem to thrive on that change?

RP: Definitely!

AR: You are a doer. Now you can see yourself in this role, all that potential is exciting to see. If I am honest, I think I have always been a leader; I always wanted to show the way. Even early in my career I took on management roles and enjoyed the challenge. Are leaders born or made? I think it is a combination. I have had some inspirational people in my life who have been great peer mentors but also leaders in their own right; I have learned and observed from them, but some of it is intrinsic.

AP: It sounds like you are continually reflecting on self but also on what makes others effective.

AR: In 2006 there was a catastrophic personal event in my family, and at that time at work we were going through a way of working that was very performance driven and quite alien. But, for me, coming into work was a relief from the personal stuff, so all my energy and my thoughts were in my work. I was able to devote my mind space to turning that failing service around. Learning to be a leader probably came from default.

AP: That is really insightful, it shows how so much of our identity is intricately tied up with work.

RP: I never saw myself as a leader, I never had any ambition and in some ways I still don't think that I am. I feel like a bit of an imposter. People think that I am cleverer than I am. I sometimes feel like it is luck that gets me through. Alison has encouraged me to take on these roles and been a mentor to me. She saw something in me I didn't see in myself. I still struggle seeing myself as a leader, and I don't know if I have the qualities that I need.

AR: I don't think I really planned my career you know, I did diabolically at school but all of my learning came in my adult life. You find yourself in situations and you learn from them and take the opportunities that come your way.

RP: I have learned so much here in the last two years and I am a better practitioner for it. We all have bad days when you think 'how did I get that so wrong?' but I am learning from it!

AR: That curiosity, that reflection, that feeling that we don't have all the answers is really empowering for your team because they can see that they are allowed to make mistakes. I can think of things we would do differently with hindsight. The team here are young but we want to be supportive, we want them to want to come to work and to do well. They have so much motivation and energy and we have the maturity and experience to balance that and to enable them to work safely.

RP: There is a framework for keeping people safe, for working things through together. We have no hesitation in saying 'we don't know, let's chat about it'.

AP: Jean McNiff talks about 'holding our knowledge lightly', because ultimately new information may challenge what we thought we know. So, we should never be too wedded to our perspectives... and our own knowledge.

RP: Yes that is really important, to allow and value uncertainty.

AR: But, as leaders, the onus is on us to be well informed. Holding knowledge lightly could be problematic – you would never make a decision. So, the onus is on you to form your knowledge and make decisions based on that; an informed and considered position. Otherwise you could be creating an unsafe workforce, if you are changing your mind at will. However, there is a skill to changing your mind when it is needed.

RP: *That comes down to competency. We need a supportive structure around us as a manager. We need mutual trusting relationships.*

AR: *I also think our leadership style is influenced by our value base. Challenging with respect and in an emotionally intelligent way, and with evidence.*

AP: *How do you develop the leadership of others in the team?*

AR: *I think it is about building confidence and making sure they know that nothing they say will be laughed at. That there is a value to what they are saying and that there is always a place for blue sky thinking, giving people opportunities to lead on things.*

RP: *Alison loves a good Task and Finish group! She will let them run with good ideas and come back with a proposal.*

AR: *Encouragement and praise is good as well, acting as a critical friend. If you could have done something differently, what would different look like? All of that brings out qualities in people.*

RP: *The practitioners are leading practice and supporting change with families. We are leading the team but they are leading practice. It is all very reciprocal. Role modelling is important too with the team leaders, letting them make their own mistakes, trying to ask questions that allow them to reflect on their leadership, supporting them to become leaders.*

AR: *I suppose we need to recognise what leadership style is needed for each situation and then be flexible and adaptive in implementing that whilst also being true to ourselves and our core values.*

RP: *Yes and it is important to recognise we can't move away from our core values. That underpinning knowledge is so crucial, as is honesty and speaking without jargon. Especially when working with families, we need to say it like it is.*

AR: *We need to understand the complexity of relationships, how social and economic factors play a part in what is going on for a family from a health perspective, from a social perspective, everything plays a part in the whole picture. So if we are going to be agents of change we need to recognise that no one person can change everything. Communication and multi-agency working may be buzzwords but they are absolutely crucial. Thinking about the strengths in the family, seeing the intricacy of the relationship, helping them to affect that change. Not just telling struggling families what they need to change but being sensitive and emotionally intelligent. We shouldn't underestimate the effects of trauma, asking the question of what has happened to you that you are behaving this way ...*

RP: *... and listening, really listening to the answers, not assuming we know.*

Case study reflections

- What kinds of leadership do Rachel and Alison demonstrate? How do their styles complement one another?
- Alison and Rachel reflect on the classic question of whether leaders are born or made. Alison makes the case that it is a combination of the two. What is your perspective and what informs your position?
- Like Emma in the earlier case study, Rachel never saw herself as a leader. What changed for her? In what ways does her view self-enable her to develop and thrive as a leader? Are there any ways in which it is potentially self-limiting?
- The leaders here talk about the importance of core values and underpinning knowledge. Why are these so important? What else, in your opinion, makes a good leader?
- Rachel and Alison candidly discuss the fact that our personal lives can impact our work and that there are emotional aspects to changes at work that need to be recognised and supported. What are the implications of this for the workplace and how can it best be managed?

Conclusion: What are the implications for practitioners arising from this chapter?

This chapter has considered the importance of leadership within the children and families' workforce. It has examined a range of leadership models and theories, arguing that leadership needs to be specific to the contexts within which it operates. Leadership therefore is situational, and the leader needs to adapt to the demands and specificities of the organisation's current circumstances. Whilst there may be particular situations (e.g. unsafe practice) that warrant a more commanding approach (Goleman, 2000), in most cases, more democratic, engaging and positive styles of leadership will deliver better outcomes. Leadership is viewed as a set of skills and qualities that can be developed by individuals in the context of their own unique personalities and ways of being. Moreover, leadership is not restricted to those who hold the title of leader but can be enabled and exercised at all levels within the organisation.

 Further reading and resources

Cain, S. (2013). *Quiet: The Power of Introverts in a World That Can't Stop Talking.* London: Penguin.
- This is a popular book aimed at a general, rather than academic audience. It provides some thought-provoking material on the potential of introverts as leaders.

Kossek, E. E., Petty, R. J., Bodner, T. E., et al. (2018). Lasting impression: Transformational leadership and family supportive supervision as resources for well-being and performance. *Occupational Health Science*, March 2018, 2(1), 1–24.
  – This journal article is written from an occupational health perspective and looks at the impact of supervisors' leadership styles on staff well-being and job outcomes.
TED talks on leadership: https://www.ted.com/playlists/140/how_leaders_inspire
  – This playlist contains some very diverse and useful ideas related to leadership.

References

Clark, R. M. (2012). 'I've never thought of myself as a leader but...': The early years professional and catalytic leadership. *European Early Childhood Education Research Journal*, 20(3), 391–401. https://doi.org/10.1080/1350 293X.2012.704762.

Goleman, D. (2000). Leadership that gets results. *Harvard Business Review*, March–April 2000, 82–83.

Hersey, P. and Blanchard, K. (1969). Life cycle of leadership. *Training and Development Journal*, 23, 26–35.

Kirkpatrick, S. A. and Locke, E. A. (1991). Leadership: Do traits matter? *Academy of Management Perspectives*, 5(2), 48–60.

Kotter, J. (1988). *Leading Change*. Boston, MA: Harvard Business Review Press.

Michelle Obama's Convention Speech, 4 September 2012. It is available on National Public Radio website: https://www.npr.org/2012/09/04/160578836/transcript-michelle-obamas-convention-speech?t=1581443195766.

Northouse, P. (2010). *Leadership Theory and Practice*, 5th ed. London: Sage.

Pervin, L. A. (1994). Further reflections on current trait theory. *Psychological Inquiry*, 5(2), 169–178.

Pound, L. (2008). Leadership in the early years. In Cable, C. and Miller, L. (eds.) *Professionalism in the Early Years*. London: Hodder Education.

Tskhay, K. O., Zhu, R., Zou, C. and Rule, N. O. (2018). Charisma in everyday life: Conceptualization and validation of the general charisma inventory. *Journal of Personality and Social Psychology*, 114(1), 131–152.

Walls, E. (2019). The value of situational leadership. *Community Practitioner*, 92(2), 31–33.

Whalley, M. (2011) *Leading Practice in Early Years Settings*. Exeter: Learning Matters.

6 THE EMOTIONALLY INTELLIGENT PRACTITIONER

Chapter outcomes

This chapter will enable practitioners to engage with the following:
- Models of emotional intelligence – 'trait model', 'ability model' and 'mixed model'
- Components of emotional intelligence
- Developing emotional intelligence
- The role and benefits of emotional intelligence in working with children, young people and families

---

Introduction

Goleman (1995, cited in Dozier, 2010, p. 130), one of the most prolific writers on EI (emotional intelligence), is famous for saying; '*If your emotional abilities aren't in hand, if you don't have self-awareness, if you are not able to manage your distressing emotions, if you can't have empathy and have effective relationships, then no matter how smart you are, you are not going to get very far*'.

Goleman, a science journalist, made the theory of EI popular, although it was developed by psychologists Salovey and Mayer in 1990. They claimed that it was a cognitive ability which is separate from, but also associated with, general intelligence. Salovey and Mayer's model of EI incorporated four different branches:

- perception of emotion

- emotional facilitation

- understanding emotions

- the management of emotions.

Goleman believes that EI (also known as EQ 'emotional quotient') is twice as important as IQ (1998, p. 31). However, the theory has its critics, with some academics suggesting that EI is 'an elusive concept' (e.g. Davies et al., 1998, p. 989), or even a myth (Matthews et al., 2002, p. 547). There has been some criticism of the model by scientists, yet there is much anecdotal and recorded evidence of the benefits of EI in people's work and personal lives.

In professions based on relationships with others, which require us to be both personally and socially competent, surely EI is crucial. Self-awareness, self-regulation, motivation, empathy and social skills are more important than ever in today's multi-professional landscape. There is evidence that EI skills can be developed and can increase. Studies researching the development of EI skills in teachers (Dolev and Leshem, 2016) and social workers (Grant et al., 2014) agree that interventions used in the training of teaching and social work students have resulted in an increase in, leading to the development of greater resilience in these practitioners. Therefore, we can see EI as a flexible set of skills, which can be acquired and improved with practice (Boddey and Hodgkins, 2015, p. 84).

Three models of emotional intelligence

Trait model

In the trait theory (Petrides et al., 2007; Petrides, 2010) EI is recognised as a personality trait, unrelated to cognitive ability or competency. Emotional thinking is seen as intuitive and automatic, rather than conscious and analytical. Petrides (2010) gives an example of a person who is reserved at work. In trait theory, this person would not be seen as having low emotional skills; instead he/she is seen as having a personality better suited to working in a quieter environment. Whilst there is some room for growth, we cannot change our personality. According to this model, there is no ideal person with excellent EI skills; rather, there are people with different personalities who are best suited to particular jobs.

Ability model

In this model, EI is seen as a type of intelligence; it involves cognitive ability as well as emotion. It is an ability that can be developed and improved. Emotions are seen as useful tools which can help us to navigate the social environment (Mayer and Salovey, in Salovey and Sluyter, 1997). The model assumes that people vary in their ability to use EI, but training can improve skills, and this is not dependent on personality. The model includes four abilities which can be developed;

- Perceiving emotions – people can be taught to recognise emotions by reading facial and body language cues

- Using emotions – learning how and when to ask for something, recognising that emotions must be considered when problem solving

- Understanding emotions – learning to understand complex emotions and nuances

- Managing emotions – we can learn ways of managing our own and others' emotions

However, there is some evidence which suggests that when developing the ability to use EI, this can become emotional manipulation, which can be identified as 'the dark side of emotional intelligence' (Grant, 2014).

Mixed model (Goleman)

This is Goleman's own model (1996), based on the work of Salovey and Mayer. The model is used widely in professional/workplace scenarios and it identifies a wide range of competencies and skills, particularly for leadership. The mixed model accepts that individuals have innate personality characteristics, but also that capabilities can be learned.

Components of emotional intelligence

EI is identified as having five major components:

- Self-awareness – the ability to 'tune into' our true feelings

- Self-regulation – the ability to control how we react to our emotions

- Motivation – the desire and energy to be interested and committed

- Empathy – the ability to 'tune into' the feelings of others

- Social skills – the ability to interact with, and communicate with others; to build relationships (Figure 6.1)

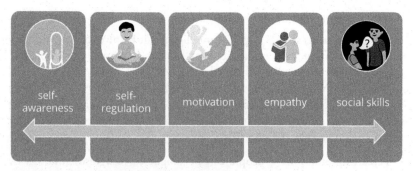

Figure 6.1 Components of emotional intelligence

How emotionally intelligent are you?

The questions on the next page are designed to help you to ascertain how emotionally intelligent you are and to identify your strengths and areas to develop. This is not an official psychological assessment; rather, it is an exploration devised by one of the authors of this book and designed to prompt reflection and discussion (Table 6.1).

Developing emotional intelligence

If we agree with the ability model (Salovey and Mayer, 1990) or the mixed model (Goleman, 1996), then we accept that EI skills can be learned and developed. In the case studies in this chapter, mental health nurse Lilly and family support workers Jade and Ruth all agree that the skill, although to some extent innate, can be developed. Supporters of trait theory (Petrides et al., 2007) also believe that there is an opportunity for growth in EI, so it is worth examining some of the ways that we can all develop our EQ. A high EQ helps us to communicate better, reduce anxiety and stress, improve relationships and overcome challenges.

Reducing negative emotions

This sounds much easier said than done, as many of us have an array of things going on in our lives that could lead to negative emotion. However, the development of a positive attitude can reduce negative emotions. Positivity increases neural dopamine levels in the body and improves creativity and attention (Ashby et al., 1999), and thinking creatively can, in turn, improve positivity. Visualisation can be a powerful tool in creating positivity. It is possible to 'choose' to be positive; the same event will affect different people in different ways, depending to some extent on each individual's attitude. Examining different ways of viewing the situation is a good way of identifying potential positives. In 1995, actor Christopher Reeve (of Superman fame) was thrown from a horse, leaving his neck broken, his spinal cord severed and his body paralysed from the neck down. Yet, he never gave up hope and he saw himself as still living a useful life. From his hospital bed in 2001, he said, 'I'm not living the life I thought I would lead, but it does have meaning and purpose. There is love, there is joy, and there is laughter' (Reeve, 2003). Many people would have given up and retreated into depression and hopelessness; attitude is everything.

Acceptance is important in reducing negativity. Everyone has negative emotions and accepting and understanding them is the first step to dealing with them. When we understand our triggers, then we can begin to take control. Anger is an intense emotion, but even this can be managed when we understand what triggers it. However, anger does not always have to be a negative response; it can be useful in identifying problems and in helping us to defend ourselves. Methods of controlling anger are widely described in therapeutic writing and self-help guides, mostly centring around thinking time and

Table 6.1 Emotional intelligence quiz

Question	Assess 😊 😐 ☹	Competence	Discussion Point
Do you ever 'pick up' negative emotion from others and feel it yourself? (e.g. stress, excitement)		Social awareness	When could this be positive? When could it be damaging?
Are you aware of times when you are beginning to struggle to cope?		Self-awareness	How is this helpful?
Do you always pause and think before you speak?		Self-management	What are the consequences of NOT doing this?
Do you ever have a feeling that someone is not ok, without them having to say anything?		Social awareness	What are the consequences of this?
Are you able to share your point of view, even if it differs from others you are speaking to?		Self-management	Why is this important?
Do you often praise others?		Relationship management	Why is this important?
Do you apologise if you have made a mistake?		Self-management	What might prevent someone from doing this?
Do you work well within a team?		Relationship management	Why is this important?

Are you able to silence your negative inner voice?	Self-awareness	What does your inner voice say? Why?
Are you able to convince others of your good ideas?	Relationship management	How?
Can you predict how others will react to something you suggest?	Social awareness	When might this be important?
Do you understand that critical feedback can be a positive thing and react positively?	Self-management	Why is this sometimes difficult?
Could you easily list your own strengths and weaknesses?	Self-awareness	What is the benefit of doing this?
Are you able to protect yourself emotionally from aggressive people?	Self-management	How can you do this?
Have others ever followed your advice or used your good ideas?	Relationship management	How does this feel?
Are you a good listener?	Social awareness	How do you know? Why is this important?
Are you aware of how others see you?	Self-awareness	How can you be sure that you are correct?

breathing techniques (MIND, 2013). Counselling can be very helpful for those wanting to let go of issues from the past which may be impacting on current emotions (see Chapter 10 for more on protecting yourself).

Managing stress

Mindfulness, relaxation and other techniques can help us to manage stress. This is discussed in depth in Chapter 11. The lower our stress levels are, the easier it is to manage our own emotions and offer support to others. Self-awareness can help us to identify times when we are becoming stressed, so that we can take action to calm ourselves before the stress reaches an unmanageable level.

Learning to be assertive

Assertiveness is a skill that can be learned, and it is important in order to preserve our own confidence. If we are passive and let people overpower us, this can lead to feelings of helplessness and stress. If we are aggressive, then we disregard the feelings of others; so, assertiveness is the balanced view that we need to try to adopt. It is about valuing yourself and your needs, recognising when you cannot change others' behaviour and learning to develop your own power to get your point across firmly, fairly and with empathy. Learning to say 'no' without upsetting others or feeling guilty is a skill that can be developed and is important in caring for ourselves (Figure 6.2).

Figure 6.2 Assertiveness

Improving resilience

Learning from our mistakes and developing the ability to 'bounce back' from adversity is another skill connected with EI. This is discussed in detail in Chapter 3. Schneider et al. (2013, p. 909) claim that the development of our EI facilitates stress resistance. This is particularly important for those of us working with children and families in stressful situations and environments.

The role and benefits of emotional intelligence

Mayer et al. (2008) identify the benefits of developing high EI to others and to ourselves. It is widely accepted that EI skills, which help us to build relationships with people, are fundamental in working with children and families. 'Making highly involved connections between children and their families is essential ... it is recognised as an inherent part of the teaching and learning process' (Lightfoot and Frost, 2015, p. 411). Mayer et al. (2016) claim that EI leads to:

- better social relations for children and adults

- being perceived more positively by others

- better family and intimate relationships

- better academic achievement

- better social relations during work performance and in negotiations

- better psychological well-being

- self-compassion.

Ultimately, EI can help us to achieve self-actualisation, the fulfilment of our potential. Being emotionally intelligent allows us to build and manage positive relationships which can generate huge benefits to both our professional and our personal lives. In the field of mental health nursing within the NHS, stress can be high and relationships key. In this case study, Lilly talks about why EI is important in her role.

Case Study: Lilly Faulkner – Therapeutic relationships in mental health nursing

Emotional intelligence is imperative for mental health nurses in order to build a therapeutic relationship with patients. It enables the patient to feel that they are able to share how they are feeling with somebody that understands what they are experiencing. However, it is also vital for mental health nurses to remain professional and not to cross professional boundaries, which I believe is another key aspect of being emotionally intelligent; knowing how much personal information to share with my patients. Patients and their families are more likely to receive better quality of care if their nurse is emotionally intelligent, as the nurse is more likely to have the ability to manage their own emotions.

Whilst it is important to maintain the trusting relationship you have as a practitioner with the children and families you are working with, it is vital to work with other professionals and attend multidisciplinary meetings. This has helped me in the past as I once had to share required information on a child I was working with who needed safeguarding intervention. I was inexperienced and did not have the capacity or knowledge to handle this situation on my own and I was able to recognise that I would need support. This was in the best interest of the child as they were able to receive the help that they needed from several different professionals. This enabled me to have support from other colleagues and to be able to not worry about the child when I went home from work. I was able to go into work the next day and offer the same level of support to the children I saw that day, as I had maintained my own emotional intelligence by not allowing what had happened the previous day to impact upon my ability to work the following day.

In order for a person to be emotionally intelligent, I believe that they have to be able to listen non-judgementally. Throughout my nursing education, I have been taught ways to manage my own emotions and I have now had the opportunity to implement this in practice, which has been beneficial. I believe that emotional intelligence is an innate characteristic that can be strengthened through learning and practice. I have worked with many nurses, who are more experienced than me, who appear to have lost their ability to be emotionally intelligent. The pressures of the ageing population and the strain on the NHS have meant that they have not been able to have time to listen to their patients; they have become disheartened and experienced burnout. This has made it difficult for them to be compassionate. I believe that a person's ability to be emotionally intelligent can be developed through experience, providing they have the necessary support and resilience to bounce back when they are finding it difficult to manage their own emotions.

When I worked as part of a school nursing team, we led high school drop-in sessions where adolescents could discuss any concerns they had about their physical and mental health. In each initial meeting, we would discuss the limits of confidentiality and provided the young person with a statement from the NHS. This stated that, as nurses, we are able to keep anything that is said confidential unless the child or another person's safety is at risk. We would then have to share the information with other professionals whilst keeping the child informed. I could imagine that this would prevent some children from telling us important information and if I was a child this would worry me. Therefore, I was able to empathise with the children and reassure them that whatever the outcome, it would be in their best interest. Being able to imagine myself in other people's difficult situations has helped me immensely in gaining patient's trust and encouraging them to discuss their worries with me.

I have found several ways to remain resilient throughout my career so far that have helped me to maintain my own emotional intelligence. I realise the *importance of mindfulness; living in the moment and not worrying about the past and the future has helped me to stay focused when listening to patient's concerns. After work, running and exercising to music are a great distraction as they allow me to focus my mind and energy on something completely different and the endorphins are a bonus! These all allow me to return to work the next day feeling refreshed and able to help patients to the best of my ability.*

Case study reflections

- At the beginning of the case study, Lilly talks about the importance of boundaries. How do you manage this in your practice? How can we balance empathy with keeping ourselves safe?
- Lilly explains that it is important to recognise your own limitations and know when you need help and support. Reflect on your own ability to ask for help.
- Lilly mentions nurses she has worked with who, as she says, 'appear to have lost their emotional intelligence'. Why do you think this could be? What could be done to prevent this from happening?
- In the last paragraph, Lilly reflects on ways of managing her own stress and building resilience. See Chapters 3 and 12 for more about these important aspects of practice.

In work with CYPF, it is likely that we will encounter some very difficult situations that would challenge any worker, however experienced they may be. Social workers, for example, may work with abused children, listen to accounts of trauma and deal with injury, death and suicide, which is particularly difficult for new, inexperienced workers, or those still in training (Grant et al., 2014, p. 875). In this case study, Jade and Ruth discuss how their own EI allows them to fulfil their roles as family support workers, working with families experiencing multiple adversity. In the interview, they talk about two specific examples of family interactions when they have needed to use their EI skills.

Case Study: Jade Maynard and Ruth Akbas – Dealing with challenging situations

AH – Angela Hodgkins
JM – Jade Maynard
RA – Ruth Akbas

AH: We've been talking about emotional intelligence and when you've found it useful or times when you've had to use those sorts of skills and you both have examples; do you want to tell us about what happened to you?

JM: I was working with a family whilst I was very pregnant, and the girl I was supporting was pregnant too, and then she lost her baby during labour. I found it really difficult, because I was thinking about my own baby and labour, and I also thought how emotionally difficult it must be for her, but I didn't want her to have to cope with my emotions as well. I couldn't cry because I needed to be emotionally strong to support her, so I had to find my own strength. Her experience wasn't mine, so I needed to put my own feelings aside. Some practitioners at the time were quite negative about the way she was behaving afterwards, but actually it is about understanding. Unless you're in that situation, you don't know how you'd feel.

AH: So how did you cope with it? How did you get though dealing with that?

JM: I had to digest what had happened and deal with my own emotions first, because actually I was upset and I'd gone home feeling very emotional, but I think it's ok to do that as long as it's dealt with appropriately. It's important to find things that help you, like having a bath or reading a book, doing something positive to take your mind off it and not carrying it, without talking about it. My manager's really good, so having that conversation with her in supervision is helpful, and so is reflecting on my own decisions. I think supervision is important, to have a conversation, to make sure that what I did for that person then was right for them and that my own emotions hadn't interfered with the support.

AH: So, would you say you are an emotionally intelligent person?

JM: Yes, I think I am, and I think you learn as time goes on. There are so many experiences you come across daily, to do with families and maybe sometimes we do react in the wrong way, but it's about reflecting on what happened at the time. Reflecting before you go in, while you're there, and afterwards. Some situations might not even be an issue to me but to the family, they might be really important. We need to show them that we empathise with their situation and their feelings.

AH: Could you have got somebody else to deal with that situation?

JM: Yes, I could have done, but because I'd got a relationship with that parent, I felt that that wouldn't have been the right decision. If she'd seen a stranger, who said 'oh sorry, Jade can't come', how would she have felt about that? Rejected maybe. So, we need to be professional and think about the families first. As much as we are important, it's about what is right for them isn't it? I suppose there are people who couldn't have dealt with the emotion, and maybe that would have been the right decision for them because if they'd have broken down, it probably wouldn't have been a good idea for them to go out, but I think if you can manage it, you should. You know yourself don't you? And I think we have to take that responsibility and be mindful of the fact that if I am doing this, I need to do it as best I can.

AH: *Thank you, and then, Ruth, your example is totally different. This is about handling a client's aggression, isn't it?*

RA: *Yes, this was a woman that I worked with who'd got two children and she had been in the care system herself as a child and had been abused. She was struggling mentally to keep herself well and she would take cannabis to help her. She had two very young children and they were neglected. I would go round to the flat and they would be drinking out of bottles when they were much too old to be doing that or they were just in the bedroom playing; she wasn't entertaining them. She was known to be quite aggressive to professionals. I think it was a defence mechanism really, for her, because she was scared. She'd been in the system all her life and she didn't want it for her children but she also hadn't been given good role models herself. She just didn't know how to parent, so rather than shout help, she would be quite aggressive. The health visitor refused to go round, because she'd been threatened, but I realised that part of her aggression was just her way of coping. I wasn't used to being brought up in a shouty, sweary environment, but it was quite normal for her so her way of behaving towards us seemed ok.*

On one occasion, I went round and she wasn't in control of herself, she was having a bit of a meltdown. She was saying 'I expect you're going to leave now, I expect you're going to walk out because I've scared you and you're going to tell your manager', so I felt at that point that I had to put her feelings before my own and recognise that she didn't mean to be aggressive and threatening, it was just her way. I felt that I owed it to her to hear her and listen to her and not do what everybody else does and run off, then make a complaint about her and say 'we have to go in twos, I'm not going on my own to see her any more'. That gained some respect between us and she did become much more respectful of me and less aggressive because I think she realised that her threatening behaviour wasn't going to make me run away. Although, I struggled with it …

AH: *Did you?*

RA: *I really struggled with it, and I actually kept thinking 'how can I get out of here?' but I thought, no, this is something I need to do for her and also, the children were there and I felt that I needed to keep the environment as calm as I could because I recognise that it is damaging to the children's emotional well-being, and I didn't want that to happen. Unfortunately, in the end the children were removed; she gave them up voluntarily one summer, she just couldn't cope with them; she had tried. They were very successfully adopted, which was wonderful. I went to see them in foster care, which was lovely. They were both quite delayed but in foster care they really thrived and the little girl was like a different child. I couldn't believe it, she was talking and I noticed things about her that I hadn't noticed before, because I was able to see her without her being oppressed by the environment she'd been in.*

AH: So in both of those stories, you both had to be really strong, emotionally, didn't you?

RA: It was really hard because it's not something I'm used to, so I had to step out of my own comfort zone to manage a situation that doesn't come easily to me at all.

JM: I think, you need emotional intelligence and you need to feel that empathy with people, because if you're cold and you've got no compassion, it won't work.

RA: Well, a lot of the professionals just walked out, because it was too much, but I had to empathise with the fact that she needed to sound off. It was her defence mechanism and it seemed justifiable to her. Because of her upbringing, that was her way of managing situations.

AH: So how have you two developed these sorts of impressive skills? The empathy, the emotional strength, how have you done that? Have you had any training?

RA: I think it came quite naturally to me.

JM: I've done some training, but I think it comes more from experience. When I first started as a practitioner doing home visits, my eyes were really opened. I was brought up in a good environment and I remember thinking 'oh my God, that poor kid' in the early days. And things still do play on my mind; we all think, you know, about that child, or that family. I think experience and reflection are really important, and learning from other people, from case discussions. It's also about your own values, beliefs and morals, they all contribute to knowing what's right.

RA: As a child, my Mom always said to me, 'walk a mile in their shoes before you judge someone'. And that has resonated in me all of my life. I'm not to judge anybody until I've been there, seen it, listened to them, understood it and I can always find some empathy. I really struggle when people say 'oh for God's sake, they shouldn't have kids' – what right do they have to say that?

*JM: That is a key thing, isn't it, being non-judgemental, because we're not there to judge, we're there to see what we can do. Everyone's life is different, we need to look and think in a non-biased way. I don't think emotional intelligence is **a** skill, is it? It's a lot of skills that hang together that make you emotionally intelligent.*

RA: I do think it is innate, to be perfectly honest. I don't think that you can develop it. It develops with you, but I think you need to have it in the first place, to a degree.

JM: I think you have definitely got to have it and then it develops, because none of us are perfect are we, in practice? You never know what you're going to get with each experience. There's nothing the same; even if it's the same issue or situation, people, families deal with things differently.

RA: *So we need to be emotionally intelligent about how we're feeling, as well as how the person you're working with is feeling. You know yourself if you're managing it ok or not. There have been times when I've been offered cases and I've said no, it's not going to work for me and it's not going to work for them, it wouldn't be fair. If things have changed or if you recognise that you're not working well with a family, you have to say.*

JM: *Yes, definitely self-awareness is important, and self-regulation.*

Case study reflections

- Jade and Ruth have both given specific examples of situations they have been in at work. What are the skills they have used in these interactions?
- Which model of EI do Jade and Ruth's views coincide with?
- Jade believes that EI is not a discrete skill, but a range of skills. Do you agree? If so, list the skills that you think make up emotional intelligent in a person.
- Ruth tells us about 'walking a mile in a person's shoes' and not being judgemental. What are some of the different ways that people could react to hearing 'they shouldn't have kids'? Which skills would you need in order to challenge this view?
- Jade claims that self-awareness and self-regulation are important; reflect on how you personally manage this.

Conclusions

In this chapter, we have examined some models of EI and the benefits of using the skill in work with CYPF. The five characteristics of EI – self-awareness, self-regulation, motivation, empathy and social skills (Goleman, 2004) – are important in any role involving working with people, as they enable us to build effective working relationships. There is evidence that EI, although to some extent innate, can be developed through managing stress, practising assertiveness and building resilience.

In the two case studies in this chapter, there are examples of professionals using EI in their interactions with others in order to empathise and consider appropriate responses. By tuning into families, we can increase our understanding of them and their lives in a non-judgemental way. In addition to improving the way we work with others, EI also helps us to regulate our own emotional responses, promoting self-actualisation and fulfilment.

Further reading

Boddey, J. and Hodgkins, A. (2015). The importance of emotional intelligence in the management of a playwork setting. *Journal of Playwork Practice,* 2(1), 57–67.

- This journal article was written by James Boddey (case study – Chapter 1) and it discusses in more detail the benefits of emotional intelligence in a playwork setting.

Goleman, D. (2004). *Emotional Intelligence and Working with Emotional Intelligence.* London: Bloomsbury.

- This chapter has referenced Daniel Goleman many times; this book is his definitive work on emotional intelligence.

Hasson, G. (2014). *Emotional Intelligence: Managing Emotions to Make a Positive Impact on Your Life and Career.* West Sussex: Wiley and Sons.

- This book is a guide to emotional intelligence in your personal life; it gives advice on how to develop your own EI skills to enhance your life.

References

Ashby, F., Isen, A. and Turken, A. (1999). A neuropsychological theory of positive affect and its influence on cognition. *Psychological Review*, 106, 529–550.

Boddey, J. and Hodgkins, A. (2015). The importance of emotional intelligence in the management of a playwork setting. *Journal of Playwork Practice,* 2(1), 57–67.

Davies, M., Stankov, L. and Roberts, R. (1998). Emotional intelligence: In search of an elusive construct. *Journal of Personality and Social Psychology*, 75, 989–1015.

Dolev, N. and Leshem, S. (2016). Developing emotional intelligence competence among teachers. *Teacher Development: An International Journal of Teachers' Professional Development*, 21(1), 21–39.

Dozier, J. (2010). *The Weeping, the Window, the Way*. Oklahoma, USA: Tate Publishing.

Goleman, D. (1996). *Emotional Intelligence: Why It Can Matter More Than IQ*. London: Bloomsbury.

Goleman, D. (1998). The emotional intelligence of leaders. *Leader to Leader*, 1998(10), 20–26.

Goleman, D. (2004). *Emotional Intelligence and Working with Emotional Intelligence*. London: Bloomsbury.

Grant, A. (2014). The dark side of emotional intelligence. *The Atlantic*. Available at: https://www.theatlantic.com/health/archive/2014/01/the-dark-side-of-emotional-intelligence/282720/ [Accessed 11 August 2019].

Grant, L., Kinman, G. and Alexander, K. (2014). What's all this talk about emotion? Developing emotional intelligence in social work students. *Social Work Education*, 33(7), 874–889.

Lightfoot, S. and Frost, D. (2015). The professional identity of early years educators in England: Implications for a transformative approach to continuing professional development. *Professional Development in Education*, 41(2), 401–418.

Matthews, G., Zeidner, M. and Roberts, R. D. (2002). *Emotional Intelligence: Science and Myth*. Massachusetts: MIT Press.

Mayer, J., Salovey, P. and Caruso, D. (2008). Emotional intelligence: New ability or eclectic traits? *American Psychologist,* 63(6), 503–517.

Mayer, J. D., Caruso, D. R. and Salovey, P. (2016). The ability model of emotional intelligence: Principles and updates. *Emotion Review*, 8(4), 290–300.

MIND. (2013). *How to Deal with Anger*. Available at: https://www.mind.org.uk/information-support/types-of-mental-health-problems/anger/managing-outbursts/#.Wwwg_ZFyAg [Accessed 11 August 2019].

Petrides, K. (2010). Trait emotional intelligence theory. *Industrial and Organizational Psychology*, 3(2), 136–139.

Petrides, K., Pita, R. and Kokkinaki, F. (2007). The location of trait emotional intelligence in personality factor space. *British Journal of Psychology*, 98, 273–289.

Reeve, C. (2003). *Nothing Is Impossible*. London: Arrow.

Salovey, P. and Mayer, J. (1990). Emotional intelligence. *Imagination, Cognition, and Personality*, 9(3), 185–221.

Salovey, P. and Sluyter, D. (eds) (1997). *Emotional Development and Emotional Intelligence: Educational implications* (pp. 3–34). New York: Harper Collins.

Schneider, T., Lyons, J. and Khazon, S. (2013). Emotional intelligence and resilience. *Personality and Individual Differences,* 55, 909–913.

7 THE COMMUNICATING AND COLLABORATING PRACTITIONER

Chapter outcomes

This chapter will enable readers to explore the following concepts:
- The vital role of communication and collaboration in working with children and families
- The importance of working in partnership with parents/carers, children and young people
- The value of integrated working across professional and agency boundaries to support children, young people and families
- The implications for practitioners arising from this chapter

Introduction

Being able to communicate effectively is one of the most important skills to have, not just for practice but also for life. However, one could argue that communicating with others is more than just a skill; rather it is a fundamental human need. In other words, it is the need to connect with others, to form relationships, to understand and to be understood. Those of us who have ever observed tiny infants, whether in practice or in family life, will recognise that even in the earliest days, weeks and months, a baby is communicating with her caregivers, making eye contact, cooing and crying, smiling or babbling. Becoming a communicator, therefore, is an innate ability, but like so many other capabilities, it is also something that can be nurtured and developed. As a practitioner, you will need to communicate effectively with a range of different individuals, whether those be children, young people, parents and carers, colleagues or partners from other agencies. Successful communication will involve tuning in to others and adapting your communication style accordingly. Importantly, we must remember that communication is a two-way process, demanding listening as well as speaking. As Susan Cain, author of *Quiet*, pointedly observes, 'We have two ears and one mouth, and we should use them proportionally'.

In the context of children and family work, it is also crucial to recognise the importance of working in partnership with others in order to achieve positive outcomes. Whilst it is important to work with colleagues and other professionals, establishing meaningful partnerships with children and young people and their parents/carers is paramount. Research identifies the importance of openness, trust, respect, shared goals and effective communication as essential elements of collaboration. Good partnership working, then, will require time, commitment and prioritising, but can deliver far better results.

The importance of communication

The word 'communication' has its origins within the Latin word *communicare*, to share or to make common. It is, by its very nature, a social process. The *Oxford English Dictionary* defines communication thus:

> Communication, n. The imparting or exchanging of information by speaking, writing, or using some other medium. The successful conveying or sharing of ideas and feelings.

Whilst this definition gives us a useful starting point, it is, perhaps, oversimplistic, in the sense that it does not recognise that communication is affected by the context and environment in which it takes place. Our past experiences, cultural terms of reference, differences in perception and physical or emotional disabilities may all affect the meaning that another person attaches to our words or actions.

Firstly, it is important to note that there are many forms of communication, and that these need to be matched both to the situation and to the audience. An important distinction to make is between formal and informal communication, and both are equally important for the practitioner. The diagram below shows some of the differences between formal and informal communication (Table 7.1).

Table 7.1 Formal and informal communication

Formal Communication	Informal Communication
Based on formal relationships between people	Mainly used with people you know well: peers, family friends
Emphasis on formal language	Uses casual language. May contain abbreviations
Oral or written (meetings, presentations, reports)	Mainly oral but could include emails
Emphasis on structure	Tends to be spontaneous and unstructured
Important for situations which need to be documented and for there to be a single agreed document to work to	Important for building relationships and engaging others

Just as we talk of 'situational leadership' (see Chapter 6), so it is important to recognise that communication is itself context-specific and situational. Within most professional relationships, there will be occasions when both formal and informal communication are necessary. So, for example, a manager may rely upon informal communication during meetings with staff to agree a vision or get ideas for a new project. However, during a staff meeting, minutes will be taken and agreed, and a staff appraisal session will be formalised through its documentation. The distinction may be even more nuanced when working with children, young people and families. Formal language and forms of documentation may well act as a barrier to engagement, perhaps particularly in cases of families who are from 'marginalised' communities, and so this will need to be carefully managed.

Also, it is important to recognise that not all communication is verbal. Non-verbal cues, as well as intonation and underlying emotional tone will all play a role in how our words are understood (Mehrabian and Wiener, 1967). Studies have suggested that non-verbal communication accounts for a large percentage of how a message is understood. One classic communication study (Mehrabian and Wiener, 1967) suggested that only 7 per cent of communication is made up of the actual words spoken, whereas body language and tone of voice account for 55 per cent and 38 per cent respectively. It is important to note, however, that body language and tone will have elements that are socially and culturally constructed. Rogoff et al. (2003) identified that non-verbal communication (e.g. gestures) can have very precise meanings, and there are often nuances across cultures in relation to how they may be understood. Moreover, certain non-verbal interactions, such as intense or prolonged eye contact, can be given completely different meanings in different cultures (Akechi et al., 2013). Awareness of non-verbal communication in self and others is an important aspect of being an effective communicator (Willis and Todorov, 2006) However, it is crucial to note that whilst we understand that others may well make assumptions about us based on non-verbal aspects such as our clothes or mannerisms, it is equally important to ensure that as practitioners, we do not make assumptions about those we are working with on the basis of external expressions like dress or hairstyle. Hence, whilst non-verbal communication is undoubtedly an important aspect of how we communicate, we must be careful to avoid stereotypical conjectures.

Bearing this in mind, the following diagram shows possible aspects of non-verbal communication, all of which may act to develop or inhibit positive communication with others (Figure 7.1).

Being aware of the subtle ways in which communication occurs allows us to ensure that our words are congruent with the other signals we are emitting. Moreover, it enables us to 'read' others' non-verbal signals and adjust our interactions to enable a better outcome.

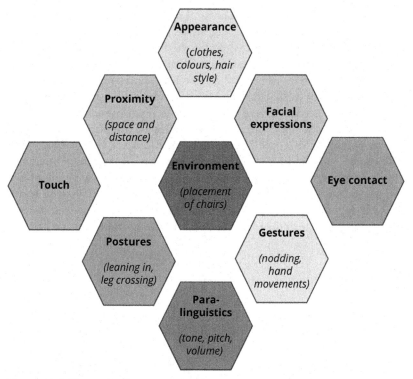

Figure 7.1 Non-verbal communication

Being an effective communicator

As we previously identified, excellent communication is concerned with listening as well as speaking. Listening is more than simply hearing the words. Rather, listening is intentional, and involves both cognitive and emotional engagement. It involves removing distractions, hearing the words, tuning into non-verbal cues, processing meaning and checking that you have understood. Listening in this way has been described as active listening (Rogers and Farson, 1957). However, it is important that active listening is not simply employed as a technique: instead, as Rogers and Farson are swift to point out, it needs to be grounded in the beliefs and values of the listener, otherwise it will present as unauthentic. Further, they contend, the basis for active listening is respect (Figure 7.2).

This kind of active listening requires commitment and practice. It is not easy and can be particularly difficult in the context of busy workloads and competing demands. A number of studies have explored the barriers to active listening and found that they are numerous. Any kind of distraction, whether physical or emotional, can act as a barrier; similarly, we can be too quick to anticipate or prejudge what is about to be said. Taylor, Nicolle and

Maguire (2013), writing in the context of nursing practice, also identify differences in language or cultural associations as potential barriers. Moreover, they assert, having insufficient time for the listening exercise can result in listening being tokenistic rather than authentic, meaningful and attuned.

A part-time student who was also a family support worker once suggested to me that the key to effective and active listening lay in the preparation. It was, she argued, about carving out the time to listen (whether to parents or to staff); it was also about creating a conducive environment, switching off devices and ensuring a lack of interruptions. Moreover, it was about being deliberately and mindfully present in the moment of listening. For anyone who has ever been subjected to a rushed supervision session or an unsatisfactory consultation with a professional, such respectful and purposeful listening will be seen as a rare gift that can help boost self-esteem, increase motivation and contribute to positive professional relationships and partnership working.

Figure 7.2 Active listening skills

Listening to children, young people and families

Regardless of your role and discipline within the children and families' work-force, it is likely that your practice will place a high value on the concept of 'voice' and listening to children and parents. In education, we often talk about 'the child's voice', notwithstanding the danger inherent within this concept of assuming that children share a homogeneous voice. Singer (2014) rightly points out that viewing children (or indeed parents/families) in this way can result in tokenistic or superficial attempts to listen to their voice. As Murray (2019) maintains, 'If we do not listen actively and attend to each child's voice, we convey to the child and others that we do not value the child's perspective, and ultimately, that we do not value the child.' The result of this can be a lack of engagement. This is equally the case with parents and families. If we believe that it is important to actively engage the voices of children and families, both within provision and interventions and also within decision making, then, as Murray asserts, several preconditions need to be met:

- We must first define what we mean by voice

- We must find suitable ways of listening to what children and parents have to say

- We must find ways to respond to parents and children, showing that their views have been listened to and taken seriously

- We need to advocate for those views within the broader policy agenda, to facilitate changes in perspective that value the views of those most affected by such policy decisions.

A privileged example of this was afforded to myself and a university colleague recently, when we were able to accompany a group of children from kinship families to give evidence to a cross-party parliamentary committee considering the needs of such families. A conducive environment was created for children to talk openly and honestly about their lives and about the challenges they face. The politicians listened attentively as the children and young people artic-ulated their experiences and the measures that might help. At the end of the session, the chairperson of the group summarised their discussion, showing clearly that their voices, both individual and collective, had been heard. I have no doubt that those present in the meeting will do all possible to work for posi-tive change to support these young people and those like them across the coun-try, but it remains to be seen whether the system is sufficiently flexible to see these views taken forward into demonstrable policy change.

The following diagram explores some basic principles for communicating with children and families (Figure 7.3).

In the following case study, we hear from Rebecca Thomas, Programme Manager for Save the Children, Wales. Her role is to work in partnership with other agencies, particularly schools, to develop supportive professional relationships and build capacity in order to transform the way children are

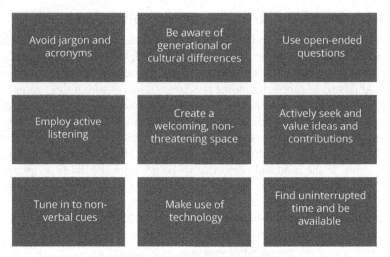

Figure 7.3 Communicating with children and families

supported in early years. Within Rebecca's work there is a strong focus upon improving outcomes for those children who are deemed vulnerable, and therefore most likely to fail to meet their potential.

Case Study: Rebecca Thomas – The importance of communication and collaboration

My role is really all about building relationships and working with others. In Save the Children, we want to transform the lives and life chances of children in this country – but we can't do this alone. We need to work in genuine part-nership with policy makers, parents and practitioners in other agencies to ensure we can give every child the best start in life. We do not seek to work in isolation; instead, our aim is to embed services into existing services and partnerships.

We talk a lot about our role as 'convening'. In other words, we are all about bringing people together, linking people with others and resources and ideas. I do not see myself as an expert, instead I am an enabler. In a school I visited recently, there was a new headteacher who was really pas-sionate about improving outcomes for disadvantaged children. I was able to send him resources to show what was out there, acting as a resource investi-gator and helping to make things happen. I do not think you can underesti-mate the importance of networking, of making time to meet, talk and explore opportunities. It is also crucial to see parents as partners and to nurture and develop their involvement, and to foster their engagement. I believe strongly in spending time with parents to help them to understand how they can work in partnership with the setting to help achieve better outcomes for their children.

I am genuinely interested in people. I am a massive believer in co-production – creating a shared agenda. I am passionate about helping parents to develop supportive home-learning environments. My values are about bringing people together, learning together. I enjoy working with others who may bring different knowledge and skills but share my passion and have a similar outlook and values. In partnership work, it is important to understand your role, and where you complement the roles of others. It is important to be clear about who you are and not try being who you are not. It is also important to recognise the strengths of others, and also the constraints they work with. Everyone is doing their best, but there may be challenges they are facing, like local systems change or funding difficulties. It is important to find people who want to work together to improve outcomes for children. We need a willingness to be flexible and adaptive to the situation. I have also learned the importance of reflection – creating space for reflection and allowing for creative problem solving. In any partnership working, good communication is vital. It is also important to know the community in which you are working. What are the community assets? What are the challenges? Take home learning, one of the challenges is parents' prior negative experiences of school. By the time their child reaches Year 3 they do not feel capable of supporting their child's learning. That is when intergenerational cycles kick in and it becomes really challenging. As someone working around this agenda, understanding the challenges is crucial and you do it through speaking with people, recognising your own assumptions and challenging them. Finally, in partnership working to tackle child poverty, I think it is so important to have optimism, to exude hope and to hold a positive view of others, recognising where skills can be built and developed for individuals and communities. I have learned so much about integrated working from this role. I have moved from a more traditional management role into convening, creating partnerships. It is less directive. It has got me thinking about power. My style has changed to be more collaborative and democratic – managing from within. I see it as having clear, shared goals to achieve. It is about communicating a vision – considering barriers and enablers, working as a team to overcome issues. Keeping a strategic head helps solve operational issues. It is about allowing and welcoming challenge, and creating space to be creative and reflexive. I also think it is important to recognise that you are working around long-term issues – investments in seeing people develop and grow. There are fewer quick wins, but ultimately this is more fulfilling than simply hitting targets. It is that reflective approach that enables us to be more strategic. What is important is building capacity in others, and developing a community of practice.

> **Case study reflections**
> - How does Rebecca collaborate with others within her role?
> - What are the key aspects of partnership working that Rebecca views as important?
> - Rebecca discusses the idea of 'convening'. Is this a helpful concept in understanding collaboration? How do you 'convene' within your current role?
> - What does Rebecca view as some of the benefits and challenges that parents experience in relation to working in partnership with schools?

Collaboration and partnership working

The case study raises some interesting points about the importance of collaboration with others. Partnership working brings together individuals, organisations or professional disciplines in order to share expertise and resources and work towards a defined shared outcome. Partnerships may be formal or informal, long-term or short-term. Whilst the terms collaboration and partnership working are often used without precision and interchangeably, Carnwell and Carson (2009) are at pains to argue that the two concepts are distinct. Collaboration is seen as a looser and less formal arrangement, which is non-hierarchical and values knowledge and expertise above role or title. Partnership working, by contrast, shares the elements of teamwork and sharing resources and a common goal, but may also be characterised by accountability and formal governance arrangements.

Regardless of these distinctions, both concepts emphasise reciprocity and joint endeavour and also prioritise service-user involvement. The benefits of working together in this way are numerous. However, there are also a multiplicity of challenges. These are summarised in the following diagram (Table 7.2).

Communities of practice as a tool for collaboration

Etienne Wenger developed the notion of the Community of Practice (CoP), defining this as a group of people with a shared interest or profession (Wenger, 1998) A CoP provides an opportunity, whether physical or virtual, to share information, ideas, experience and learning, in a way that facilitates personal and professional development. It thus has three important facets: a domain (or defined body of knowledge, a community (essential for sharing learning), and practice (the focus around which the community shares and develops knowledge). Communities of Practice, then, have the potential to contribute to quality improvement in organisations through the generation

Table 7.2 Benefits and challenges of collaboration

Potential Benefits	Potential Challenges
It is not within the gift of one single agency or professional discipline to meet the needs of an individual of family	Communication – need for information-sharing protocols, often agencies use different technologies or systems
Avoids duplication and addresses gaps in provision	May be time-consuming
Makes better use of resources and expertise	Differing professional cultures, constraints, language
Fosters better professional understanding, relationships and respect	Geography – if not co-located
Engages the family	Lack of coherence of aims, objectives, roles and accountabilities
Potential for improved outcomes	In some cases, partnership working is advocated even where it makes more sense to provide a single agency response

of new ideas, in order to identify solutions to challenges and to support the identification, evaluation and replication of good practice. An additional benefit of CoPs lies within their potential to enhance individuals' continuous professional development and reflective practice.

Collaborating with children and families

Participation Works (2010) defines children and young people's participation thus:

> Participation is a process where someone influences decisions about their lives and this leads to change.

Hence, participation is more than just 'allowing children a voice', it also concerns the way in which children's contributions are heard and acted upon.

Hart (1992) developed a ladder of participation (or indeed non-participation) to consider the extent to which organisations sought and acted upon the participation of children and young people. The rungs on his ladder ranged from situations where children's participation was manipulated, used as window dressing only or tokenised (rungs 1–3), through information and assignation, consultation (rungs 4–5), to more meaningful participation in adult-led contexts or with children initiating and leading (rungs 6 and 7) and finally to rung 8 which epitomises genuine co-construction within a respectful, democratic and equal relationship.

There is evidence from research that even very young children can be meaningfully engaged in decision making. Clark and Moss (2011) developed the innovative Mosaic Approach, a multi-method framework for listening to children. Inherent within this approach is a recognition of diversity of expression and an offer of a variety of enticing ways for children to express themselves (e.g. verbally, through artwork, photographs or made objects). This multifaceted process enables adults to create a rich picture of children's perspectives. The approach is not without its critics, with some arguing that the process is time-consuming and that despite the importance of dialogue and conferencing between adults and children, the findings are open to too much adult inference and interpretation. However, the creativity of the approach can allow for interesting data be collected which provides insight into children's perspectives and could have potential for replicating this approach beyond very young children, to engage older siblings and parents. It is easy to imagine how such engagement can be very powerful at an individual-setting level.

However, it is important that young people's voices are heard at all levels of decision making, including on very strategic issues. ENOC (the Europe-wide network of Children's Commissioners) has developed a European Network of Young Advisors (ENYA) which enables young people to come together from across Europe in order to express their views regarding their rights, make their ideas heard and develop joint recommendations for decision makers. Focusing upon topical issues which affect young people's lives (such as young people in a digital environment), such initiatives offer ways for children and young people's voices to be heard and acted upon. The extent to which the recommendations from such initiatives are actually implemented will determine whether they go beyond tokenism (Hart, 1992).

The following case study was written by a speech and language therapist who is also a lecturer, Hazel Richards. Within the case study, she firstly articulates the context and value base within which she operates. She then goes on to explore a critical incident, which identifies the importance of collaboration and integrated working.

Case Study: Hazel Richards – Theoretical explanations of a critical incident

This vignette uses a case study to consider the contribution of Speech and Language Therapy in an example of collaborative working. Speech and Language Therapists (SLTs) provide treatment, support and care for children and adults who have difficulties with communication, or with eating, drinking and swallowing (RCSLT, 2019). Joint working is central to this, since multiple skills, interactions and contexts are involved with these difficulties. Speech and Language Therapy can therefore be regarded as a 'connected specialism' (Norwich, 1996, p. 100), in that what is specialised about it is also interdependent on others (i.e.

other professionals and indeed children and families). *A holistic approach, that recognises the importance of the whole and the interdependence of its parts, in terms of the individual, is therefore preferable. Indeed, connectedness, supportiveness and working with and valuing difference mark productive, holistic pedagogies (Hayes et al., 2006). Furthermore, provision that is adjusted, that extends to principles of respect, care and compassion (Boylan and Woolsey, 2015) and has a holistic conceptualisation of well-being (Bottery et al., 2012) is a necessary part of additional needs provision.*

Multidisciplinary teams involve personnel working for different institutions and organisations, who have separate finances, purposes and values. This contributes to the co-existence of different understandings and practices within the team. *Current legislation and policy (Children and Families Act* 2014, *SEND Code of Practise, DfE and DoH,* 2015) *include a mandate for increased collaboration, driven by the competing rationales of holistic support and cost-effective, efficient provision (Bernardes et al., 2015; Curran et al., 2017). However, capacity issues, exacerbated by economic cuts, create challenges for collaboration, including different priorities, resource limitations, training cuts and staff turnover (DCSF, 2008). Moreover, the market economy means agencies can be competing rather that co-operating (McConkey, 2010; Ekins, 2015).*

Although there is no comprehensive model of the factors that influence the success of joint working (Salmon, 2004), time and trust are central to the 'complex alliances' involved (Allan and Youdell, 2015, p. 7). The work of SLTs involves 'mediating between different ways of being in the world' with Butler (2019) coining the term 'pastoral labour' to capture this (p. 1). This has links to research demonstrating that professionals are driven by altruism and that they place children's well-being at the centre of their practice. It also coheres with the increased focus on pupil voice (Bernardes et al., 2015; DfE and DoH, 2015) which has long been at the heart of SLTs' work (Gallagher and Chiat, 2009).

A working knowledge of processes and systems, and knowledge of other roles and personnel, are also known to enhance collaborative working (Salmon, 2004; Lindsay et al., 2008). Since education, and language and communication skills, are so mutually involved, it would make sense for initial teacher training, and the education of professionals such as SLTs, to include more of each 'domain' in their course of study. Indeed, collaboration is enhanced by mutual regard and positive relationships (Burton and Goodman, 2011), with these being central to the promotion and development of interaction that is the crux of the SLT role.

Critical incident

The next section provides the context and description of a critical incident, followed by questions to allow the specific issues, and consequences of these, to emerge. Critical incidents are significant moments that act as 'turning points' in that they contribute to personal, institutional or 'social phenomenon' change (Tripp, 2012, p. 24). At the time of this incident I had been working as a SLT for

18 years. Significant changes to service delivery in terms of case load size, resourcing and staffing, and institutional reorganisation had taken place during these years. As a result, certain areas of the caseload had been prioritised (e.g. early years, to give precedence to early identification and intervention), in comparison to others. Changes had also taken place in my working life, in that I now worked part-time due to family obligations, and was responsible countywide for supporting colleagues with complex cases. That is, individuals whose speech, language and communication needs and/or eating drinking and swallowing difficulties involved numerous, sometimes difficult, issues.

As an experienced SLT with specialist skills, including dysphagia (eating, drinking and swallowing difficulties), alternative and augmentative communication, neuro-developmental disorders (including, for example, specific learning, social communication, attentional and attachment difficulties) and acquired brain injury, I was allocated Sam (pseudonym), on his transfer from hospital to community care. Sam, a sociable, sporty 12-year-old, had sustained a significant head injury as a result of a cycling accident, and had spent six weeks in specialist hospital provision, first in intensive care, then in a multidisciplinary rehabilitation ward. On discharge to the community, Sam had a hemiplegia (weakness down one side of the body), was on a thickened modified diet due to eating, drinking and swallowing difficulties, needed assistance and adaptations to support his personal care, experienced fatigue and epilepsy, and had memory, processing and concentration difficulties, as well as difficulties understanding and using written and spoken language.

Many professionals, including paediatricians, physiotherapists, occupational therapists, educational and clinical psychologists, peripatetic learning support teachers and SLTs, were therefore involved in his care. Due to neuroplasticity being higher in younger ages (the brain's ability to adapt by reorganising its networks of nerve cells to compensate or recover), and recognition of the benefits of early, intense rehabilitation to outcomes (Carson, 2019), including their cost-effectiveness in the long term, Sam needed a level of therapy input higher than that provided by the SLT service specified for children of statutory school age attending mainstream settings (which was one visit per term). In addition to this, Sam's difficulties meant that sustained sessions were contra-indicated and that liaison with others was a priority to ensure a joined-up approach to his rehabilitation. Also, his current placement at home meant that his parents, who were separated, were the principle implementers of therapy and care programmes.

I therefore argued his case with my SLT line managers, securing weekly visits for the first half-term, followed by half-termly visits, and twice-weekly visits by an SLT assistant, with liaison after every visit, until his return to school. During this time, joint visits were also made with the physiotherapist, whom I had worked with on other cases, and with the learning support teacher to ensure a consistent approach was taken. Indeed, the learning support teacher had a higher level of contact so was able to incorporate some of Sam's SLT targets and approaches into her sessions. Normal eating, drinking and swallowing skills were regained a fortnight after discharge and Sam made gradual improvements with his understanding and use of written and spoken language. Sam and his family then expressed their desire for a quick return to school, so a phased return was initiated after a term. This had implications for his reha-bilitation in that SLT therapy was reduced to the mainstream model level of input, which was not adequate to support contact with the range of staff Sam was involved with in high school, and all professionals had to consider the other demands that Sam was now under including the fatigue he experienced after a full day of concentration. Input in the early stages of Sam's return to school therefore involved support and advice about Sam's care to his parents. Sam has experienced persisting difficulties with processing, higher level-comprehension and some motor skills and subsequently he attended a further education set-ting, where he trained to be an outdoor activity support worker.

Case study reflections

Consider the following questions in order to explore the multiple fac-ets present in this scenario:
- What connected specialisms were involved in Sam's care?
- Which two conflicting mandates affected Sam's rehabilitation?
- What preference did Sam and his parents express (parent and pupil voice)?
  a) What do you think motivated this choice?
  b) What possible impact did this have for his rehabilitation?

- What evidence of pastoral labour is there?
- Is there any evidence of
  a) System knowledge and the impact of systems?
  b) The existence/contribution of working relationships?

1. Do any of the factors in this case surprise you? Take time to reflect on the conflict this may create for the values, principles and focus of Speech and Language Therapy (and other professionals' practice).
2. What would have improved this scenario, in your view? (Consider both macro- and micro-level factors.)

Conclusion: What are the implications for practitioners arising from this chapter?

This chapter has considered the importance of communication and collabo-ration. Both are viewed as important skills and attributes for the practitioner. Positive communication and active listening are presented as essential com-ponents of developing trustful and constructive relationships with children, parents/carers and colleagues. Moreover, collaboration with others, despite its many challenges, can prove an effective way of delivering improved out-comes for children and families.

Further reading

Clark, A. (2005). Listening to and involving young children: A review of research and practice. *Early Child Development and Care*, 175(6), 489–505.

- This explores approaches to listening to and involving children in the early years. Some of the approaches explored can be applied in middle childhood and beyond.

There are a wealth of online resources supporting young people's participation. Here are some examples:

- www.youthscotland.org.uk
- www.youthworkwales.org.uk
- www.ukyouth.org
- www.youthaction.org
- www.ukyouthparliament.org.uk

Walker, G. (2018). *Working Together for Children: A Critical Introduction to Multi-agency Working*. London: Bloomsbury.

- This accessible textbook provides an overview of the importance of working across organisational boundaries to improve outcomes for children, young people and families

References

Akechi, H., Senju, A., Uibo, H., Kikuchi, Y., Hasegawa, T. and Hietanen, J. K. (2013). Attention to eye contact in the West and East: Autonomic responses and evaluative ratings. *PloS One*. https://doi.org/10.1371/journal.pone.0059312. Available at: https://journals.plos.org/plosone/article?id=10.1371/journal.pone.0059312 [Accessed 7 August 2019].

Allan, J. and Youdell, D. (2015). Ghostings, materialisations and flows in Britain's special educational needs and disability assemblage. *Discourse: Studies in the Cultural Politics of Education*, 37(1), 70–82.

Bernardes, E., Shaw, B., Menzies, L. and Baars, S. (2015). *Joining the Dots: Have Recent Reforms Worked for Those with SEND?* Driver Youth Trust [online]. Available from: https://www.lkmco.org/wp-content/uploads/2015/10/DYT_JoinTheDotsReportOctober2015-2.pdf [Accessed 11 April 2019].

Bottery, M., Wright, N. and James, S. (2012). Personality, moral purpose, and the leadership of an education for sustainable development. *Education*, 40(3), 3–13.

Boylan, M. and Woolsey, I. (2015). Teacher education for social justice: Mapping identity spaces. *Teaching and Teacher Education*, 46, 62–71.

Burton, D. and Goodman, R (2011). Perspectives of SENCos and support staff in England on their roles, relationships and capacity to support inclusive practices for students with behavioural, emotional and social difficulties. *Pastoral Care in Education,* 29(2), 133–149.

Butler, C. (2019). Working the 'wise' in speech and language therapy: Evidence-based practice, bioploitics and 'pastoral labour'. *Social Science and Medicine*,

230, 1–8. Available at: https://doi.org/10.1016/j.socscimed.2019.03.038 [Accessed 22 May 2019].

Carnwell, R. and Carson, A. (2009). The concepts of partnership and collaboration. In Carnwell, R. and Buchanan, J. (eds.) *Effective Practice in Health, Social Care and Criminal Justice: A Partnership Approach*. Maidenhead: Open University Press.

Carson, A. (2019). Early, intense rehabilitation helps recovery after serious traumatic head injury. *National Institute of Health Research*. Available at: doi:https://doi.org/10.3310/signal-000604 [Accessed 22 May 2019].

Children and Families Act 2014. Available at: http://www.legislation.gov.uk/ukpga/2014/6/contents/enacted [Accessed 11 April 2019].

Clark, A. and Moss, P. (2011). *Listening to Young Children: The Mosaic Approach*, 2nd ed. London: National Children's Bureau.

Curran, H., Mortimore, T. and Riddell, R. (2017). Special educational needs and disabilities reforms 2014: SENCos' perspectives of the first six months. *British Journal of Special Education*, 44(1), 46–64.

Department for Children, Schools and Families. (2008). *2020 Children and Young People's Workforce Strategy: Report of the Children's Workforce Practitioners Workshops*. Nottingham: DCSF Publications. Available from: https://webarchive.nationalarchives.gov.uk/20130321051911/https://www.education.gov.uk/publications/eOrderingDownload/CYP_Workforce-Strategy_Report.pdf [Accessed 12 April 2019].

Department for Education and Department of Health. (2015). *Special Educational Needs and Disability Code of Practice: 0 to 25 Years. Statutory Guidance for Organisations Which Work with and Support Children and Young People Who Have Special Educational Needs or Disabilities*. Available from: https://www.gov.uk/government/publications/send-code-of-practice-0-to-25 [Accessed 12 April 2019].

Ekins, A. (2015). *The Changing Face of Special Educational Needs*. London: Routledge.

Gallagher, A. and Chiat, S. (2009). Evaluation of speech and language therapy interventions for pre-school children with specific language impairment: A comparison of outcomes following specialist intensive, nursery-based and no intervention. *International Journal of Language and Communication Disorders*, 44, 616– 638.

Hart, R. (1992). *Children's Participation*. Florence, Italy: UNICEF International Child Development Centre.

Hayes, D., Mills, M., Christine, P. and Lingard, B. (2006). *Teachers and Schooling Making a Difference: Productive Pedagogies, Assessment and Performance*. Sydney: Allen and Unwin.

Lindsay, G., Desforges, M., Dockrell, J., Law, J., Peacey, N. and Beecham, J. (2008). *The Effective and Efficient Use of Resources in Services for Children and Young People with Speech, Language and Communication Needs*. Monograph. Nottingham: DCSF-RW053. Available at: http://wrap.warwick.ac.uk/45063/ [Accessed 3 June 2019].

McConkey, R. (2010). Promoting friendships and developing social networks. In Grant, M. G. and Ramcharan, P. (eds.) *Learning Disability: A Life Cycle Approach to Valuing People*, 2nd ed. Maidenhead: Open University Press, pp. 329–341.

Mehrabian, A. and Wiener, M. (1967). Decoding of inconsistent communications. *Journal of Personality and Social Psychology,* 6(1), 109–114.

Murray, J. (2019). Hearing young children's voices. *International Journal of Early Years Education*, 27(1), 1–5.

Norwich, B. (1996). Special education or education for all: Connective specialisation and ideological impurity. *British Journal of Special Education*, 23(3), 100–104.

Rogers, C. and Farson, R. E. (1957). *Active Listening*. Chicago: Industrial Relations Center, University of Chicago, p. 25; also in Newman, R. G., Danzinger, M. A. and Cohen, M. (1987). *Communication in Business Today*. Washington, DC: Houghton Mifflin.

Rogoff, B., Paradise, R., Arauz, R. M., Correa-Chavez, M. and Angelillo, C. (2003). Firsthand learning through intent participation. *Annual Review of Psychology,* 54(1), 175–203.

Royal College of Speech and Language Therapists. (2019). *Speech and Language Therapy*. Available at: https://www.rcslt.org/speech-and-language-therapy [Accessed 22 May 2019].

Salmon, G. (2004). Multi-agency collaboration: The challenges for CAMHS. *Child and Adolescent Health*, 9(4), 156–161.

Singer, A. (2014). Voices heard and unheard: A Scandinavian perspective. *Journal of Social Welfare and Family Law*, 36(4), 381–391.

Taylor, S. P., Nicolle, C. and Maguire, M. (2013). Cross-cultural communication barriers in healthcare. *Nursing Standard*, 27(31), 35–43.

Tripp, D. (2012). *Critical Incidents in Teaching: Developing Professional Judgement*. London: Routledge.

Wenger, E. (1998). *Communities of Practice: Learning, Meaning and Identity*. Cambridge: Cambridge University Press.

Willis, J. and Todorov, A. (2006). First impressions: Making up your mind after 100-ms exposure to a face. *Psychological Science*, 17(1), 592–598.

8 THE CREATIVE AND PROBLEM-SOLVING PRACTITIONER

Chapter outcomes

This chapter will enable practitioners to engage with the following:
- Examining creative thinking and how this skill enhances work with children, young people and families
- Developing solution-focused approaches to empower others
- Analysing transferable skills for today's workforce

Introduction

Creative problem-solving skills are becoming more and more important in today's workplaces, as we progress further into the twenty-first century. We can only guess what the world will be like in a few decades' time and, as we have discussed already in this book, we need to develop skills that are flexible and transferable, preparing us as best we can for the future. In working with children, young people and families, this is particularly important, as services and provisions are changing and developing at a rapid rate. Cuts in finance and services have led to practitioners needing to think up creative solutions to problems. The NHS is currently struggling to cope with funding cuts (Campbell, 2018). The latest DfE figures show that local authority spending on early years services has fallen by more than £650 million since 2010 (Morton, 2017), and in social services, there has been a 25 per cent cut in spending on children's services since 2010 (NCB, in Carson and Stephenson, 2017). Although ultimately this cannot go on indefinitely, these austerity measures have led to staff having to devise short-term creative solutions to overcrowding and to lack of equipment and resources.

In this chapter, some of the ideas around creative thinking and problem solving will be examined. How can we become more creative in our thinking? What motivates us to make a change? How can we use the full range of skills we have developed throughout our careers? A case study detailed within this chapter illustrates some of these ideas in practice; in particular, a solution-focused approach to problem solving within a community. Steve

Jobs, entrepreneur and co-founder of Apple, used creative approaches throughout his career and saw creativity and intuition as essential in today's technological world. He famously said: 'Creativity is just connecting things. When you ask creative people how they did something, they feel a little guilty because they didn't really do it; they just saw something. It seemed obvious to them after a while. That's because they were able to connect experiences they've had and synthesise new things' (Wolf, 1996).

Examining creative thinking

Creativity, to the majority of people, is concerned with art, with creating something tangible out of media such as paint, textiles, clay, music, etc. However, creativity in the context of this chapter is concerned with creative thinking. Ingledew describes creative thinking as 'the process of generating the ideas that make breakthroughs possible. These breakthroughs can lead to solutions to seemingly irresolvable problems or can bring completely new things into existence' (2016, p. 7). In an interesting study by Zedelius and Schooler (2015, p. 1), they identify two stereotypes of creative people; those who exhibit high levels of concentration and attention, and those who are volatile, with 'scattered minds'. There is some debate over what makes one person more creative than another and 'mindfulness vs. mind-wandering' are opposing ideas within the debate. Creative ideas can be developed by concentration on the task at hand, or they can spring forth randomly when we are least expecting it! Have you ever suddenly had a 'eureka' moment whilst trying to get to sleep at night? Or whilst driving the car? Working with children can enhance your ability to develop creative thinking, as their imagination and problem solving within their play can spark ideas in us. Craft et al. (2008), developer of the term 'possibility thinking', saw this as an everyday and an inherent capability in everyone, rather than a few gifted people. Her work with children in the early years evidences creative thinking in very young children. Possibility employs the imagination and encourages us to consider 'what if?' and consider 'as if'. This enables us to think about all possibilities; for example, thinking about your own future: 'What if I retrained as a social worker? Or an astronaut!' Looking at things 'as if' can open up possibilities we may not have thought of, e.g. 'What if we imagine organising this classroom as if money were no object?'

Other types of creative thinking (see Figure 8.1) are divergent thinking, lateral thinking and 'blue sky thinking'. Each of these approaches encourages us to look at situations or problems in a different way, in order to inspire a spark of creativity. De Bono's Six Thinking Hats approach (a lateral thinking theory) can be very useful in group meetings, with each person taking on a role and looking at the issue from a unique angle (e.g. wearing the metaphorical yellow hat means looking at benefits, wearing the white hat means looking at the facts, etc.). Divergent thinking is a playful approach where the participants think of as many ideas as possible. Imagine a group of young

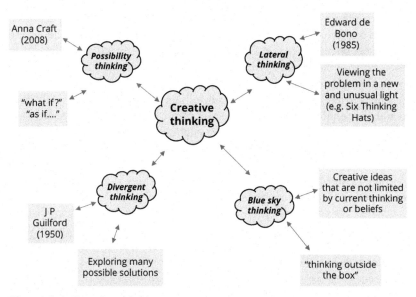

Figure 8.1 Creative thinking

children with a pile of boxes and you will see a great example of divergent thinking, as they imagine the boxes to be cars, boats, houses, spaceships, etc.

Creativity, however, is only the start. From a creative idea, we then need innovation to realise that idea (Sloane, 2006). We also need the skills to recognise the issue, create a plan and then carry out the plan. Education guru Ken Robinson (2006), who speaks and writes about creativity skills in schools, says: 'you can't just give someone a creativity injection. You have to create an environment for curiosity and a way to encourage people and get the best out of them.' This, then, is a lesson for managers and leaders, who should provide encouragement and an environment conducive to creativity. An example of a company that does this exceptionally well, having won numerous awards for its company culture, is Google (Forbes, 2018), with its flexibility, fun environment and freedom to be creative. It even encourages employees to bring their dogs to work! Google employees take less holiday and fewer sick absences than most companies because their staff are so well looked after and happy. Creativity can be very enjoyable and can produce a great sense of achievement and self-actualisation (Maslow, 1970).

Developing solution-focused approaches

Taking a solution-focused approach is about allowing others to find solutions to problems, rather than making assumptions about what people want and need. It is about communities developing their own services with support, rather than outsiders creating what they think the community needs. The idea of using the strengths and skills of the people involved is one that has been around for a while, and it is being increasingly used in work with children and young people. Lohuis et al. (2017) describe the benefits of this approach in their study of its use with people with learning difficulties, a service in which professionals often assume what people need, as there is a belief that the people (clients) themselves will not be capable of identifying this. In the study, they define the solution-focused method as 'a future-oriented and pragmatic work approach encouraging simple, adaptive solutions based on "doing what works" and using people's own strengths and resources'. The study found that there were benefits to the approach, but they also highlighted some difficulties, some tension between professionals knowing what works from experience, and empowering clients by accepting their ideas.

When adopting a solution-focused approach, it is important to foster a positive attitude and to empower people to believe that they can make a change for themselves. This has been proven to be more effective than focusing on problems and difficulties (Morgan, 2016, p. 142). It is vital for professionals to listen and to learn about the issues from the people involved themselves. This sort of 'bottom-up' approach ensures that interventions arise from the people themselves. In solution-focused therapy, the therapist encourages their client to find areas of strength, and this can work very well with children and families too. For families suffering multiple adversity, there will always be things that have kept the family going this far; there will always be strengths somewhere, which can be developed, **and this** will allow the family to feel that they have been able to help themselves.

Analysing transferable skills

The term 'transferable skills' is usually connected with career development; we identify our transferable skills in order to show what we could bring to a new role. This, then, is a useful thing to consider, as roles are constantly changing and developing, and people are less likely to stay in one role for life than in previous decades. The latest statistics show that a UK worker will change employer every five years on average (Hope, 2017) and in many careers involving working with children and families, job roles within the workplace change, as legislation and policy changes. There are numerous skills that can be transferred to different situations (see Figure 8.2), but the following are particularly relevant to the creative practitioner.

Problem solving

Problem solving is enormously significant in today's world, as we have previously explored. In schools and colleges, problem solving and problem-based learning is now given more emphasis than it received in the past. Indeed, the computer software company, Adobe (2018), says that there is 'an urgent need for these skills to be taught in the classroom to prepare students for jobs

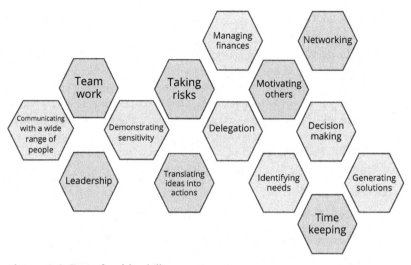

Figure 8.2 Transferable skills

of the future'. Pinar et al. (2018, p. 144) researched the problem-solving skills of student midwives and found that 'as psychological resilience and self-confidence levels increase, problem-solving skills increase', so this would suggest that we need to be resilient and self-confident in order to be able to solve problems in our work. The ability to see a problem, to identify a goal, to formulate a solution and to implement it is a complex undertaking, but problem-solving skills can be developed. One method of doing this is to follow the IDEAL model (Bransford and Stein, 1984);

- Identify the problem

- Define the problem

- Explore the options

- Act on a plan

- Look at the consequences

Problem-solving skills can be developed through the use of mind puzzles, computer games, DIY, etc., which allow us to 'practice' solving problems in the real world. Academic study also encourages the use of problem-solving skills, particularly when researching and planning assignments or engaging in problem-based learning scenarios. Stadler et al.'s (2018) study of complex problem-solving skills within higher education programmes showed that this helps students to 'handle the complexity of University study' and so increases students' success.

Decision making

Making decisions is part of the creative problem-solving process, and being confident in decision making demonstrates competence and assertiveness. Decisions are a part of our everyday lives but they range from minor decisions, such as deciding what to wear in the morning, to making crucial decisions that impact on other people's lives. Decision making is a process which can be undertaken by an individual or a group and there are many variables, for example the environment you are working in and the people around you. Guo's (2008) DECIDE model of decision making provides an explanation of the process:

1. **D**efine the problem

2. **E**stablish or **E**numerate all the criteria (constraints)

3. **C**onsider or **C**ollect all the alternatives

4. **I**dentify the best alternative

5. **D**evelop and implement a plan of action

6. **E**valuate and monitor the solution and examine feedback when necessary

Although decision making involves the examination of facts, intuition or 'gut feeling' also plays a part in the process, and this is just as valid. Atkinson and Claxton's (2000) work on intuition is fascinating; they describe intuition as a 'holistic way of knowing' and argue that trusting in your own judgement is an effective way of working. Intuition involves both cognitive and emotional processes and draws on past experiences and knowledge. Just as we don't always have to concentrate and think about how to drive a car every time we drive to work, we can sometimes make decisions which are based on what we intrinsically 'know' without consciously examining all aspects. Cook (2017, p. 431) writes about the importance of social workers listening to 'gut feelings' in home visit situations, as these feelings are usually linked to experience and therefore useful in identifying risk. Cook sees intuition as 'an essential part of the social worker's decision-making toolkit'.

Case Study: Adam Taylor – Problem solving in community development

Here, I talk to Adam about his journey towards setting up a youth club and range of other services on an estate within an area of deprivation in the West Midlands.

AH – Angela Hodgkins
AT – Adam Taylor
AH: What led to setting up your youth group here, on this estate?

AT: At the time, I was working in Social Services, as a project coordinator as part of what was called the outreach team within Children's Services, so my job was to get groups of kids to come up with ideas of things to do, then go away and find the funding, put it all together, get the people I needed, get the kids to be involved, and then to make things happen.

I've lived on this estate for over 30 years. When my kids were growing up here, the police ran a Friday night disco down at the Community Centre and there were voluntary youth groups. I didn't really pay much attention to it because I was busy earning money to pay the bills. It was only when the grand-kids were born that I started noticing things around the estate. When they were born, I got an allotment and started getting involved in the group there; as I was walking to the allotment, I started talking to the local shopkeepers and they were telling me 'it's really awful round here, there's all sorts of destruction going on'. So, I started looking into it because I thought 'hang on, my grandkids are growing up on this estate, is it really that bad?' I realised that the police at the time had got a dispersal order on the local kids. If there were two kids hanging around together, they were moved on, but there was nowhere to move them on to, and I thought 'hold on, what's going on here? there's nothing happening here for them'.

Then I thought, well I've been running clubs where I work, I've been doing all this stuff; managing funding, surely I've got the skills to set something up, and because I knew how to handle council bureaucracy, I knew how to get the ball rolling. So, I sent an email to all the local councillors saying, 'I want to start a youth club in the area, a voluntary one, how do I do this?' Only one of the six replied and she invited me to a meeting with the local neighbourhood police squad and youth services and I had a chat with them. They had been trying to work with the Scouts to set something up there, but it wasn't happening. My view was that it was always the 13–19-year-olds that they targeted, and I think that's the wrong age to do it. I always wanted to set something up for the 7–12s because that's when, if you get them, you can influence them, so that then they become less trouble when they're 13–19s.

I started talking to Youth Services and said 'this is what I want to do, set up a young group. If you want to set up an older group, I'll help you do that if you'll help me do this'. The guy at the time who was leading it was brilliant. He took me along to meet up with the Scouts for a meeting. The leaders were both old guys and they both were keen to have an injection of new thoughts and new blood.

Anyway, we started; Youth Services had done a deal with the Scouts, they were going to open a youth club on a Friday night there, and they were going to staff it, so I became a volunteer. To start off with, to draw interest, we started doing what's called a 'walkabout', walking round the estate. The youth workers' term was 'engaging with young people'. In my words, that sort of engagement is rubbish because what we were doing is we were walking around, finding the kids, filling in a form with them and then walking off, and that's what they called engagement, because they've got a piece of paper.

None of them knew the area, so I ended up having to take them to the back roads, where I knew the kids hung out. We ended up meeting up at the park and we'd go in and there would be 10–20 kids there, all ages, and I'd go in and start playing football with them, and the youth workers, who were being paid, stood outside and called them out one at a time to fill the forms in, then sent them back in to me. Then I said, 'we could go over the other side of the park, and round that estate, and they said 'no, that's not in our remit, that's not in our area'. I said, 'but all of those children come to the park and they all come to the youth club', and they said 'yes but we don't go down there because that's out of our boundary'. Kids don't have boundaries! And that really, really bugged me. I know [how] all that bureaucracy and the council work, it's like 'that's not our problem, that's somebody else's problem', and I wanted to get rid of all that.

I also noticed that the police at the time were the only ones who were actually doing anything with the kids. They were organising barbecues in the park, so I started going along and helping them. They'd get a barbecue set up in the park for all the kids to come along and they'd play football with them and give them burgers. Eventually, we started on a Friday night at the Scout Hall and there were four leaders and me as a volunteer. All the leaders were employed, and they wanted me to become a paid member, and I refused, because as soon as I was employed, I would be governed by them, and I didn't want to be. I said I'd volunteer happily but then they wouldn't be able to tell me what to do, and they agreed to that arrangement. I've got to give a little to get a little. I got the Scouts on board and agreed to being in control of the garden plots because I wanted to create a community garden. We got somebody to come and knock all the garages down which is where there were problems with drugs and then build garden plots out of the garages themselves. It was fantastic, and we were getting the kids involved.

One day, I was digging the plots, and a couple of girls came over and said 'What are you doing?' and I said 'Grab that fork and that spade and I'll show you, come on' so we started digging it over and then we planted some stuff and then they came back and they watered it; eventually it got to the point where they could harvest it, so we harvested it and then I went and showed them how to cook it and we made soup out of it and the one girl said 'Oh yeah, brilliant, I want to take some home for my Dad, to show him what I've done' so of course I put some in a pot and she took it home. Then, the leader of the Friday night youth services group said 'we've got this paperwork, we need to get the child and fill it in'. Of course, this is where me being a volunteer and not being paid meant I could say to him 'On your bike, if you want it done, you do it with her, because I'm not doing it. I know what I've got out of it, she knows what she got out of it, we don't need paperwork.' Paperwork is designed to provide somebody else with evidence that something has happened, I know that because I worked for Social Services, so I've always wanted to get past that.

All the time I was doing this, I was pushing to try and get a younger group set up. So, youth services found some money to do it, paying four members of staff, and it was costing them £200 a week. They weren't charging the kids to come in, so £200 a week was just not sustainable at all. It lasted for about 6 months and we had a group of kids doing all sorts of stuff and they got young kids up to the age of twelve coming off the streets. The group came to an end because they ran out of money, and on the very last night, I had a parent come in saying 'My daughter has just started coming and you're stopping it. What's going on?' and I said to the parent 'I want to start something up, but I can't do it on my own, I need some help. Would you like to help me?' Fortunately, she agreed, and I'd got the skill set to go and get funding and we'd also got the two members of the Scouts Association involved, so we started having regular meetings. I think it took almost 18 months to get everything sorted to start it up, that's how long it takes. We had to set up a committee, and we had to have a constitution and we had to have various other things in place. We got in touch with the Community Voluntary Service because they had some attachment to the Scouts and so we got involved with them. They were very helpful in producing lots of stuff for us to use, which was great. Again, all this networking is important. So, we got it all set up and eventually we started. The first night, we got six kids and we got those kids to create the rules.

AH: *How long ago was this? How long has it been running now?*

AT: *The club is just into our ninth year now. The first year was difficult and it got to the point during the second year where we'd got about 20 kids and we were having to think of things to do all the time with the kids, so it got to the point where there were about 15 kids, then only 10 kids, and Kerry, the other person, said 'I don't want to do this anymore; if we don't get any more kids, I want to give it up' because we were having to find subsidies to cover the cost of the hire of the hall. We were charging, and we have always charged. The reason for that is, if the kids have to pay for it, there's an investment in the club. It then becomes theirs, so they're more likely to respect it. The idea of this youth club was to make it so that it was sustainable and pays for itself and nobody has to keep going and looking for funding and there's as little paperwork as possible, most of which I do.*

AH: *So how did you get from there to where you are today?*

AT: *Well, I went into the local primary school and I met with the headteacher and I asked him if I could talk to the kids. I ended up with the whole school in front of me, showing them a video we'd made of the group, with kids having water fights and stuff. The music to the video was 'Gangnam Style', because that was the thing at the time and all the kids were doing the moves to 'Gangnam Style', it was brilliant. Then I did a Q & A and some of the kids there who went to the group answered the questions. We don't really plan activities now, it's just a place to chill, a place for them to be with their friends and just hang out. We* *have strong links with the Scouts, who have also gone from strength to strength now they've got a new leader, and the centre is being used regularly by the community. I am a Scout leader and I tell the kids about the youth club and how it's different. We have over 60 kids most weeks now, and at one point last year, we started having to lock the gates as soon as we'd got 70!*

AH: *And the estate is much better now, isn't it? I don't know whether you know how much of a part this has played, but it's definitely better. There are no dispersal orders any more.*

AT: *Yes it is, because now we are classed as a low-crime area. The police's view has changed massively over the years. We had a local neighbourhood squad who we got really friendly with and we used to get them to come up a lot with their van and they'd be serving the kids at the tuck shop and they'd go outside and play basketball with them, so suddenly they had names. They were John and Steve and Rob, rather than 'the pigs' or 'the filth'. It's my belief that when the kids are out there, doing whatever they're doing, the police neighbourhood squad turn up and say 'Oi, Johnny!' and he says 'Alright Rob!' and Rob says 'What do you think you're doing?' and the kid says 'Oh sorry Rob' because there's a relationship going on, so you can do something better. The police know this, it's just bureaucracy that stops them doing it. So that's become part of it, the police come up whenever they can and build those relationships. We still have the police coming to the youth club now sometimes. They know that we've done some good work on the estate and we've really built up these relationships within the community. It's all about those relationships.*

There was also the idea of turning the plots down by the shops into something useful with the income. I spoke to the shopkeepers, and we agreed that I was going to make a community herb garden. We would plant herbs and the local community could have them. Everybody said, 'it won't work, they'll just trash it', but we took the kids down there on a Saturday morning, when everybody was around, and we started digging it over and planting herbs and everybody saw that the kids were doing it; their kids were doing it, so suddenly they had an investment in it because it was their kids' work. So, when the parents are sitting over in the pub garden opposite, having their fag and their pint and they see some little oik riding their bike over the garden, they come over and shout 'Oi, get off! My Johnny did that!' and that was the theory behind it, and it seems to have worked.

It's just about thinking about what needs to be done; there's so much that we can all do. And also, the reason behind it has always been selfish. It still is completely selfish on my part. I don't want my grandkids growing up on that estate, where it's risky and dangerous for them. I would rather create a community around them that will look after them. That might mean that I have to look after other people's children at the same time but at least my children are safe.

Case study reflections

- Reflect on the ideas on creative thinking used in this chapter and how they relate to Adam's experiences.
- What has influenced the approach taken by Youth Services and the approach taken by Adam in this example?
- Consider the transferable skills that Adam used in this example – can you identify your own transferable skills from previous jobs/roles?

Conclusion

This chapter has discussed a range of creative and problem-solving approaches and analysed the importance of transferable skills. For those of us working in diverse ways with children, young people and families, it is important to build up a toolkit of skills that stand us in good stead for the roles we may find ourselves in as our careers progress. Often, situations call for us to stand back and look at the problem and to examine creative ways of dealing with it using the skills and experiences at our disposal. In this way, we can produce and manage services which are appropriate for the particular needs of children, young people and families.

 Further reading

Blumenthal, K. (2012). *Steve Jobs: The Man Who Thought Different*. London: Bloomsbury.
  - There are a few books about Steve Jobs, some more recent than this one, but this details the benefits of his creative thinking.
Trott, D. (2016). *One Plus One Equals Three: A Masterclass in Creative Thinking*. London: Pan Macmillan.
  - An accessible, enjoyable and humorous book about creative thinking.

References

Adobe. (2018). *Creative Problem-Solving Skills Are Key to Tomorrow's Jobs, But Today's Curricula Are Leaving Students Behind*. Available at: https://news.adobe.com/sites/adobe.newshq.businesswire.com/files/press_release/additional/012418CreativeProblemSolvingSkills.pdf [Accessed 8 August 2019].
Atkinson, T. and Claxton, G. (2000). *Intuitive Practitioner: On the Value of Not Always Knowing What One Is Doing*. Maidenhead: Open University Press.
Bransford, J. D. and Stein, B. S. (1984). *The Ideal Problem Solver – A Guide for Improving Thinking, Learning and Creativity*. New York: Freeman.

Campbell, D. (2018). Hospitals struggling to afford new equipment after NHS budget cuts. *The Guardian* [online], 22 May 2018. Available at: https://www.theguardian.com/society/2018/may/22/hospitals-struggling-to-afford-new-equipment-after-nhs-budget-cuts [Accessed 8 August 2019].

Carson, G. and Stephenson, L. (2017). Social care's funding pressures in numbers. *Community Care*, 21 November 2017. Available at: http://www.communitycare.co.uk/2017/11/21/social-cares-funding-crises-numbers/ [Accessed 8 August 2019].

Cook, L. (2017). Making sense of the initial home visit: The role of intuition in child and family social workers' assessments of risk. *Journal of Social Work Practice*, 31(4), 431–444. https://doi.org/10.1080/02650533.2017.1394826.

Craft, A., Gardner, H. and Claxton, G. (2008). *Creativity, Wisdom and Trusteeship*. London: Sage.

Forbes Technology Council. (2018). *13 Reasons Google Deserves Its 'Best Company Culture' Award*. Available at: https://www.forbes.com/sites/forbestechcouncil/2018/02/08/13-reasons-google-deserves-its-best-company-culture-award/#5dd423e83482 [Accessed 8 August 2019].

Guo, K. (2008). DECIDE: A decision-making model for more effective decision making by health care managers. *The Health Care Manager*, 27(2), 118–127. https://doi.org/10.1097/01.HCM.0000285046.27290.90.

Hope, K. (2017). How long should you stay in one job? *BBC News*, 1 February 2017. Available at: https://www.bbc.co.uk/news/business-38828581 [Accessed 8 August 2019].

Ingledew, J. (2016). *How to Have Great Ideas: A Guide to Creative Thinking*. London: Laurence King.

Lohuis, A., Van Vuuren, M., Sools, A. and Bohlmeijer, E. (2017). Ambiguities of 'doing what works': How professionals make sense of applying solution-focused support for people with intellectual disabilities. *International Journal of Developmental Disabilities*, 63(3), 170–183. https://doi.org/10.1080/20473869.2016.1198102.

Maslow, A. H. (1970). *Motivation and Personality*. New York: Harper & Row.

Morgan, G. (2016). Organisational change: A solution-focused approach. *Educational Psychology in Practice*, 32(2) 133–144. https://doi.org/10.1080/02667363.2015.1125855.

Morton, K. (2017). Spending on early years cut by £650m. *Nursery World*, 11 December 2017. Available at: https://www.nurseryworld.co.uk/nursery-world/news/1163096/spending-on-early-years-cut-by-gbp650m [Accessed 8 August 2019].

Pinar, S., Yildirim G. and Sayin, N. (2018). Investigating the psychological resilience, self-confidence and problem-solving skills of midwife candidates. *Nurse Education Today*, 64, 144–149. https://doi.org/10.1016/j.nedt.2018.02.014.

Robinson, K. (2006). Do schools kill creativity? TED 2006. Available at: https://www.ted.com/talks/sir_ken_robinson_do_schools_kill_creativity?language=en [Accessed 10 February 2020].

Sloane, P. (2006). *The Leader's Guide to Lateral Thinking Skills*. London: Kogan Page.

Stadler, M., Becker, N., Schult, J., Niepel, C. et al. (2018). The logic of success: The relation between complex problem-solving skills and university achievement. *Higher Education*, 76(1), 1–15.

Wolf, G. (1996). Steve Jobs: The next insanely great thing. *Wired*. Available at: https://www.wired.com/1996/02/jobs-2/ [Accessed 8 August 2019].

Zedelius, C. M. and Schooler, J. W. (2015). Mind wandering "Ahas" versus mindful reasoning: Alternative routes to creative solutions. *Frontiers in Psychology*, 6, 834.

9 THE REFLECTIVE AND ETHICAL PRACTITIONER

Chapter outcomes

This chapter will enable readers to explore the following concepts:
- Values and beliefs and how these inform our personal philosophy
- The difference between espoused and lived values
- What it means to be an ethical practitioner
- The importance of reflective practice for those working with children, young people and families
- Reflective activism – making changes to benefit people's lives

Introduction

Reflective practice is widely accepted as an essential aspect of professional practice for those working with children, young people and families. This chapter outlines the importance of reflective practice and the deeper dispositions of reflexivity and reflective activism. Reflecting on our own values and principles is essential in order to understand ourselves and our personal philosophy. The role of personal values and principles are examined and analysed, in relation to professional ethics.

Values

Whilst there is a general consensus about the importance of values, there are a multiplicity of different definitions and categorisations that could be applied. In its most basic construction, a value could be defined as the measure of worth we attach to something, but more often when we talk of values, we are referring to a deeply held, important and lasting ideal. Values may well be shared with others within a particular cultural context and could also be seen as broad-based guidelines to live our lives by. Our own personal value base (shaped by our experiences and environment) will inform the professional values we espouse, but there is also a growing recognition in many workplaces of the importance of having 'shared values', which are agreed through meaningful dialogue and 'signed up to', sometimes as part of a formal mission statement.

Some examples of values suggested by practitioners we have asked are shown in the diagram below. What values would you add to this? (Figure 9.1).

It is important to recognise that values do not develop in a vacuum; they are shaped by our experiences and by the society around us. They will also be influenced by beliefs and ideologies.

Take the following scenario:

These are two separate descriptions of a child, written by a nursery practitioner. Look at Child A only and decide how you as a practitioner would welcome this 3-year-old child to the nursery you work at. Consider what you might need to do in order to prepare for this child joining you.

Now do the same with Child B (alternatively, carry out this activity with a colleague, taking one child each) (Table 9.1).

The truth is that Child A and Child B are the same child; the descriptions are simply different ways of looking at the child. It is likely that if you are presented with the description of Child A, your thoughts would centre around support needed and problems to be solved; a deficit model. In contrast, Child B is presented as a child who is loving and fun, yet it is still evident that some support may be needed.

This example shows how two practitioners can both have the interests of the child at heart but, through the prioritisation of different values

Figure 9.1 Examples of values

Table 9.1 Child A and Child B

Child A	Child B
Is not yet toilet trained	Points to his bottom when he needs to go to the toilet
Cannot talk	Beginning to use some signs to express himself
Cannot sit still for more than a few minutes	Enjoys physical activity
Has difficulty understanding social rules	Runs up to staff excitedly to cuddle and kiss them
Cannot recognise his own written name	Responds to a photograph of himself with glee
Displays inappropriate behaviour with other children	Tries to make friends but needs support with this
Has attachment issues	Finds it difficult to separate from his loving parents

(and perhaps coming from different ideological starting points), they can arrive at very different perspectives on how a situation can be handled.

It is also fair to say that our own values can often present dilemmas for us as practitioners (and indeed as human beings). For example, the professional and/or organisational goals we are expected to work to may sometimes conflict with personal values we hold. When one of the authors of this book was working as a department head in a large secondary school, the curriculum management team was directed to 'concentrate on getting D-grade GCSE students up to a C grade'. This conflicted with her own values related to supporting *all* children to meet their potential and also esteeming those students for whom getting a D would be a real achievement. Moreover, constraints within organisations, often related to time or resources, can sometimes make it difficult to adhere to our core values.

> The conditions created in the new, re-structured work organisation place workers in an extremely painful psychological situation, one which throws them out of kilter with values of high-quality work, their sense of responsibility, and professional ethics. (Dejours, 2009, p. 37)

A good example of this would be a mental health practitioner having a deeply held value related to the importance of early intervention but then undertaking an assessment with a young person who was not hitting the threshold for interventions. The practitioner firmly believes the young person would benefit from a particular service but cannot offer support until things are close to crisis point.

Yet another such dilemma is where two of our own values come into conflict. For example, a nursery manager values the parents' voice in decisions affecting their children's care. She also believes strongly in giving staff equal opportunities and ensuring fair and equal divisions of tasks. A parent then tells her that she does not want a male practitioner changing her child's nappy. In this case, the manager has two deeply held values in direct conflict with one another. This can be psychologically uncomfortable for the manager, who is only able to resolve the situation by acting against one of these deeply held values; in other words, the manager experiences cognitive dissonance (Festinger, 1964). Whilst psychologists have identified that some individuals can live with significant amounts of dissonance, for others it is highly uncomfortable, resulting in stress and attempts to reduce the dissonance experienced. This usually involves one of three strategies: firstly, alter one of the beliefs or values to reduce the distance between them and create greater congruence; secondly, acquire new information that outweighs the dissonance; or thirdly, reduce the importance attached to the values. In the case of our nursery manager, however, none of these strategies are likely to reduce the dissonance experienced or provide a resolution.

Espoused values

Perhaps a final dilemma is the congruence between espoused values and enacted or lived values (Schein, 2010). Put simply, espoused values are those we *claim* to hold whilst enacted values are those we live by. In an ideal world, espoused values would also be those that are enacted by individuals and by the organisation as a whole. However, all too often there is a mismatch between these two elements. Take, for example, the organisation that advocates children spend quality time with their parents yet seems incapable of supporting staff's requirements to work flexibly. On an individualised basis, an example would be a family support worker, who espouses a philosophy of empowerment, whilst taking actions that contribute towards creating dependence on the practitioner.

As Slovenko and Thompson (2015) suggest, shared values can change over time, but this should be in response to robust values-based debate between scholars and practitioners and not as knee-jerk reactions to policy, ideology or societal change.

It is important for the practitioner to reflect upon their values and also, within teams, to explore the values they hold and the extent to which these are shared, to interrogate those values and to explore the nuances of our understandings of them. It is important that such reflection is not simply seen as a paper exercise but as something that is core to helping practitioners and teams to work out who they are, what they are about, what matters, how they enact what matters and how they present themselves to the world. Osgood (2010) sees reflective practice as an important aspect of 'your professional self'.

Self-reflection

In order to be able to understand our personal and professional self, we need a good amount of self-knowledge. Reflecting on ourselves is as important as reflecting on what we do. The Johari window model, developed by Joseph Luft and Harrison Ingram (Jo and Hari) in 1955, aimed to help people to better understand themselves and their relationships with others. The model has four quadrants:

- Open – This represents things that you know about yourself and which are obvious to others around you (e.g. skin colour)
- Blind – This represents things about you that you are not aware of, but which others are aware of (e.g. passive aggression)
- Hidden – This represents things about you that you know, but that you keep hidden from others (e.g. your past school experience)
- Unknown – This represents things about you that you are not aware of and that others are not aware of (e.g. the potential to become a good parent).

The idea of the model is that, by increasing your 'blind' and 'hidden' areas, you will uncover more of the 'unknown' area, which houses your future awareness and potential. Here is an example of the Johari window model as used by one of the authors (Table 9.2).

In order to 'open up' the blind area, you should find ways of obtaining feedback from others. This helps you to gain more self-awareness. In order to 'open up' the hidden area, you could talk to people and be open with them; sharing experiences can help others to understand more about the real you. This can help to increase intimacy and to build friendships and better working relationships.

Table 9.2 Johari window examples

Open	Blind
I am a woman, I am English and I have brown hair	People have told me that I sigh a lot, which I didn't realise
Hidden	**Unknown**
There are things about my past private life that the people I work with do not know	I do not know what the success of this book might be or where else it may lead

Being an ethical practitioner

Within all areas of work with children, young people and families, ethicality is deemed of utmost importance. However, defining what we mean by ethicality is a little more difficult. Social pedagogy (a holistic approach concerned with well-being, learning and development) includes the principle of *Haltung*, which Eichsteller and Holthoff (2012) describe as an ethos or mindset and concerns the extent to which actions are congruent with one's core beliefs and values. This rich concept is related not only to our ideas of self but also to how we construct others. It is, as Slovenko and Thompson (2015) argue, affirming of individuality and personhood, with a focus on developing potential. Based on authentic and positive relationships, social pedagogy places ethicality at its heart.

There are a number of ethical considerations that are common to all roles and disciplines within the CYPF workforce. As Stonehouse (2012) points out, such ethical considerations require reflection and will lead to better decision making. Some of these are shown below:

• Ensuring confidentiality

• Exploring consent

• Avoiding harm

• Respecting autonomy

• Avoiding oppressive practice.

There have been several attempts to create ethical frameworks in order to support practice. The following table considers two such attempts, placed side by side for comparison (Table 9.3).

Unsurprisingly, there are a number of criticisms of such frameworks: for example, that they place too high an emphasis on outcomes (harm vs. good) rather than the action itself. This suggests that the same act could be considered ethical in one context but not in another. Also, how do you balance good and harm in real-life situations? Consider the practice example below:

As part of a drive to improve school attendance (a measure which is known to contribute to better outcomes) a primary school arranges a special visit to a theme park for all students with attendance over 98 per cent. This is clearly very motivating to the children who benefit. However, it potentially harms the children who do not qualify for the treat, causing disaffection and isolation. In this case, does the good achieved for some children outweigh the harm for others? Practitioners face ethical dilemmas such as this one on a daily basis.

Table 9.3 An ethical framework using the ideas of Rowson (2006) and Beauchamp and Childress (2009)

Rowson (2006) developed an ethical framework for practice, based on the mnemonic FAIR		Similarly, Beauchamp and Childress (2009) proposed four ethical principles.	
Fairness	This is linked to the concept of social justice and rights	Justice	Aligned to ideas of fairness (opposite). This embodies the idea of social justice and equal treatment
Respect for Autonomy	Enabling others to make autonomous decisions and not preventing people from acting on those decisions about their own lives, their choices, their data.	Respect for autonomy	Respecting other people's wishes and supporting them in their decisions (this aligns closely with A opposite)
Integrity	Seeking congruence between values and actions	Beneficence	Going beyond non-maleficence, beneficence embodies the idea of actively bringing about good
Seeking the most beneficial and least harmful consequences, or Results	Producing the maximum benefit possible as well as preventing as much harm as possible	Non-maleficence	This complements beneficence, my argument that we should avoid doing harm (see R opposite)

Stonehouse (2012) argues that the frameworks alone are not sufficient to ensure ethicality. Rather he proposes two additional concepts: veracity (being honest and truthful) and fidelity (being trustworthy, maintaining confidentiality and keeping promises). To an extent this concurs with the principle of integrity proposed by Rowson (2006) above, and adhering to these principles certainly leads to greater congruence for the practitioner.

Reflective practice

Reflective practice is an important transferable skill in working with CYPF. It enables us to develop greater understanding of our own practice and so increases self-awareness. Leitch and Day (2000) suggest that what defines an effective reflective practitioner is 'a thorough understanding of oneself, the values and "moral purpose" that underpin practice'. Philosopher Paolo Freire was an advocate of reflection in all things, saying; 'Reflection and action must never be undertaken independently.'

Reflecting on our own practice is something that most practitioners do instinctively. Schon (1983) wrote about 'reflecting in' and 'reflecting on' practice, meaning that we reflect whilst engaged in work activities and again after the event. Many of us can identify examples of this within our practice. When engaged in an activity with a group of children, for example, we observe and think about what we are experiencing, often changing our plans in small ways according to what we see. We then reflect afterwards about how the activity went, in order to use the information in future plans.

Evaluating an activity by considering how well it went is a basic reflection, but there can be much more to 'critical reflective practice'. There is a clear link between reflective practice and quality improvement. Appleby and Andrews (2012) explain that quality improvement is 'best served by practitioners who apply key principles of reflective practice but also have the capacity to consider and understand their own reflective activity'. Quality improvement should include everyone, not just managers. All practitioners can play a role in changing things for the better; we can all be 'agents of change'.

It is helpful, when reflecting, to consider the perspectives of others involved. In order to reflect effectively, Brookfield (2017) recommended that we examine the issue in question using four different 'lenses', these lenses being autobiographical, peer, student and theoretical. Brookfield's theory originally related to the teaching profession, so we can substitute 'student' for 'child/young person'. Using the example of the children's activity above:

Autobiographical lens – this involves thinking about yourself and your own feelings about the activity, considering your values and beliefs and how these may be affecting it. For example, if the activity is based on mathematics and you believe that this is something that you are not confident with, this may well affect the way you present the activity.

Peer lens – this might involve talking to a colleague, reflecting on how the activity went with another person who can add their point of view.

Child/young person lens – observations of the children/young people will help you to reflect on the activity from their point of view, by putting yourself in their position.

Theoretical lens – reading about the activity, similar activities or associated theories will give a theoretical viewpoint on the activity.

Reflection using all of these lenses will provide a critical holistic view of the activity, and a much richer reflection than a simple 'How did it go/how could it have been improved?' Brookfield's model is just one of a multitude of published reflective practice models: other popular models include Gibbs (1988), Kolb (1984) and Rolfe (2001).

Being a critically reflective practitioner

As Brookfield's model demonstrates, looking at an issue through alternative perspectives enables the practitioner to be more critical in their reflection. Being critical involves examination of your own views and openness to ideas. Policy transforms provision and new ideas/theories are developed, so practice needs to evolve. It is important that we, as practitioners, are open to adjusting our perceptions. McNiff (2014, p. 106) proposes that we should:

> Be aware ... that things will continue to change; this includes your knowledge claim. You should always hold your knowledge lightly and be aware that what you know today may change tomorrow. Always remember that you may, after all, be mistaken.

'Holding our knowledge lightly' is the key to cultivating a critically reflective disposition. The following case study demonstrates the importance of reflecting and considering your viewpoint and looking critically at the situation that you are presented with.

Case Study: Chloe Jones – Whose feelings are these? Reflecting on conflicting emotions in child-centred practice

As a newly qualified social worker, reflection is a skill I am constantly working on. The often unpredictable and emotionally charged nature of social work can sometimes lead to conflicting feelings and emotions, so effective reflection on the part of the practitioner is key. During a particularly ethically complex placement, I found myself actively aware of my 'reflection in action' for one of the first times. I was working in a local authority's children's services, with a team responsible for recruiting, assessing, training and supervising foster carers. In this particular case, the foster carers were contemplating adopting a child in their care – a child of 18 months with a history of multiple caregivers and placement breakdown. As a practitioner, I was confronted by conflicting emotions, needing to balance the personal with the professional, along with the interests of the child himself and the other actors involved.

It is important to note that, in this particular case, the multiple adversities experienced by the child, including being placed in foster care shortly after birth, being neglected and experiencing placement breakdowns, had impacted the child's social, emotional and attachment need, creating some challenges. Upon arrival at his current placement, he had been labelled as 'lacking in emotional warmth', 'hard to comfort' and overly comfortable with strangers. However, the foster carers worked therapeutically to support the formation of secure attachments with the child. This included practising the positive interaction cycle to ensure positive social interactions for him, for example through playing and singing. Under this care, the child was thriving and making positive social and emotional steps. It was clear to me, as a practitioner, that these foster carers had made a tangible positive change in this child's life and would likely go on to do so should they care for him in the longer term.

Bearing these important contextual details in mind, I was faced with a real internal conflict when faced with the foster carers' desire to adopt. The psychodynamic approach is relevant here, holding that both conscious and unconscious struggles can exist and that recognition of and reflection upon these conflicting emotions is vital. Upon hearing the news, my immediate reaction was one of excitement for the child's future, he had thrived so well under the care of his current placement. However, it was here that it was critical to practice 'reflecting in action', being aware of my reaction and how it may impact my professional approach towards both the child and the foster carers. While excitement and joy may have been my initial emotions, it was important for me to consider both the practicalities of the potential adoption and the impact the adoption may have on the carers' roles within the wider agency and on the child.

In terms of practicality, I had to reflect upon the context of legislation and policy within which we were working. Under the current system, any relative, if deemed viable, can apply to care for the child under a special guardianship order (SGO), even if they have had no contact or existing relationship with the child. As a practitioner, I can be critical of this where there is no existing relationship, particularly given the context of the child in question who had already experienced placement breakdowns and had flourished with his current carers. However, despite my personal fears and criticisms, it was my professional and ethical responsibility to give appropriate advice surrounding the court proceedings in order to effectively manage expectations.

Similarly, I was also experiencing feelings of fear in terms of the loss of those effective therapeutic foster carers for future children needing intervention, should they proceed with the adoption. I was faced with an ethical dilemma, weighing up the interests of this particular child, who was benefiting so greatly from their care, versus the potential interests of any future children who may go on to benefit from them. Alongside this conflict, I also considered the great loss to the agency itself should these foster carers adopt the child. It was here that I experienced a feeling referred to in social work literature as 'helicoptering', whereby the practitioner is able to reflect on the situation from an external position. In my care, I felt as though I had two distinct voices helicoptering above the interaction, one of excitement for the child and one of fear of losing the foster carers, yet was able to manage these internal voices and provide professional advice that was in the best interest of the child. Reflection is key here in order to weigh up these competing emotions and help reach the most effective and child-centred solution.

As a social worker, it is essential to constantly ask and reflect upon the question, 'Whose feelings are these?' Are they my own? Are they projected by the foster carers? Are they influenced by the agency's narrative? Social workers also have the responsibility of listening to the child's wishes through observation, ensuring the child is not invisible. However, especially in preverbal children, it is imperative that this is done as ethically and professionally as possible. Reflection is a central part of this process, and is essential in maintaining a professional, ethical and child-centred practice.

Case study reflections

- What can you learn from this case study about being an ethical and reflective practitioner?
- Chloe talks about the first time she became aware of herself 'reflecting in action'. Can you think of examples from your own practice where you were reflecting in action? What was the impact of this?
- Another way of thinking about the perspectives that Chloe considers (child, practitioner, and personal) is as lenses (Brookfield, 2017). Which lenses do you need to consider within your own role? How do you ensure the authenticity of these lenses and, in cases where they may be saying different things, how do you balance these perspectives within your decision making?
- Chloe is very aware of the need to acknowledge, understand and manage her own (sometimes conflicting) emotions. How does reflection support this?
- How does Chloe's case study relate to the ideas about ethical practice presented above?
- How does your organisation support you in being a reflective and ethical practitioner?

Reflective activism is an operational form of reflective practice, a proactive skill. If we define 'reflection' as looking at ourselves and our practice, and define 'activism' as taking direct action, then 'reflective activism' is reflection, followed by action. The term 'reflective activist' is akin to reflection resulting in change/improvement. Reflection is only the first stage; if we are to improve and transform practice, then action is essential.

Case Study: A reflective conversation with Dr Karen Hanson [Interviewer: Karen Appleby]

KA: Can you offer a general introduction to your professional role as a reflective practitioner?

KH: That's quite a challenging question in some ways. I have a reflective disposition so it's difficult to distinguish between my professional reflective practice and my personal way of being. However, if I contextualise my professional role, I have adopted certain principles that are intrinsically linked to reflective practice. For instance, my leadership approach is based on the appreciation of my team members' skills and strengths. This requires a desire to relate to others and engage in their professional development, recognising strengths through observation and reflective discussions, and then seeking opportunities for their growth. Active engagement, ethical practice, curiosity and a genuine desire to make changes for improvement are all some of the basic principles at the root of my professional role as a reflective practitioner.

KA: Can you remember the first time you heard the term 'reflective practice', and explain the context?

KH: It was a long time ago when I was training to be a primary school teacher in the 1990s, when there was a lot of emphasis on being a reflective teacher. I was introduced to reflective practice as a technical process used to evaluate the effectiveness of your teaching and the success of the children. We were encouraged to use Gibbs' (1988) reflective cycle model as a framework, and at that time it was really useful and enabled me to look for improvements both in my practice and the children's experiences. However, with time and experience, I realised that I was focusing too much on my own perspective in order to make judgements and changes. This is extremely limiting as it fails to consider the perspectives of others. How did the teaching assistant view the situation? What was it like for the children? Had they gained more from an experience than I had observed? What did experts have to say about it? I was not making informed evaluations and my practice was confined to the institutional and professional codes of practice and regulatory expectations. I wasn't looking at the bigger picture.

KA: What qualities do you believe are most significant for the developing reflective practitioner?

KH: In simple terms, I think the most important qualities are curiosity, interest, honesty, ethicality, inclusivity, open-mindedness and creativity.

KA: If anything, what has been the catalyst for any transformation in your thinking and practice?

KH: I was introduced to the work of Brookfield (2017). I was searching for institutions offering professional doctoral courses. I found one basing its learning and teaching approach on a social constructivist model, discussing the work of Brookfield and the importance of using a multi-perspective approach to learning. This was the catalyst that transformed my thinking and went on to inform both my research and practice.

KA: *What is your current 'theory' of reflective practice?*

KH: *It's interesting to ask about my current theory, as I believe that the nature of reflective practice requires re-evaluation of existing 'frames of reference', and adjustment according to ecological changes. That's really what prompted me to develop the theory of evolutionary reflective practice (Hanson, 2012). It expands on the thinking of Brookfield (2017) and his theory of the four lenses, autobiographical, literature/theory, colleagues and students. I developed a fifth dimension, the 'peripheral sociocultural lens', aiming to widen and enrich critical reflective processes. The additional lens prompts us to consider the sociocultural context in which we are working. Each situation and each cause for reflection will be influenced by a variation of contextual issues. It could be environmental, socio-economic/political, or impacted by an individual's diversity, gender or ability. So, to go back to the question, I believe my definition of reflective practice is relevant today:*

> Critical reflection is an active engagement in continual review and repositioning of assumptions, values and practice in light of evaluation of multiple perspectives, including the wider socio-cultural perspectives influencing the context; transforming and transcending self and practice in order to effect change and improvement.

Case study reflections

- Karen talks about important qualities connected to being a reflective practitioner. How do curiosity, interest, honesty, ethicality, inclusivity, open-mindedness and creativity help support reflective practice? Are there any other qualities you think are important?
- Karen considers her current 'theory' for reflective practice, acknowledging that this is continually being re-evaluated in the light of changing knowledge and understanding and external influences. What has informed (and is currently informing) your own 'theory' of reflective practice?
- How does Karen's conception of a wider peripheral sociocultural lens support a multi-perspective approach to reflection?
- Karen provides a definition of critical reflection that is informed by her doctoral research. She sees reflection as intrinsically linked to action and ultimately to quality improvement. Do you agree? Can you think of examples from your own practice where you have demonstrated reflective activism?

Reflecting as part of a Community of Practice (CoP)

Whilst it is important to reflect as an individual practitioner, there is also much value in reflecting collectively, thus enabling multiple perspectives to be interrogated. Such reflection can be formal or informal.

Action learning sets, reflective fora and facilitated or self-facilitated reflective practice groups can all serve to enable practitioners to develop richer understandings of practice issues as well as to provide a useful vehicle for exploring ethical professional dilemmas, considering critical incidents and ultimately improving services and outcomes for children, young people and families.

Conclusion

This chapter has considered the importance of ethicality within all aspects of our work as practitioners. We have explored the significance of values and some of the challenges associated with acting in accordance with them. We have considered why reflection is so important and what it means to be an ethical practitioner. The case studies have provided rich insights into both the theory and the practice aspects of critical reflection. We have explored what it means to be a reflective activist, focusing once again on the positive difference a practitioner can make within their role.

 Further reading

Bassott, B. (2015). *The Reflective Practice Guide*. London: Routledge.
  – This book covers a range of reflective practice theories and supports the development of critical reflection.
Bolton, G. and Delderfield, R. (2018). *Reflective Practice: Writing and Professional Development*, 5th ed. London: Sage.
  – Gillie Bolton believes that writing is key to developing reflective practice. In this book, she and Delderfield examine reflective writing and present writing activities to support this development.
Lees-Oaks, R. (2012). *Johari Window*. Available at https://youtu.be/c7rlCgy6i88 [Accessed 21 October 2019].
  – A video by a counselling/teaching lecturer, explaining the model in simple terms.

References

Appleby, K. and Andrews, M. (2012). Reflective practice is the key to quality improvement. In Reed, M. and Canning, N. (eds.) *Implementing Quality Improvement and Change in the Early Years*. London: Sage.
Beauchamp, T. L. and Childress, J. F. (2009). *Principles of Biomedical Ethics,* 6th edn. New York: Oxford University Press.

Brookfield, S. (2017). *Becoming a Critically Reflective Teacher*, 2nd ed. San Francisco: Jossey-Bass.

Dejours, C. (2009). *Souffrance en France: la banalisation de l'injustice sociale.* Paris: Editions du Seuil.

Eichsteller, G. and Holthoff, S. (2012). The art of being a social pedagogue: Developing cultural change in children's homes in Essex. *International Journal of Social Pedagogy*, 1(1), 30–46.

Festinger, L. (ed.) (1964). *Conflict, Decision, and Dissonance*, Vol. 3. Stanford: Stanford University Press.

Hanson, K. J. (2012). 'How can I support early childhood studies under-graduate students to develop reflective dispositions?' EdD thesis, Exeter University. http://hdl.handle.net/10036/3866.

Leitch, R. and Day, C. (2000) Action research and reflective practice: Towards a holistic view, *Educational Action Research*, 8(1), 179–193.

McNiff, J. (2014). Chapter 8, p. 106 in Walker, R. and Solvason, C. (2014). *Success with Your Early Years Research Project.* London: Sage.

Osgood, J. (2010). Reconstructing professionalism in ECEC: The case for the 'critically reflective emotional professional'. *Early Years*, 30(2), 119–133.

Rowson, R. (2006). *Working Ethics: How to Be Fair in a Culturally Complex World.* London: Jessica Kingsley Publishers.

Schein, E. H. (2010). *Organizational Culture and Leadership.* San Francisco: Jossey-Bass.

Slovenko, K. and Thompson, N. (2015). Social pedagogy, informal education and ethical youth work practice. *Ethics and Social Welfare*, 10(1), 19–34.

Stonehouse, D. (2012). The support worker's guide to ethical practice. *British Journal of Healthcare Assistants*, 6(5), 249–250.

10 THE INCLUSIVE, HOPE-INSPIRING PRACTITIONER

Chapter outcomes

This chapter will enable readers to explore the following concepts:
- The importance of understanding inclusion, equality and diversity
- Anti-discriminatory and anti-oppressive approaches to practice
- Unconditional positive regard as a key principle for working with families
- The practitioner as architect of hope-inspiring relationships
- The implications of the chapter for practice

Introduction

Working in services for children, young people and families brings the practitioner into contact with people from many different cultural, social, economic and religious backgrounds. Being aware of our own prejudices is essential. Children, young people and families will present with different needs, strengths and abilities and all must be appropriately included, valued and supported. Developing inclusive practice requires practitioners to accept the responsibility for creating environments and practices in which *all* children can flourish and feel they belong. Moreover, this chapter also considers the importance of inspiring hope with individuals or families who may have lost it.

Unconditional positive regard

This chapter begins with the premise that trust, respect, unconditional positive regard (Rogers, 1951) and reciprocity are central to developing positive working relationships with children, young people and families (Prowle and Musgrave, 2018). So, what do we mean by unconditional positive regard, and why is this so important in helping practitioners to establish trustful relationships? The term 'unconditional positive regard' was first coined by Stanley Standal and then further developed and theorised by psychologist

Carl Rogers (1951). It embodies the idea of fundamental acceptance and support of an individual regardless of their words, actions or attitudes. This acceptance, Rogers argues, is essential in providing the conditions in which human beings can flourish, change and develop where necessary, and ultimately meet their potential. Rogers argues that the therapist (or, in our case, the practitioner) needs to put aside personal perspectives and biases in order to demonstrate that unqualified acceptance of the other person's humanity. This represents a positive and affirming view of human beings as having within themselves the resources for change and growth and emphasises the constructive role practitioners can have in supporting that growth within a relationship of acceptance. Myers (2007) defines this as an act of grace, valuing another despite knowing their failings, which can have a positive effect on creating the opportunity for positive change.

This philosophy underpins much practice within education, health, social work and early years; these are all disciplines in which it is viewed as important to separate the child from any behaviour that is considered undesirable (recognising that what is determined 'undesirable' is itself largely culturally and socially constructed). In other words, the positive regard for the **person** remains unchanged despite their actions. Some critics of the theory have suggested that the concept of unconditional positive regard can only flourish where there are meaningful one-on-one relationships (for example, a family support worker working intensively with a parent), and that it works less well where relationships are casual or short term (or indeed where a practitioner is working with large groups, such as in a classroom context). Other critics have argued that as a concept, unconditional positive regard requires more research into its impact and the contexts in which it can be helpful. What is interesting, though, is the way that it values the trustful practitioner/client relationship as a core part of the intervention, thus lending support to the importance of practitioner time spent engaging and developing such relationships (see Chapter 4).

The importance of hope-inspiring relationships

Madsen (2009) argues that the development of a real partnership with families is the foundation of effective practice. This is certainly evident within the family support area but has equal applicability in other contexts of working with children, young people and families, such as health or education. Writing in the context of child protection, Turnell and Essex (2006) argue that the best outcomes occur when strong working relationships exist between a family and its helpers. Of necessity, this relationship demands mutual trust and valuing, within an approach that seeks to identify and build on strengths and 'locates workers as agents of hope and support' (Institute of Public Care, 2012). This strength-based approach, advocated by many (Saleeby, 2013; Featherstone et al., 2014) sits in stark contrast to traditional strategies, which are perhaps more risk-averse and emphasise the difficulties and challenges rather than any assets and potencies within the family and community.

It is important to note that establishing these positive and hope-inspiring relationships with children, young people and families will be easier for some groups of practitioners than others. Pott (2017), for example, explains why it may be difficult for some families to trust statutory services who have legal obligations and public responsibilities that emphasise the need to protect children from harm, arguing that this may inhibit attempts by social worker to create those supportive relationships. In such cases, a family support service that is seen as separate from the social worker may be able to strengthen the support around the parent, and act as a buffer so that the parent can engage more confidently with child protection systems (Darlington et al., 2010). Similarly, in a school-based context, the teaching assistant working intensively and individually with a child may have more capacity to establish that hopeful relationship with parent and child than the teacher. Such a recognition is an excellent starting point for effective collaboration between practitioners (see Chapter 7) and also challenges traditionally construed professional hierarchies and power structures.

The practitioner as architect of hope-inspiring relationships

There is a growing recognition that relationships are an important aspect of our lives and can affect our well-being, our ability to cope and the extent to which we experience belonging and feel connected to others. Whilst this is true of all relationships, it is perhaps even more pertinent when applied to relationships between practitioners and the families they work with, especially in contexts where the families themselves may be isolated or marginalised.

In a thought-provoking article for *The Guardian* (2017), Gillingson talks about the importance of putting relationships at the heart of practice, and enabling families to work with practitioners to create individual solutions to the challenges they are facing, to build resilience and to manage areas of risk. Gillingson identifies that this needs culture change, with priority given to developing positive relationships and moving away from tick-box processes into more meaningful dialogues that really engage the voices of children and parents/carers.

The point above illustrates that relationships and relationship building needs to be promoted not just by the individual practitioner, but, equally importantly, supported by the organisation, allowing time and capacity to be allocated to this crucial aspect of practice and realising that this will pay dividends in the long term. The following diagram explores some of the considerations necessary in building positive relationships that inspire hope (Table 10.1).

Table 10.1 Developing positive relationships

Before visit/first meeting	Think about where the visit will take place – ideally you want somewhere comfortable and non-threatening for the individual/ family. Who will be present? In the case of a referral, you may want that person to do the introductions. How will you help put the individual/family at ease? What do you want the meeting to achieve? How will you find out what the individual or family hopes for from the meeting?
First visit/meeting	Think carefully about layout of the room if you can influence this. Consider aspects like clothing and bags – not too formal. Introduce yourself and your role. Be clear about your involvement and how long it will last. Take time to listen to what the individual/family feels is important and what they want to achieve. Be clear about what the next steps are.
As the relationship progresses	Avoid jargon. Use active listening techniques. Follow through on commitments. Do not over-promise. Take time to review progress and identify any further.
Closing the relationship	Ensure appropriate exit strategies are in place. If possible, leave a slightly 'open door' to enable further contact if needed. Celebrate the progress made.

Hope-inspiring relationships will depend very much on the context in which they are developed. In a school, it may be about enabling a student to envisage their own successful educational outcomes. In a challenging article about paediatric palliative care, Smith et al. (2018) explores how parents of children with life-limiting illnesses can be ethically supported to foster appropriate hopes, enabling them to cope and to strive to improve the quality of their family time together even in very challenging circumstances.

In the following case study, Martha Sercombe, a Specialist Health Visitor, talks about helping the parents that she works with to rediscover hope. Many of the parents that she supports have survived traumatic experiences in their own lives. They are often finding it hard to move beyond those experiences and, as a result, have little confidence in their own ability to parent. Using strength-based approaches, Martha helps the parents to recognise what they are doing well and begin to enjoy and celebrate their relationship with their child, with the aim of building stronger relationships, breaking unhelpful cycles of thought and behaviour and ultimately envisioning a more positive and hopeful future. Here, Martha reflects on her work with a number of families where hope has played an important part in supporting them in achieving achieve positive outcomes.

Case Study: Martha Sercombe – Helping families to rediscover hope

In my role as Specialist Health Visitor working with vulnerable families, I have often found myself supporting families who appear to have lost all hope. My work has brought me into contact with people from all walks of life and some of them have lived through really difficult experiences.

For example, a few years ago I was working with a mum who was an asylum seeker. She had two little girls and had just left an abusive relationship and was so concerned for the future of her daughters if she returned to her country of origin. When she had originally left her country the girls were left with a relative. Then they were placed in an orphanage where they were severely neglected. She was fearful at that time they might be subjected to female genital mutila-tion, but fortunately this was not the case. However, if they returned the oldest child would be forced to enter the sex trade at eleven, because as she had flat feet she would not be considered marriageable. At the point I met her she was living in Wales but was very isolated, very afraid and had little recourse to pub-lic funds. Despite all this, she was still able to meet the children's needs. But she felt so desperate, so powerless and far too indebted to us as practitioners. When I went to her house she would get down on the floor and try to kiss my feet. I used to get down beside her and explain that she never had to do that; that she was a human being and valued in her own right. Eventually after two appeals she did get her leave to remain but remembering that lady in the early days of my time with her; that is what lack of hope looks like! So, for me, lack of hope is about wanting change but feeling powerless, no sense of purpose, no self-belief, not having anyone to believe in you.

As a practitioner, one of the best things I can do is have faith in the parents, belief in their ability to change, seeing their humanity and helping them to believe in themselves and hope for a better future. I want to help them to know that they do not have to remain stuck; that they can make positive changes and that they can enjoy a positive relationship with their children. It is not inevitable that they repeat the patterns of their past; they can move forward into a more hopeful future. A good example of this was a young woman that I was supporting, who was in a women's refuge. A care leaver herself, she had had four children removed and when I worked with her she was pregnant again. The work I did with her was helping to put things in place to keep herself and the baby safe,

Another example was a young mum whose baby was 15 months old when I started working with her. Mum had a history of being sexually abused. She was agoraphobic and just could not believe in her ability to be a good parent to her child. One of the first questions I asked myself, was 'How can I help her believe in herself?' One of the tools I find most helpful for this is Video Interaction Guidance (VIG). This has been recommended by the National Institute for Clinical Excellence (NICE) for children with emerging needs as well as for attachment difficulties/issues. The way VIG works is to take a 10-minute video clip of (another) parent and child interacting and then edit down until it contains only the positive interactions. You show it to the parent and then use it to explore that positive interaction. For example, 'Look, she is smiling at you now. What was it you did that she liked? What did you do well?'

I used it with this mum, who had totally lost faith in herself. She did not understand how her child could possibly love her. On seeing the video and watching her child gaze at her so trustingly she broke down watching that lovely interaction. She said, 'it looks like she really loves me'. She was amazed. In that first clip she was wearing pyjamas. The next time I went back, she was dressed and by the third visit she had been going out to the corner shop and was even taking the little one to the park. At first she couldn't see beyond her history, but through the videos and the shared reviews she made that shift. She began to understand her child better and to become more attuned. She realised that she could be a good mum and meet her child's needs; that she could have that loving relationship. The families keep the videos and sometime later her health visitor told me that this mum is still watching hers and finding it helpful.

Another family I worked with was a lady with four children. She was a care leaver and had her first baby at age 16 when she was still in foster care. There were lots of strengths there, she had been supported by her foster parent to keep that first child and she was still with the baby's father 10 years later when I worked with her. But she was living with poor mental health and struggling to move beyond her past. She had been abused as a child and in her first foster placement. Having a little girl brought it all back to her.

I used Watch Wait and Wonder, a child-led psychotherapeutic approach that uses the infant's free play activity in order to enhance the parent–child attachment relationship, whilst also developing the child's emotional regulation and sense of self and enhancing maternal responsiveness and attunement. It really allowed the child to explore difficult emotions through play and the parent was able to watch and understand her child better. She was amazed to see her daughter play so carefully, and found herself valuing things about her that she had not noticed before. Soon, the situation at home was much calmer, the child was more settled even though we did not do any conventional 'behaviour management'. Sleep had improved despite not doing any formal work on routines. Mum was living more in the moment and enjoying her relationship with the children more, realising that she was protecting her children and keeping them safe. She realised that despite the fact that she was *not herself protected as a child, she could be that good parent that her children needed. She had hope for a more positive future for her family.*

Ultimately, some of the parents need us to show that we have trust in them, especially when they do not yet have faith in themselves. So often they have been labelled, and even practitioners can make too many assumptions and just expect parents to be able to move on or be able to put the child's needs first. I think we just need to show kindness, to be trauma aware and to recognise the impact of trauma and its effects on a child's neurological development. We need to focus on positive relationships and help parents to become more responsive and attuned to their children. Tools like the Solihull Approach and VIG can help but ultimately we need to present that possibility of change and growth, to be inspiring of hope.

As a practitioner we can help spark that hope, but it is the families themselves that do the hard work. We just help them recognise all the positive aspects of what they already do and to make those positive changes when needed. It has been so positive over the last few years to watch our transition as services to a kinder, more understanding model of support, that is trauma informed and recognises the difficulties people may face in moving beyond their past whilst also giving them the tools to begin making positive changes. I think that hopeful approach is a hallmark of all that I do as a practitioner and as someone responsible for training staff.

Case study reflections

- Martha paints a powerful picture of what it looks like when an individual has lost hope. This lack of hope manifests itself in multiple different ways as Martha describes. Can you think of a situation in your own practice where hope was a factor? How did you support the individual to rediscover hope and how did this manifest itself in their life?
- Martha discusses the importance of having trust in parents within a strength-based approach. What considerations need to be made in order for this be achieved safely and in the interest of the child?
- This case study emphasises the importance of practitioners being trauma aware. To what extent is this a feature of your practice/your organisation's practice?
- How can you inspire hope with the children and families that you work with?

Inclusion, equality and diversity

The term inclusion refers to engaging and involving everyone irrespective of ethnicity, gender, disability, sexuality or religion. It embodies ideas of removing barriers to engagement and providing equal access to opportunities and resources, as well as tackling areas of intolerance or discrimination. Inclusion is often seen as a rights-based issue (Equality Act, 2010). Booth and Ainscow

(2011), writing in an education context, helpfully summarise some aspects of inclusion, some of which are highlighted below:

- Viewing every life and every death as of equal worth.
- Helping everyone to feel that they belong.
- Reducing exclusion, discrimination, barriers to participation.
- Restructuring cultures, policies and practices to respond to diversity in ways that value everyone equally.
- Linking provision to local and global realities.
- Learning from the reduction of barriers for some children in order to benefit children more widely.
- Viewing differences between children and between adults as resources for learning.

Nutbrown and Clough (2013) explore the ways in which inclusion can sometimes be construed in a tokenistic way, for example as purely based on location. In an early years setting, for example, this would suggest that as long as children share the same physical space, all are included. This overly simplistic view does not account for the subtleties of what it means to be excluded, or indeed what Graham and Slee (2008) describe as the 'politics of identity' which permeate so much of our culture and perhaps unconsciously our practice. Of course, there are issues for inclusion of staff as well as children, young people and parents, and writing this book we have become very aware of the gender and ethnicity balance within our own professional networks. Clough (1999) identifies potential 'arenas of inclusion and exclusion', which can serve to impact on the multiple aspects of the lives of children and their families.

The diagram below identifies just some of these arenas (Figure 10.1).

Writing this chapter, 20 years after Clough's study was published, it could be argued that these arenas, whilst protected to an extent in law, are still relevant and that, moreover, insidious discrimination is still present. In some cases, one could argue there is actually an increase in potential exclusion, precipitated by factors such as in-work poverty, changes to benefits that

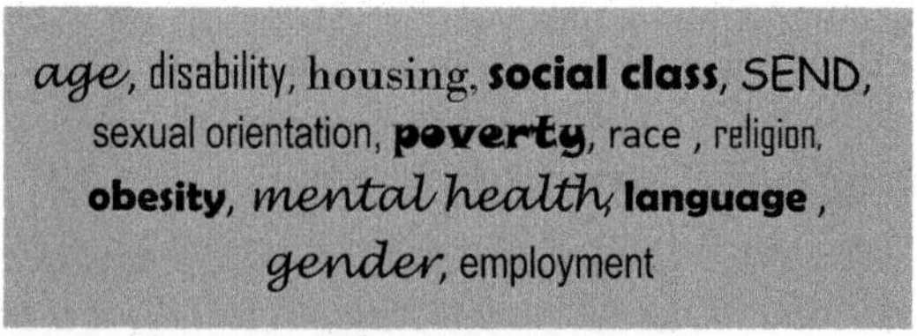

age, disability, housing, **social class**, SEND, sexual orientation, **poverty**, race , religion, **obesity**, *mental health*, **language** , *gender*, employment

Figure 10.1 Arenas of inclusion and exclusion

disadvantage many, and regressive housing policies. However, one could also argue for additional arenas that are perhaps less recognised or acknowledged, such as geographical inequalities experienced in so-called 'left-behind communities', and issues surrounding migration and Home Office status. Whilst, as in other areas of this book, individual practitioners and settings can help to mitigate disadvantage and promote opportunities, they cannot address some of the structural barriers that exist for individuals and groups subject to wider multiple disadvantage (this relates back to our discussions of adversity and intersectionality in Chapter 2). It could be argued that addressing these structural issues is something that only government can do, using the levers of legislation, policy and resourcing. It is important, though, that practitioners can continue to advocate for children and families and raise awareness of these barriers, challenges and inequalities where they arise, as well as undertaking compensatory action to address inequalities. In other words, for marginalised groups or individuals, practitioners may need to go beyond simply ensuring access to services, and actively promote their inclusion.

Equally contentious are the concepts of equality and diversity. The former entails ensuring everybody has an equal opportunity and is not treated differently or discriminated against because of their characteristics. These characteristics as defined by the Equality Act (2010) include specific protections related to age, marriage, disability, pregnancy/maternity, race, religion, sexual orientation, sex and gender reassignment. Diversity is about recognising and celebrating differences between people and groups and treating those differences with respect. Such differences might include beliefs, values and cultural practices. Moreover, how do we make provision for individual psychological differences, for example, the quieter child, the introverted team member? How do we ensure that the approaches that we use genuinely engage everyone? It is also important to note that the concepts of inclusion and diversity will have different nuances in different areas of practice.

In practice, it is all too easy to pay lip service to these principles without really challenging ourselves and our practice. What does equality really mean for the families we work with? Is it really about giving everyone the same treatment, or does it involve compensatory action? Can we really say we value diversity when presented with statistics that show clearly that outcomes between individuals and groups are so vastly divergent?

Take child poverty for example. CPAG (2018) has identified that 4.1 million children (or 30 per cent) in the UK are living in poverty for the second year consecutively (as defined as families living below 60 per cent of the median household income after housing costs). The negative impacts of growing up in poverty are well documented and are summarised here by the Children's Society (2019) (Table 10.2).

One could also argue that there are examples of practitioners managing the fallout from this kind of disadvantage, by, for example, opening food banks in schools to support hungry children. Clearly, in these challenging contexts, simply having an inclusion policy is not going to cut it.

Table 10.2 Effects of growing up in poverty

Children living in poverty are more likely to:
• Have poor physical health
• Experience mental health problems
• Have a low sense of well-being
• Underachieve at school
• Have employment difficulties in adult life
• Experience social deprivation
• Feel unsafe
• Experience stigma and bullying at school

Similar correlations have been identified for other characteristics, and it is important to note that poverty does not happen in a vacuum but is often part of a toxic mix of adversities that impact simultaneously on families. All too often, this kind of disadvantage can be transmitted intergenerationally, resulting in cycles of deprivation that are hard to break or to change.

One of the most powerful moments in my teaching last year occurred whilst facilitating a group of Level 5 Early Childhood students within a privilege walk. Throughout this activity, participants were invited to confront the ways in which society privileges some individuals over others. The discussion that followed fostered better understanding of one another but also of the lives of children that the students may work within the future. However, some educators have criticised the approach, which, they argue, relies on people with marginalised identities to self-declare as a prerequisite of the learning experience and in doing so, can actually underline social divides. An alternative approach involves a 'privilege sale', an activity which helps participants explore notions of privilege by inviting them to identify what privileges they find personally important. This could be seen as a less threatening option as it is one step removed from our own lived identities. However, we would argue that however the discussion takes place, it is essential for practitioners within the CYPF workforce to engage with social justice issues in a meaningful way, and then to apply the lessons learned to their practice.

Within education, consideration has been made of how best to work inclusively. This has led to the development of philosophies and systems such as Universal Design for Learning (UDL). This represents a move away from traditional models whereby learning opportunities were differentiated to meet individualised needs and instead focuses on making the very construct of learning accessible to all. Working on evidence from neuroscience, UDL seeks to provide multiple means of representation, multiple means of expression to enable students to demonstrate what they know, and multiple means of engagement to tap into interests, strengths and motivations and enable appropriate challenge. This is a different way of thinking about inclusion, equality and diversity issues, with interesting potential applicability to other disciplines.

Anti-oppressive Practice (AoP)

The concept of anti-oppressive practice originated in social work as a way of understanding, challenging and ultimately eradicating the power imbalances inherent in organisations and wider sociocultural contexts that serve to disadvantage marginalised groups and individuals. Advocates of AOP are keen for practitioners to reflect upon the care versus control dynamic that is inherent to an extent in all practitioner–client relationship. A useful first step in this process of reflection is to be able to understand and recognise oppression when we encounter it. Barker (2003) powerfully defines oppression as:

> The social act of placing severe restrictions on an individual, group, or institution. Typically, a government or political organization that is in power places these restrictions formally or covertly on oppressed groups so that they may be exploited and less able to compete with other social groups. The oppressed individual or group is devalued, exploited, and deprived of privileges by the individual or group who has more power. (pp. 306–307)

For the practitioner it is essential to be cognisant of discourses and practices that serve, whether knowingly or unconsciously, to perpetuate oppression, and to be critically reflective in interrogating one's own role within that oppression. Moreover, it is important for the practitioner to challenge perceived 'truths' about identities, to validate diversity and celebrate difference (Dominelli, 2002).

Thompson (2016) argued that practitioners need to be aware of and sensitive to the oppression and discrimination that is evident all around us. He argues that it is impossible to be neutral on this matter; practitioners are either part of the solution, or part of the problem. In order to address oppression and discrimination, three things are necessary: justice, equality and participation. Practitioners need to look carefully at their practice to identify elements of oppression and discrimination (which may be explicit or implicit) and to change their practice accordingly.

Whilst AoP was developed within social work, it has been widely used in other practice arenas such as youth work, mental health and education. In an ideal world a commitment to anti-oppressive practice would underpin all our work with children young people and families, be prevalent within our multi-agency discussions and inform our reflections as individuals, as organisations and as partnerships.

Non-judgemental, non-discriminatory approaches

Over the years, I have been privileged to research with families as part of service evaluations. I often ask, 'What is it that you value most in a practitioner?' Very often, the first response is 'He didn't judge me' or 'I didn't feel judged'. Closely aligned to the idea of unconditional positive regard (explored above), a non-judgemental approach requires the practitioner to put aside personal perspectives and to accept the person's reality without criticism and judgement. Whilst it is easy to talk about a non-judgemental approach, this is much harder to achieve in practice, and demands self-awareness and reflection on the art of the practitioner. It also requires empathy and compassion. As Martha pointed out in the case study above, part of being non-judgemental is about understanding the impacts of adversity the person we are working with may have faced. It is also about working with people 'where they are' in their personal journey and helping them to envisage a hope for the future.

In the following case study, Lauren Evans, an early career physiotherapist, explores her commitment to the inclusion of children and families and how she achieves this in practice.

Case Study: Lauren Evans – Inclusion for all

I was first drawn to physiotherapy through my keen interest in healthy living. I am passionate about the role of physical activity in supporting people's well-being, and so I decided to train as a physiotherapist. I currently specialise in the outpatients musculoskeletal sector with patients over 16. However, I qualified in 2016 and worked initially as a rotational physiotherapist covering inpatient and outpatient departments in both adult and child care.

Working in this kind of setting involves a very rich and diverse workload and brought me into contact with people from all walks of life. I quickly realised the importance of being very open-minded and non-judgemental, and also of avoiding making assumptions and really engaging with the individual to find out what was important to them. I found that involving the child and family was particularly important when working with children and young people.

My work with children specifically has varied from respiratory management with acutely ill children to rehabilitating children after various injuries or accidents, and I have supported children of all ages, from very small infants through to adolescents and young adults.

When starting rehabilitation, it is so important to involve children and parents in the process equally. Particularly with young children, it can be tempting to discuss treatments just with the parents (as the responsible adults), and not discuss it with the children themselves, or equally discuss plans with the child and not incorporate needs and concerns of family members. It is a balancing act and getting the child and family on board with the treatment plan and feeling some ownership of it is so important for a good outcome.

This is illustrated by some work I did with the family of a 7-year-old girl, who came into the hospital after breaking her leg. She ended up requiring an open reduction internal fixation operation in order to repair the fracture. This is where the bone has separated to the point that it would not repair itself, and an operation is needed to generate the healing. Children can find surgery very traumatising and it can have a larger impact than adults experience, which should be taken into account. The parents were also shocked and anxious. They shared some of the difficulties they were facing as a family, of which the girl's condition was just one. It was clear that, in order to get a good outcome, I needed to work closely with the family, engaging them and building trust whilst also liaising closely with the consultant and nursing staff to build a picture of the child's recovery post-surgery, her mood, pain relief and complications I needed to be aware of. In this particular case, the rehabilitation was not straightforward as the patient developed a psychological barrier to full recovery. Through active listening and relationship-building with the child and family, I was able to develop a very flexible support package, which enabled me to visit the patient at home and at school. I was able to give her teachers strategies to support her and enable her inclusion in school activities. Prior to this, the child's attendance had been a concern, so the teachers were pleased that the physiotherapy made her excited to go to school, as I had incorporated lots of fun-based approaches into her treatment. Liaising with School Services enabled the family to access wider family support, and the outcome of this case was a good recovery for the child. However, without really tuning into the child and the family and adapting my approaches to meet their individual circumstances, the outcome may have been less successful.

This particular case really highlighted to me just how important effective communication is with family members and other members of the health and social care sector for the overall care and best interests of the patient.

When I work with families, I am always very mindful of the language I use. It's important to avoid jargon and, without being patronising, presenting things simply and clearly to ensure everyone understands. I may use games to engage children or even encourage the family to join in. As physiotherapy is, by its nature, physical, it may involve touch and sometimes a degree of discomfort. It is really important to communicate why I am doing things and exactly what will happen to the child, and to ask their consent. I also need to be really attuned to non-verbal communication and body language, particularly where there may be language barriers. Working with families has also shown me the importance of being socially and culturally aware. Some treatments will require partial undress and for some cultures this can be uncomfortable. It is important to be aware of cultural and religious issues that may be present, and to adapt treatment plans where appropriate. For example, if the patient is really uncomfortable about undressing, I may suggest wearing a thinner top so that I can treat through it.

It is also important to recognise that we all have different personalities. Some people may need continual reassurance, others may be tempted to push too hard and do too much, so I need to encourage them to slow down. Still others may need a firm and honest approach outlining the potential consequences of not engaging with the physio process. So, inclusion is not just about race, class, age, religion and gender; it is about seeing the individual and their needs and being flexible in our approach.

Ultimately, in all cases, it is about ensuring a good outcome from the treatment, and also making sure that the child and the family feel respected, listened to and involved. Achieving this aim requires emotional intelligence, sensitivity, creativity and adaptability and a real passion for working with people and helping them to achieve the best possible recovery.

Case study reflections

- Why does Lauren see inclusion as so important?
- What practical approaches does Lauren use in order to ensure the inclusion of children and families?
- Lauren talks a lot about tuning in to the individual. Why is this so important? What are the potential barriers to tuning in to individuals? How does this contrast to the theory of UDL explored above?
- Lauren also explores the need to involve both the child and the parent/carer. How do you ensure the child's voice is heard within your setting?
- How does your setting ensure the inclusion of all?

Conclusion: What are the implications for practitioners arising from this chapter?

This chapter has considered the importance of recognising and celebrating the diversity of the individuals that we work with. We have explored the importance of unconditional positive regard and how this can underpin positive approaches to working with children, young people and families. As well as the traditional domains of diversity, we have considered individual psychological differences and the impact of trauma. Hope has been presented as an important aspect of how we engage with individuals and families, particularly those who may see themselves as marginalised or powerless. It is now important for the individual practitioner/student to examine for themselves what inclusion means in the context of their own work, and to look critically at how they are demonstrating unconditional positive regard, celebrating diversity and inspiring hope in the children, young people and families with whom they work.

 Further reading and resources

Privilege Sale – https://thesafezoneproject.com/activities/privilege-for-sale/
  – An alternative approach to the Privilege Walk which provides opportunities for reflection and discussion.
The Privilege Walk – https://edge.psu.edu/workshops/mc/power/privilege-walk.shtml

- Not without its critics, the privilege walk offers an experiential opportunity to explore the ways in which society privileges some individuals over others.

Thompson, L. (2016). *Anti-discriminatory Practice: Equality, Diversity and Social Justice* (Practical Social Work Series). Basingstoke: Palgrave.

- A useful and thought-provoking overview of anti-discriminatory practice, written from a social work perspective.

References

Barker, R. L. (2003). *The Social Work Dictionary*, 5th ed. Washington, DC: NASW Press.

Booth, T. and Ainscow, M. (2011). *Index for Inclusion: Developing Learning and Participation in Schools*. Bristol: Centre for Studies on Inclusive Education.

Clough, P. (1999). Exclusive tendencies: Concepts, consciousness and curriculum in the project of inclusion. *International Journal of Inclusive Education*, 3(1), 63–73.

Darlington, Y., Healey, K. and Feeney, J. (2010). Challenges in implementing participatory practice in child protection: A contingency approach. *Children and Youth Services Review*, 32, 1020–1027.

Dominelli, L. (2002). *Anti-oppressive Social Work Theory and Practice*. New York: Palgrave.

Featherstone, B., Morris, K. and White, S. (2014). A marriage made in hell: Early intervention meets child protection. *British Journal of Social Work*, 44, 1735–1749.

Graham, L. J. and Slee, R. (2008). An illusory interiority: Interrogating the discourse/s of inclusion. *Educational Philosophy and Theory*, 40(2), 277–293.

Institute of Public Care (2012). *Early Intervention and Prevention with Children and Families Getting the Most from Team Around the Family Systems*. Available at: https://ipc.brookes.ac.uk/publications/Early_Intervention_and_Prevention_with_Children_and_Families_June_2012.pdf [Accessed 12 June 2019].

Madsen, W. (2009). *Collaborative Helping: A Practice Framework for Family-Centered Services*. TAOS Institute. Available online at https://www.taosinstitute.net/files/Content/5693194/Madsen-Collaborative_Helping-Family_Process.pdf [Accessed 12 February 2020].

Myers, D. G. (2007). *Psychology*, 8th ed. New York: Worth.

Nutbrown, C. and Clough, P. (2013). *Inclusion in the Early Years*. London: Sage.

Prowle, A. and Musgrave, J. (2018). *Utilising Strengths in Families and Communities to Support Children's Learning and Wellbeing in Pedagogies for Leading Practice. Thinking About Pedagogy in Early Childhood Education*. London: Routledge.

Pott, R. (2017). Delivering social work services in collaboration with the legal representation for individual clients: An effective, ethical and economical approach to supporting families in child abuse and neglect legal proceedings. *Child Abuse and Neglect*, 73, 24–29.

Rogers, C. R. (1951). *Client-Centred Therapy: Its Current Practice, Implications and Theory*. Boston: Houghton Mifflin.

Saleeby, D. (2013). *Strengths Perspective in Social Work Practice*, 6th ed. London: Pearson.

Smith, R. J., Bally, J., Holtslander, L., Peacock, S., Spurr, S., Hodgson-Viden, H., Mpofu, C. and Zimmer, M. (2018). Supporting parental caregivers of children living with life-threatening or life-limiting illnesses: A Delphi study. *Journal for Specialists in Pediatric Nursing*, 23(4).

Thompson, L. (2016). *Anti-discriminatory Practice: Equality, Diversity and Social Justice* (Practical Social Work Series). Basingstoke: Palgrave.

Turnell, A. and Essex, S. (2006). *Working with Denied Child Abuse: The Resolutions Approach*. Maidenhead: Open University Press.

11 THE IMPORTANCE OF PRACTITIONER SELF-CARE AND SELF-MANAGEMENT

Chapter outcomes

This chapter will enable practitioners to engage with the following:
- The role and importance of self-assessment and self-care when working with children, young people and families
- The effects of stress and burnout on practitioners
- Coping mechanisms and resources to promote mental and social well-being
- Support services and professional supervision

Introduction

The Buddha once said, 'if your compassion does not include yourself, it is incomplete' (Kornfield, 1996). As we have explored previously (see Chapter 1), working with children, young people and families can be emotionally demanding. Using advanced empathy skills and working with a wide range of children and families can lead to practitioner stress and 'compassion fatigue' (Taggart, 2013). There is an emotional cost to practitioners, with many practitioners struggling to find a work–life balance (Hodgkins, 2019, p. 46). Therefore, there is a need for practitioners to be able to identify, and find ways of managing, the effects on themselves in a positive way. Mechanisms to help practitioners cope with stress can be personal strategies, e.g. developing a 'mental health toolkit' (Hodgkins and Watson, 2017) or professional strategies, e.g. clinical supervision.

Mental well-being is more than the absence of mental ill health; it encompasses feeling happy, being able to contribute productively and realising our potential. Keeping mentally well enables us to cope with daily stresses and to adapt and manage in times of change and uncertainty (MIND, 2017). The majority of people who work with children, young people and families give as a reason for choosing the career, 'the opportunity to make a difference'

(Atkinson and Claxton, 2000). The reward for many of these professionals is intrinsic and the personal reward is in making a difference for others. When giving *of* ourselves, however, we must not neglect care *for* ourselves.

Stress

Public Health England (2017) defines stress as 'the feeling of being under too much mental or emotional pressure, and pressure turns into stress when you feel unable to cope'. It is important to differentiate between 'pressure', which can be motivating and positive, and stress, which can harm us. The feeling of strain and pressure can be beneficial in certain situations, e.g. in sport, but it is when there is too much pressure that it can become negative, causing the body to go into 'fight, flight or freeze' mode. In an acute stress situation, the body activates the sympathetic nervous system and hormones such as adrenaline and cortisol are released in order to prepare the body for action. Impairment of the prefrontal cortex causes difficulty in thinking logically, which can affect our work as well as our home lives. Prolonged stress can affect resilience and can lead to burnout (Persson and Zakinsson, 2016). Stress is not an illness in itself, but it can cause illness if it is not managed. The effects of acute and chronic stress can be wide-ranging:

> Acute stress responses promote adaptation and survival via responses of neural, cardiovascular, autonomic, immune and metabolic systems. Chronic stress can promote and exacerbate pathophysiology through the same systems that are dysregulated. (McEwen, 2007)

In trying to alleviate stress, people often turn to negative 'crutches' to help them cope (e.g. smoking, overeating, drinking too much alcohol), but these activities can cause yet more harm, as the combination of chronic stress and changes in lifestyle leads to an increase of wear and tear on the body, called 'allostatic overload' (McEwen, 2007), which can then lead to 'burnout'.

Burnout

Burnout is different to stress; it can be defined as a loss of enthusiasm for work, cynicism, and a low sense of accomplishment. Where stress causes emotional overreactions, burnout causes a lack of emotion; where stress causes urgency and hyperactivity, burnout makes us feel helpless and hopeless. The factors leading to burnout include prolonged stress with no improvement in circumstances. The writers of the original study into burnout (Maslach and Jackson, 1986) developed a scale to assess the three dimensions of burnout, which they defined as: emotional exhaustion; depersonalisation (becoming emotionally detached); and diminished personal accomplishment.

Various writers have studied the phenomenon of burnout within their profession and have identified factors that they believe contribute to the condition. Research relating to medicine, teaching, social work and nursing identifies common themes, such as increased workload and organisational factors. There is little research into other areas, such as early years, family support or youth work, but any profession that involves caring for vulnerable people is likely to include some of these factors. The caring professions appear to suffer from burnout more than most. Taggart (2011, p. 86), writing about early years practitioners, talks of a caring 'vocation' being 'a double-edged sword, often synonymous with self-sacrifice or burnout rather than job satisfaction'. Ingram and Harris (2001) coined the term 'the kipper effect' to describe the way that youth workers are affected by pressures from all sides, causing the well-rounded person to be squashed flat (like a kipper).

Perceived factors leading to burnout (Table 11.1):

Table 11.1 Perceived factors leading to burnout

Profession	Factors	Sources
Medicine	Increased workload Repeated reorganisation A culture of blame and fear	Orton and Pereia-Gray (2015) Wilkinson (2015)
Teaching	Time demands Workload Student disruptive behaviour Organisational factors Increased scrutiny Accountability to standardised tests	Flook et al. (2013)
Social Work	Poor working conditions Excessive paperwork Increasingly long working hours Little opportunity for advancement Ineffective bureaucratic structures	McFadden et al. (2015, p. 1548)
Nursing	Supporting others through loss, illness and pain Recent austerity measures Absenteeism Staff shortage	Brennan (2017)
Youth Work	Emotional exhaustion Depersonalisation Lack of a sense of personal accomplishment Secondary trauma	Bradford (2016) Steinlin et al. (2017)
Early Years	Compassion fatigue Emotional closeness Financial concerns (managers)	Taggart (2011, 2016) Elfer (2012) Elfer et al. (2018)

Self-assessment

The Holmes–Rahe Stress Inventory (AIS, 2018), first published in 1967, identifies the stresses in people's lives and rates them, giving a score which distinguishes a person's likelihood of becoming ill with a stress-related illness. Changes at work, and changes in responsibility at work, score relatively highly on the scale, which supports some of the above research. The stress index, although somewhat dated, is still a useful tool.

The Health and Safety Executive (HSE, 2017) states that employers have a legal duty to protect employees from stress at work, and they suggest that workplaces should carry out risk assessments and identify measures that should be put in place to protect workers. The HSE's latest research (2019) shows that stress-related illness costs Britain over £5 billion per year, so employers are also invested in tackling the problem. The HSE (2019, p. 4) identifies six 'management standards' which, if not properly managed, can lead to work stress. These are: demands, control, support, relationships, role and change. The way that an organisation manages these areas can make all the difference to the mental well-being of the employees. However, it is still important for people to tune into their own emotions and recognise signs of stress in themselves. Signs of stress are different for different people, so it is important to recognise your own warning signs (Figure 11.1).

Self-reflection is key to being able to assess our own well-being and identify ways of managing difficulties (see Chapter 1). When engaged in reflective practice, professional and personal identities combine, and emotion is an important part of the cognitive process. Taking the time to think about how we are coping is central to managing our workload and work experience.

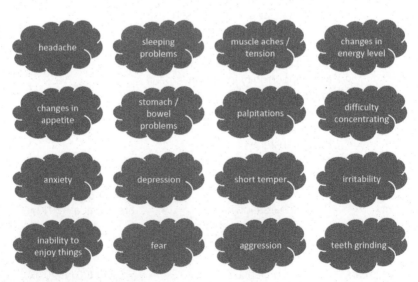

Figure 11.1 Warning signs

Time management

Good time management skills can make a huge difference to a busy life, and organisation usually means less stress. If you find that you have masses to do, and you are not sure where to begin, write all of the tasks down on pieces of paper and divide them into four piles, labelled in terms of urgency and importance. Place each of the tasks onto a coloured square; decide how important and how urgent each task is. Then, deal with them accordingly. Some things are both urgent and important, e.g. an email to your manager about a complaint needs to be answered; this needs to be done straight away and should take priority over everything else. A task that is important, but not urgent, e.g. planning for a future event, should be scheduled, so make a note of a day and time when you will do it, and stick to that. A task that is urgent but not important, like answering the phone for example, could be delegated to another person. Then there are things that are not important or urgent, like watching TV; these are the things that can (and should) be ignored (Figure 11.2).

We can learn to move some items into other areas, with practice. Something that is important but not urgent will become urgent if we do not plan effectively. Covey (2000) says that we should spend most of our time on 'important but not urgent' tasks, as these are likely to be the tasks that bring the most enjoyment. Delegation is an important skill to develop. In the example above, if we answer the phone ourselves, we may think that we are handling an important and urgent task when actually it is urgent, but seldom likely to be important. The danger area is spending time on 'not important and not urgent' activities. By procrastinating, spending lots of time idly surfing the web or on social media, we can use up a huge amount of available time. However, that doesn't mean that we don't sometimes need 'time out' to relax. Things like a day out with family should also be in the 'important' sections, not just work activities.

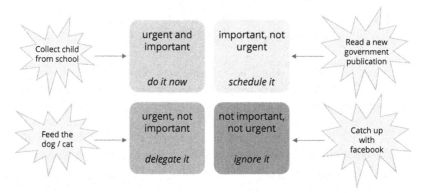

Figure 11.2 Time management

Coping mechanisms and resources

If we accept that stress is a part of working with children, young people and families, and that burnout is a potential risk, then we need to identify what we can do to manage stress effectively. The first step is identifying the problem. In order to do that, we need to be both self-aware and aware of others who may be struggling to cope. The ways in which people cope with stress depend on their particular personalities and motivations. What is seen as 'coping' for one person may not appear so in another person's eyes. People react to situations in different ways; for example, two people may react very differently to being criticised by their manager. Whilst one person might 'shrug it off' another may argue with the manager, and another may dissolve into tears. Aldwin and Werner (2014, p. 357) say that 'Coping must be seen as a means for human development whether that development is viewed in terms of mastery, ego integrity, individuation, wisdom or free will. In order to accomplish this, we must facilitate communication and mutual respect.' Open communication and empathy with our colleagues and work teams are the keys to a supportive community that looks after its members.

Duran and Huckerby's (2015) work on nurses' stress management techniques include three different methods: work directed, person-directed and holistic interventions.

Work-directed interventions – support services and professional supervision include strategies put in place by the organisation for the purpose of alleviating stress and pressure, e.g. psychological debriefings, clinical supervision and respite rooms (staff rooms). Providing resources to increase teachers' sense of personal efficacy and ability to manage stress may reduce burnout (Flook et al., 2013, p. 182).

Person-directed interventions – self-management include strategies that people organise for themselves when they identify their own need for stress relief, e.g. making lifestyle changes, reflection time, peer support, time management.

Holistic interventions and well-being – these are general strategies which are perceived to be helpful in relieving stress and having a lifestyle conducive to all-round wellness, e.g. meditation, healthy eating, exercise, getting adequate rest.

A holistic intervention which has become very popular in recent years is mindfulness. Mindfulness is not a new idea, however; it has its roots in Hinduism and Buddhism and it is an important part of practising yoga. It is a mental state achieved by focusing one's awareness on the present moment, whilst calmly acknowledging and accepting one's feelings, thoughts and bodily sensations. It is a therapeutic technique that many people find useful in combatting the stresses and strains of life. The NHS (2016) claims that 'Paying more attention to the present moment – to your own thoughts and feelings, and to the world around you – can improve your mental wellbeing.'

Mindfulness is recommended by the National Institute for Health and Care Excellence (NICE) as a way to prevent depression in people who have had three or more bouts of depression in the past. Mindfulness practice contains three elements:

- The development of awareness – through systematic mindfulness activities

- A particular attitudinal framework – kindness, curiosity and a willingness to be present

- An embodied understanding of human vulnerability – developed through exploring personal experience through mindfulness practice; we learn that suffering is an intrinsic part of experience and that we can learn to recognise and step out of habitual patterns (taken from Crane, 2017)

There are many websites and self-help books dedicated to mindfulness, and classes are available through GP surgeries and large organisations who increasingly provide mindfulness training for their staff.

Support services

There is a wealth of support available to help people suffering stress, or stress-related illness, and if self-care is not working or is not sufficient, then it is important to seek advice and support from elsewhere. It is important to know where to go/who to speak to if you feel that your mental health is becoming a concern.

Your GP – a doctor can make suggestions of ways to manage your stress or he/she can refer you for other services, such as counselling.

Cognitive Behaviour Therapy – CBT is a talking therapy which can be useful in helping to change patterns of thinking and behaviour. The therapist can help people to manage situations better and avoid a stress response. This is available through the NHS but there may be a long waiting list.

Private counselling – there are lots of counsellors and therapists offering a range of talking therapies which will help people to manage stress. These are easy to find but can be expensive. Choosing a counsellor who is registered with the BACP (British Association of Counsellors and Psychotherapists) is advisable.

Helplines – There are many telephone helplines (e.g. Samaritans, MIND, Supportline, Lifeline), some available 24 hours a day, and these can often offer immediate support to those in need of someone to talk to.

Websites – As with helplines, there is also a wealth of support available via websites, which can be very reassuring and helpful. The MIND website, for example, has information, guides, links to support services, tips and stories from people going through similar situations.

Suicidal feelings – Many people have suicidal feelings at some point in their lives, and when stress and pain become overwhelming, it is crucial to talk. Problems can be overcome, and people do get through this, so please do talk to someone, whether it is a friend, family member, doctor or helpline (Samaritans telephone number: 116 123).

Professional supervision

In most professions involving working with children and families (social work, counselling, etc.) supervision is an important part of the working relationship. It should be a two-way process between an employee and someone within the organisation who is able to support the employee emotionally. Supervision is good practice, and good-quality, reflective supervision supports practitioners in developing their practice, knowledge and skills, 'helping us to make difficult decisions and ultimately keep children safe' (Clayton, 2017).

Supervision is an aspect of performance management, but it is much more than this. Supervision should not only evaluate performance but should also be about sharing good practice and supporting each other emotionally. Inskipp and Proctor (2003, in Creaner, 2013, p. 7) identify three domains of supervision (Table 11.2).

Each of these domains requires reflection, and this should be a foundation of supervision meetings (Wilkins et al., 2017). The relationship between supervisor and supervisee is crucial, with practitioners needing to feel safe to express their feelings, concerns and fears in a non-judgemental atmosphere (Remez, 2016). Supervision, for those working with children, young people and families, is inconsistent (Hodgkins, 2019, p. 54), with some workplaces offering little in the way of emotional support. The following two case studies give accounts of the importance of support and the importance of looking after our own emotional health as professionals.

Table 11.2 Domains of supervision

Formative (Educative)	This relates to learning, skills development and professional identity development
Normative (Managerial)	This refers to accountability, developing best practice principles, ethical and legal considerations, compliance with agency and organisational procedures and professional standards for the well-being of clients
Restorative (Supportive)	This considers the impact of the work on the supervisee and the necessary psychological support and scaffolding required to offer professional support to the supervisee. This function can help mitigate the stresses and impacts of the work and promote practitioner well-being.

Case Study: Wendy Neale – Counselling in a police protection team

My work is about keeping people safe to be at work and identifying where they may be struggling within the role. With child protection work particularly, people used to only be allowed to work for five years in child protection, before they moved on, but they've stopped that now. Some people can work in there for years and they're fine, but other people do find it quite exhausting mentally, physically and emotionally.

What I end up doing is giving them tips on how to keep themselves safe, telling them how I keep myself safe as a counsellor. I've found that the police often don't have an outlet to talk about their work; if they take it home, family say 'we don't want to hear about this, it's not very pleasant', so they carry it with them. One of the tips I use is that I 'carry' those issues in a rucksack and I leave the rucksack at a certain point on my journey home. It will be there to pick up again in the morning but when I walk through the door, I'm not carrying that rucksack on my back. When I walk in, I can be Mom, partner, all those other things. I allow that journey time between work and that space to mull over work, that's fine, but then when I've reached that particular place in my journey, that's my time to say 'that's it now, I've left it there and I'll pick it up again in the morning.' I've found that that's been really helpful to people.

Because I understand, I give them examples, I'll tell them what works for me. If I've had a really bad day, I'll go home and the first thing I'll want to do is have a shower to cleanse the day off. I just want to be clean and out of the clothes I've been in. That's something that's changed in the police because before, they all had lockers but now a lot of them tend to go home, just to put a coat on and go home in their uniform, because there's no storage space, but if you can take that uniform off, then that role that you've been playing all day can be put away. All of these little things psychologically help you to feel better.

The other thing I do, when I come home and I am thinking about things is to write the thoughts down, put them in a jar and then that's my to-do list, and it's out of my head. 'I can't think about this now, so I'm leaving in that jar and I'll come back to it.' For me, the written word is powerful because people need to get the thoughts out of their head. We carry out a questionnaire when people come in to receive counselling, asking things like 'how have you felt in the last 7 days' the general one you get at the GP, but that list often makes people cry because it's the first time they've acknowledged it, it's the first time they've seen it written down.

One of the biggest problems regarding self-care is that people don't take breaks, so they sit at their desk, they eat at their desk, but you need to stand up, walk away, have a change of air, a change of environment and a 15-minute walk away can make such a difference to your day. In an office environment, if you all do it, it makes life easier.

What we have to look out for is compassion fatigue, where people have just reached the limit of being able to have empathy, it's like they've shut down to everything. They can become too desensitised and in the end it's like they've got no care, it hardens them. If they've got the victim in mind, but they're interviewing the suspect, it's about keeping that emotional control about what you know the victim has said has happened. It really is a tough job, it's been an eye-opener for me, in terms of how they cope. Because I did EMDR training and rewind technique training, I'm considered the trauma person. It has become a buzzword at the moment so everybody wants EMDR. It's really just giving people tips and making sure that they do take care of themselves.

One of the things we implemented as a change happened because some-body came to see me who had suddenly started to struggle with work. It was a typist, who typed up all the interview notes. Previously, a file would come in and someone might type up the witness statements and someone else would type up the interview or victim statements, but they started to give people the whole file, and some people really struggled with that because when you've got the whole thing you start to build up a picture of the whole story and that impacted on quite a few of the people when they started to get more emotion-ally involved in the case. They have now reverted to the old system, because they realised that so many people were struggling.

I absolutely love my work. It's tough but I've had massive support with my supervision, which I have every four weeks for about two hours, that's important for me because that's where I can question how I'm doing and how I'm feeling. A couple of years ago, I was off work for a while and although they let me go back to work, my supervisor said I wasn't fit to see people. She made sure I started by just doing some telephone assessments and once I'd done that she said 'ok you can see two or three clients a week' and then I built it up.

It's important because I need an outlet to talk through times when I feel like I'm struggling. If I've got a client or a situation and I think 'I don't know where to go with this', that's what I use my supervision for. Sometimes my supervisor will point out times when I am taking things personally, and I think 'yeah ok, I'll put that in my rucksack and leave it here'. We're all human, aren't we? And that's what I tend to say to people, none of us are perfect every day.

I worry more about people who say that nothing affects them, because if you're saying that the things you're dealing with don't affect you then that does worry me because it should, because we're all human beings. So for me it's all about self-care. Sometimes when I come home and I'm tired and I have arranged to go out and I don't feel like it, I know that if I go, I'll feel better because I'll feel uplifted by seeing my friends and then I'll come away thinking 'that was great'. Having hobbies as well, things that help you to relax. I used to bake a lot but then if you're baking a lot, you're overeating, which is no good, so I've taken up knitting which is great for me because it's good for clearing your mind.

> **Case study reflections**
>
> - Consider what Wendy has to say about the importance of self-care. What lessons can you take from this for your own practice?
> - Reflect on the strategies that Wendy has described. Would any of these be useful for you? How do you de-stress and care for your own emotional health?

Mental health toolkit

Some organisations develop a 'mental health toolkit' (mentalhealth.org, annafreud.org) which is comprised of resources which support good mental health. As an individual, it can be a useful exercise to create your own virtual mental health toolkit to consult if you are aware that you are becoming stressed (Figure 11.3).

Support services – know where to go/who to speak to if you feel that your mental health is becoming a concern.

Enjoyable activity – know which things you enjoy doing and which will 'take you out of yourself' for a while. Do things that you are good at to increase your self-esteem.

Communication – talk about how you are feeling; ignore the perceived social stigma and be open about your feelings, as others are likely to be dealing with similar emotions.

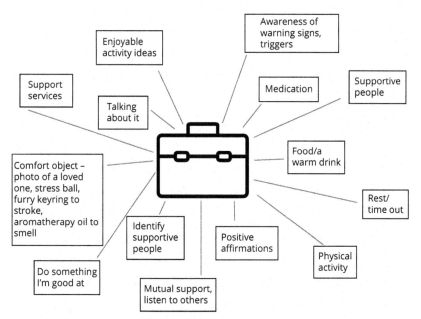

Figure 11.3 Mental health toolkit

Supportive people – learn which people in your life support you and build you up and spend time with them. Avoid negative people who drain you, especially when you are feeling vulnerable.

Warning signs – know your own warning signs; you may have physical symptoms which can warn you that you are becoming mentally unwell. Recognising these signs is half the battle.

Triggers – be aware of things and situations that are likely to trigger anxiety and deal with them only when you are feeling emotionally strong enough.

Mutual support – create an environment at work where you can talk to each other and listen to others non-judgementally.

Activity ideas – physical activity is always helpful for our mental health, so find something that you enjoy and that suits you. For some it will be running, for others, dancing, and for others, a gentle stroll outside. All of these will make you feel better.

Food and drink – eat and drink well and try to make healthy choices; eating lots of comforting chocolate and drinking heavily may have a short-term gain but will not be helpful in the long run. Nourish your body as if you really care about it.

Comfort object – this might be a photo of loved ones that you keep with you, a furry keyring to stroke, a stress ball, aromatherapy oil to smell, or even an outfit that you find comforting to wear.

Positive affirmation – find things about yourself that you like, that make you feel good, and treasure them. Tell yourself that you deserve to do things for you, in the words of L'Oréal, 'because you're worth it!'

Case Study 2: Erica Brown – Coping with palliative care

Many years ago, I received a phone call from the Chairman of a voluntary organisation where I had applied to become a trustee. She opened the conversation with the statement, 'You have a remarkably eclectic CV' and then invited me to expand on my letter of application by telling her how my professional experience might be beneficial to the charity. This was just one of many occasions when I have concluded that I am unable to separate my personal story from the course that my professional journey has taken me on.

I remember interviewing a mother of a child born with complex needs who had died 25 days after his birth. As a bereaved mother, I discovered a connection with her story which became the catalyst for what I later discovered was my first foray into autoethnographic research. Post-bereavement life posed perplexing conundrums in understanding existential questions such as:

Who am I at this moment?

How are my personal and professional paths related?

How am I viewing other peoples' situations in relation to my lived experience?

After my own twins died, for months I was unable to think coherently or to do even simple tasks. I existed in a world of emotional pain and brokenness.

Then, just before the first anniversary of their birth, I realised that my babies' legacy to me was that gradually I could reframe my life and work with children who had complex needs. At first, I was unsure how to combine my previous experience as a reception class teacher with new roles in special education and higher education. I wanted to develop an approach which enabled me to use rigorous reflexivity, which would help me to meet the individual and very complex needs of families and their children. But I was aware that I often listened selectively, recalled conversations fragmentally and recounted things in ways that best suited my own purpose. So, I resolved to help families create meaning through encouraging them to talk about their experiences of despair, chaos and the disruption of hope for their child's future. I discovered that families needed to grieve old dreams before they could take the first steps in a previously unimagined world. Perhaps most important of all, I learned that a person's ability to be strong in response to one situation does not mean that they will remain resilient for their next challenge.

Working with 'special' children and their families requires special skills that demand that we listen with more than an open heart and the finesse of active listening, and also think about how to help people find hope when the stability of their world is shattered.

According to recent research by Bell and Romano (2015) and Hurley et al. (2015), supportive relationships are pivotal to how well people develop coping strategies. Against all the odds many parents do 'bounce back' and develop the ability to cope with challenging experiences both publicly and privately (Brown et al., 2018). Resilience is a contested concept. It is, however, fundamental to professionals understanding how families can thrive despite adverse circumstances (Shean, 2015).

In recent years, my work in higher education research and in children's hospices has been firmly grounded in constructive interpretivism or how people create meaning from their lived experience (Thanh and Thanh, 2015). People enter the caring professions with a wide range of motives and ambitions. Most have a deep vocation, but they are human, and if the ideals and expectations become jaded under the stress of caring, negative responses may come into play. People who give care, need to receive care. The quality of care that families receive is highly dependent on the quality of support that staff receive. Over the years I have learned to develop strategies that safeguard myself against burnout.

An old Indian proverb likened the need for human holistic care to a house with four rooms. Each room is an important element of holistic care and every person should take responsibility for each dimension of care:

- *A physical dimension*
- *A spiritual dimension*
- *A cognitive dimension*
- *An emotional dimension*

The proverb teaches that unless a person commits to opening each door of their house every day, the rooms will become dusty, stale and unloved. I ask students and colleagues at CPD events to reflect on how they care for themselves holistically and to record in each quadrant what they do to fulfil each element of their care.

There is no single way to support people in distress. Yet there are avenues open to each one of us. Keep travelling alongside those who hurt and listen to the words they speak and ways in which they choose to communicate. Pace yourself in your work with children and families and be sensitive to their need to play an active part in what is happening. Give support, but do not intrude. Care, but do not lose sight of the emotional price you pay for your own commitment. Seek solace, guidance and comfort for yourself. But most importantly, be there, and trust children and families to be your guides.

Case study reflections

- Erica said that she is unable to separate her personal story from her professional journey; is this the case for many of us in the caring professions? What are the implications of this?
- In her work with life-limited children, young people and their families, Erica says that it is important to encourage them to talk about their experiences of despair and chaos. How difficult would this be for you? How might you handle this?
- Erica explains that people who give care need to receive care and that the quality of care that families receive is highly dependent on the quality of support that staff receive. Do you agree? Think about the setting/organisation that you work in. How could support for staff be improved?

Erica talked about the 'house with four rooms' (Godden, 1990). Try the activity for yourself; identify the things that you do in each area of your life. Here are some ideas (Table 11.3).

Table 11.3 'Four rooms' ideas

Mental	Emotional
Learn new vocabulary	Listen to uplifting music
Read a book	Surround myself with positive people
Watch a documentary on TV	Spend time with beloved pets
Learn a new skill or craft	Do a random act of kindness
Learn a new language	Connect with family
Write to-do lists	Express emotions
Play games	Hug, cuddle and kiss your loved ones
Research an interest	Have fun with friends
	Watch some comedy

Table 11.3 (continued)

Spiritual	Physical
Practise meditation/mindfulness	Eat a healthy balanced diet
Use a reflective journal	Drink plenty of water
Help someone	Walk whenever you can
Watch the sea	Find an exercise activity that you enjoy
Look at the stars	Dance
Do yoga or Tai Chi	Get plenty of sleep
Spend time in nature	Get a massage
Go to church/temple/mosque	Do some gardening
Be silent	

Conclusion

In this chapter, we have explored the effects that working with children, young people and families can have on our mental and physical health. It is clear to see that working with vulnerable people, and taking on the emotional strain of doing so, creates a strain that must be acknowledged and addressed. The case studies by Wendy and Erica have explored challenging aspects of their work and have given us practical suggestions and resources to help us to take care of ourselves.

With all of the evidence about stress and burnout in work with people, it is vital that we build resources to protect ourselves; whether this is by creating our own support mechanisms or asking for help and support from others. It is only when we truly nurture ourselves that we can care for others effectively.

 Further reading

Bell, T., Romano, E. and Flynn, R. (2015). Profiles and predictors of behavioural resilience among children. *Child Abuse and Neglect*, 48, 92–103.
  - A good article to read if you want to find out more about how children develop resilience.
Brown, E. (2018). *Life Changes 2: Loss, Change and Bereavement for Young People Aged 11–16 Years*. Manchester: Lions International.
  - A very useful book by the author of the case study in this chapter.
Clance, P. and Imes, S. (2003). The imposter phenomenon in high achieving women: Dynamics and therapeutic intervention. *Psychotherapy: Theory, Research and Practice*, 15(3), 241–247.
  - Find out possible reasons why you don't feel worthy of the position that you are working in!

References

Aldwin, C. and Werner, E. (2014). *Stress, Coping and Development*. London: The Guildford Press.

American Institute of Stress. (2018). *Holmes–Rahe Life Stress Inventory*. Available at: https://www.stress.org/holmes-rahe-stress-inventory [Accessed 9 August 2019].

Atkinson, T. and Claxton, G. (2000). *The Intuitive Practitioner*. Buckingham: Open University Press.

Bradford, G. (2016). Achievement, wellbeing, and value. *Philosophy Compass*, 11(12), December 2016, 95–803. https://doi.org/10.1111/phc3.12388.

Brennan, E. (2017). Towards resilience and wellbeing in nurses. *British Journal of Nursing*, 26(1), 43–47.

Clayton, S. (2017). *Reflective Supervision: The Cornerstone of Good Social Work Practice, Research in Practice*. Available at: https://www.rip.org.uk [Accessed 9 August 2019].

Covey, S. (2000). *The Seven Habits of Successful People*. London: Free Press.

Crane, R. (2017). *Mindfulness-Based Cognitive Therapy*. Oxon: Routledge.

Creaner, M. (2013). *Getting the Best Out of Supervision in Counselling and Psychotherapy: A Guide for the Supervisee*. London: SAGE Publications Ltd. https://doi.org/10.4135/9781473914896.

Duran, L. and Huckaby, S. (2015). Current trends in stress management. *Journal of the Academy of Medical-Surgical Nurses*, 24(2), Suppl. 7.

Elfer, P. (2012). Emotion in nursery work: Work discussion as a model of critical professional reflection. *Early Years*, 32(2), 129–141.

Elfer, P., Greenfield, S., Robson, S., Wilson, D. and Zachariou, A. (2018). Love, satisfaction and exhaustion in the nursery: Methodological issues in evaluating the impact of Work Discussion groups in nursery. *Early Child Development and Care*, 1–18.

Flook, L., Goldberg, S., Pinger, L., Bonus, K. and Davidson, R. (2013). Mindfulness for teachers: A pilot study to assess effects on stress, burnout, and teaching efficacy. *Mind, Brain & Education*, 7(3), 182–195.

Godden, R. (1990). *A House with Four Rooms*. London: Corgi.

Health & Safety Executive. (2017). *Stress at Work*. Available at: http://www.hse.gov.uk/stress/risk-assessment.htm [Accessed 9 August 2019].

Health & Safety Executive. (2019). *Tackling Work-Related Stress Using the Management Standards Approach*. Available at: http://www.hse.gov.uk/pubns/wbk01.pdf [Accessed 9 August 2019].

Hodgkins, A. (2019). Advanced empathy in the early years – A risky strength? *NZ International Research in Early Childhood Education Journal,* 22(1), 46–58.

Hodgkins, A. and Watson, N. (2017). Learning to learn in the HE context. In Musgrave, J., Savin-Baden, M. and Stobbs, N. (eds.) *Studying for Your Early Years Degree*. London: Critical Publishing.

Holmes, R. (1967). The social adjustment rating scale. *Journal of Psychosomatic Research*, 11, 213–218.

Hurley, D., Alvarez, L. and Buckley, H. (2015). From the zone of risk to the zone of resilience: Protecting the resilience of children and practitioners in

Argentina, Canada and Ireland. *International Journal of Children, Youth and Family Studies*, 6(1), 17–51.

Ingram, G. and Harris, J. (2001). *Delivering Good Youth Work: A Working Guide to Surviving and Thriving*. Dorset: Russell House Publishing.

Kornfield, J. (1996). *Buddha's Little Instruction Book*. Chicago: Ebury Publishing.

Maslach, C. and Jackson, S. E. (1986). *Maslach Burnout Inventory: Manual*, 2nd ed. Palo Alto, CA: Consulting Psychologists Press.

McEwen, B. (2007). Central effects of stress hormones in health and disease: Understanding the protective and damaging effects of stress and stress mediators. *European Journal of Pharmacology*, 583(2–3), 174–185.

McFadden, P., Campbell, A. and Taylor, B. (2015). Resilience and burnout in child protection social work. *British Journal of Social Work*, 45(5), 1546–1563.

MIND. (2017). *How to Improve Your Mental Wellbeing*. Available at: https://www.mind.org.uk/information-support/tips-for-everyday-living/wellbeing/#.WetRTLpFyUl [Accessed 9 August 2019].

NHS. (2016). *Mindfulness*. Available at: https://www.nhs.uk/conditions/stress-anxiety-depression/mindfulness [Accessed 28 January 2018].

Orton, P. and Pereia-Gray, D. (2015). Burnout in NHS staff. *The Lancet*, 385(9980), 1831.

Persson, P. and Zakinsson, A. (2016). Stress. *Acta Physiologica*, 216(2), 149–152.

Public Health England (2017). *Stress and You*. Available at: https://www.nhs.uk/oneyou/stress#DZwhMTtilLmzu8d2.99 [Accessed 28 January 2018].

Remez, A. (2016). The building blocks reflective supervision model. *Journal of Infant, Child & Adolescent Psychotherapy*, 15(2), 120–123.

Shean, M. (2015). *Current Theories Relating to Resilience and Young People*. Melbourne: Victorian Health Promotion Foundation, pp. 29–32.

Steinlin, C., Dölitzsch, C., Kind, N., Fischer, S., Schmeck, K., Fegert, J. M. and Schmid, M. (2017). The influence of sense of coherence, self-care and work satisfaction on secondary traumatic stress and burnout among child and youth residential care workers in Switzerland. *Child & Youth Services*, 38(2), 159–175.

Taggart, G. (2011). Don't we care?: The ethics and emotional labour of early years professionalism. *Early Years*, 31(1), 85–95.

Taggart, G. (2013). The importance of empathy. *Nursery World*, 14 May 2013. Available at: https://www.nurseryworld.co.uk/nursery-world/opinion/1106788/importance-empathy [Accessed 9 August 2019].

Taggart, G. (2016). Compassionate pedagogy: The ethics of care in early childhood professionalism. *European Early Childhood Education Research Journal*, 24(2), 173–185. https://doi.org/10.1080/1350293X.2014.970847.

Thanh, N. and Thanh, T. (2015). The interconnection between interpretivist paradigm and qualitative methods in education. *American Journal of Educational Scien*ce, 1(2), 24–27.

Wilkins, D., Forrester, D. and Grant, L. (2017). What happens in child and family social work supervision? *Child & Family Social Work*, 22(2), 942–951.

Wilkinson, E. (2015). UK NHS staff: Stressed, exhausted, burnt out. *Lancet*, 385(9971), 1831.

12 THE CONTINUALLY DEVELOPING PRACTITIONER

Chapter outcomes

This chapter will enable practitioners to engage with the following:
- The importance of CPD in careers with children, young people and families
- Methods of continuing your professional development
- Motivation to improve and succeed
- Personal development and self-appraisal
- Career development and employability in the twenty-first century

---

Introduction

This chapter considers the importance of continual professional development for practitioners working with children and families. It highlights the need for self-appraisal and self-development as well as career development. The links between research/reading and good practice will be examined, with currency being important for practitioners' well-being and for the ultimate benefit of the children and families we work with. The workforce today is not static, and so we need to be ready to adapt and grow in our roles. Career changes are more prevalent today and this will also be examined.

The importance of CPD

Professional development should be a continuous process throughout our careers. It ensures that we remain competent in our profession and keeps us up to date with our practice which, in the children and families' field, is ever-changing. CPD helps us to stay interested and opens up new and creative possibilities for change and development. 'Professional development has the potential to motivate, refresh and above all to help people get better at what they do' (Bubb and Earley, 2013, p. 244).

Alsop (2013, p. 77) suggests that 'in engaging in activities at work that further their knowledge and experience ... professionals are also taking steps to develop themselves as professional artists'. 'Professional artistry', a phrase first coined by Schon (1987, p. 22), describes the professional competence that practitioners display in unique, uncertain and conflicted situations of practice.

> Professional artistry is evident in those moments of highly effec-
> tive or beautiful practice which, when witnessed, may seem inex-
> plicable or even magical. It involves a complex blending of what
> the professional knows (in diverse ways), senses (in the here and
> now and in terms of possibilities) and is capable of. (Frost and
> Titchen, 2010)

The standard for teachers' professional development (DfE, 2016a) states that 'High-quality professional development requires workplaces to be steeped in rigorous scholarship, with professionals continually developing and support-ing each other ...', and the Teachers' Professional Development Expert group (DfE, 2016b) add that it should be available and accessible to every-one in the teaching profession, with staff given 'clear opportunities to develop their careers and be recognised for greater knowledge and expertise' (DfE, 2016b, p. 1).

In the teaching profession in England, since the Teachers' Pay and Conditions Act in 1987, all teachers have been given five INSET (In Service Training) days per year with no pupils on site. However, a study by Bubb and Earley (2013, pp. 242–243) found evidence that much of this allocated time is spent on admin and classroom preparation. The study showed that secondary teachers, in particular, reported some dissatisfac-tion with the relevance of training provided. They found that these days were often used for introducing new initiatives, when staff wanted person-alised training to be made available to them which met their individual needs. In many professions, CPD is an obligation. In other sectors, it is less formal and driven by individual motivations. It is important to add that there are some differences in CPD requirements within the countries of the UK (Figure 12.1).

CPD, for some, is a luxury; with cuts to Local Authority funding and to staffing ratios, there is less time and opportunity for additional courses, training events and opportunities to share experiences and good practice with others. In the following creative story, Annie recounts her early days as a nursery nurse, at a time when CPD was not seen as important for these 'lowly' professionals.

Teaching	• Although it is a professional duty for all teachers, there is no legal minimum number of hours for teachers' CPD; however the Teachers Standards state that teachers should ' take responsibility for improving teaching through appropriate professional development' (DfE, 2011)
Social work & Care	• To meet the standards of the Health & Care Professionals Code, all practitioners must keep a CPD profile, which evidences regular learning activities of different kinds. A record must be kept and an audit is carried out with a randomly selected sample each year. (HCPC, 2018)
Nursing and Midwifery	• All nurses and midwives must complete a minimum of 35 hours of CPD every 3 years, to comply with the Nursing and Midwifery Council. 20 of these hours must include preparatory learning. (NMC, 2019)
Early Years	• Through the EYFS, providers are required to support staff to undertake appropriate training and professional development opportunities. Providers must ensure that staff have up to date knowledge of safeguarding and child protection, health and safety, paediatric first aid, food hygiene and the administration of medicine. (DfE, 2017: p29)
Youth Work	• One of the National Standards of Youth Work states that they must 'Take appropriate action to maintain continuous professional development'(NYA, 2019) although there are no formal requirements outlined.

Figure 12.1 CPD requirements

Case Study: Annie Pendrey – 'Cinderella, you will go to the CPD!'

Once upon a time in a land not so far away was a nursery nurse. Her main purpose in her career was to take the chairs from off the tables at the beginning of her day, prepare art and craft activities and assist the young children with taking off their coats and hanging them up. When it was time for PE, her sole responsibility was to push, tug and slide little hot sweaty feet into rubber plimsolls. In addition, this nursery nurse was never allowed in the staff room for a tea break as she was always on First Aid duty and was armed with a huge supply of wet paper towels and plasters which treated everything form a bumped head to a knee full of gravel. This nursery nurse was me!

The National Nursery Examination Board (NNEB) was set up in 1945 by the Ministry of Health offering childcare qualifications. In 1985, I qualified as an NNEB nursery nurse and began my career in education, with my first role in a reception class. At the end of a busy day in reception, I would wash the paint pots, bulldog-clip clean newspaper to the painting easel and guillotine buff-coloured kitchen paper ready for another round of free expressive painting the following day. Meanwhile, the other guests at the ball (the REAL teachers) would leave me to go into the staffroom to reflect, have learning conversations and engage in Continuous Professional Development.

Today witnesses me wearing glass slippers and spinning round and round in my gown with the responsibility of planning and delivering CPD in my capacity as Professional Development Manager in an FE institution. It is in this capacity that I reflect continuously and embrace my grass roots as an NNEB and ensure all the Cinders of the education system are invited to the ball.

Whilst there is an ongoing shift towards enabling educators to own their professional development, the work of Lave and Wenger (1990) purports that CPD is best achieved when all educators work together in a community of practice. The work of Knipe and Speck (2005) also asks us to consider how CPD needs to be realistic and personally relevant and have real application to the world and the context of early years education. This suggests that the Cinderellas of the education system leave the paint pots to soak, and attend the CPD ball and dance with clear, personal and professional aspirations.

There is a plethora of reasons why the early years practitioners of today need to be part of CPD, not only to keep current but to increase job satisfaction, complement their CVs and increase individuals' scope for promotion. The early years practitioners' aspirations need to celebrated and aligned with the ever-changing landscape of the field and, as Lave and Wenger (1990) suggest, should be situated in the here and now.

Reflecting upon my own professional journey from NNEB to Professional Development Manager, I have never lost sight of humanism and how positive self-regard (Rogers, 1951) for all educators is imperative. Treating early years professionals as equals within our communities of practice, our situated learning and our learning conversations only lead us all to outstanding practice for our young children's hearts and minds. And to any teacher who leaves me washing the paint pots I would say, 'but you see … I have the other slipper so I must attend the CPD'.

Case study reflections

- What does Annie's story say about the relationship between professional and personal development?
- What do you think are the benefits of engaging in CPD as a group or team?
- Would this work for you?
- What does Annie's story have to say about the relationships between professionals within a school? What does this mean for integrated working?

Table 12.1 CPD plan

What CPD do I have to do? (legally or contractually)	
What do I want to do? What interests or fascinates me?	
What do I need to know to get where I want to be?	
Do I need to work towards a formal qualification?	
Can I learn alone? Or would I prefer to learn with others in a group?	
Where can I find information about possible opportunities?	
Who can help/advise/support me?	

In the early years sector, where there has been a professionalisation of the workforce, this has actually increased *control of*, rather than *empowerment for*, practitioners (Osgood, 2010). Demands are made on workers who, as Annie's case study (above) depicts, were previously somewhat powerless. Research has evidenced the fact that outcomes for young children are higher if the staff working with them are well qualified and skilled (Department for Education, 2014, p. 10). Therefore, CPD has to be a priority for all childcare providers. As Annie suggests in her case study, professional development should be collegial, with each person being a member of a learning community (Frost, 2014, cited in Lightfoot and Frost, 2015, p. 415).

There will be other factors influencing your CPD plans, such as opportunity, availability, cost, etc., but spending some time carefully considering what you want/need to do and how you might go about it is helpful. Ask yourself these questions to help you to formulate a plan (Table 12.1).

Methods of continuing your professional development

As evidenced in several studies (e.g. Bubb and Earley, 2013; Lightfoot and Frost, 2015), it is clear that CPD needs to be personalised, relevant, sustained, supported and collaborative (ATL, 2015). No one method will suit all professionals; we all have different needs, interests and learning styles, and all have our own motivations and ambitions. Using the three learning styles identified by Fleming (1995), a visual learner might enjoy reading, whereas an auditory learner might learn better attending lectures. A kinaesthetic learner may need to physically try things out. Honey and Mumford's (1982) work, which describes four learning styles, also gives a range of learning activities suitable for each 'type' of person. There has been some criticism of learning styles in recent years (Fleming, 2012; Newton and Miah, 2017), amidst claims that there is a lack of empirical evidence to support the theory. Even so, research by Newton and Miah (2017) found that a substantial number of academics continue to find them useful. Therefore, it may be worth considering finding out and making our own minds up about whether they are something we may find helpful.

There are a multitude of theories concerned with learning styles (Honey and Mumford (1982), Kolb (1984), VAK Fleming (2011), Multiple Intelligences Gardner (1983, 2003), etc.) and each of these attempts to describe variations on how people learn best. The following diagram uses a range of theories to present an overview of some of the ways that people learn. It can be useful to know how best you personally learn, so that you can plan training and study times accordingly (Figure 12.2).

How do you think you learn best? Are there several learning styles that resonate with you? You can find many learning-style tests online – search for 'Honey and Mumford Learning Style Questionnaire', 'the VARK questionnaire' or 'Myers–Briggs personality type questionnaire'.

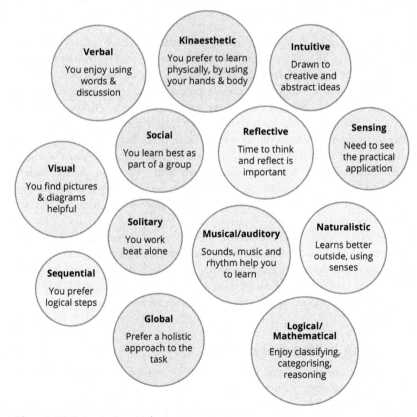

Figure 12.2 Learning styles

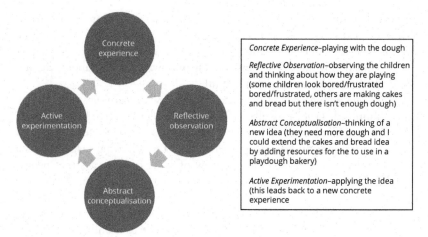

Concrete Experience–playing with the dough

Reflective Observation–observing the children and thinking about how they are playing (some children look bored/frustrated bored/frustrated, others are making cakes and bread but there isn't enough dough)

Abstract Conceptualisation–thinking of a new idea (they need more dough and I could extend the cakes and bread idea by adding resources for the to use in a playdough bakery)

Active Experimentation–applying the idea (this leads back to a new concrete experience

Figure 12.3 Experiential learning cycle

Experiential learning, or 'learning through experience', is, according to Kolb (1984, p. 38), 'the process whereby knowledge is created through the transformation of experience'. Kolb's model is a four-stage learning cycle, in which the learner engages in concrete experience, reflective observation, abstract conceptualisation and active experimentation. Although we all have our own preferred ways of learning, Kolb's model suggests that the four learning styles are all important to use in order for real learning to take place. Variations of this model are used throughout the practice of working with children and families, observation and reflection being widely accepted as key aspects of professional practice. To explain the stages, imagine that you have set up a playdough activity with a group of children (Figure 12.3).

The model is a cycle, so the learning gained from an experience because a new concrete experience and so the cycle begins again, with improvements and new thinking and understanding continuously being developed. This model goes a long way to explaining how valuable experience is in practitioners. Qualification and training are important, but experience cannot be underestimated.

Learning in the workplace

Much professional CPD takes place within the workplace, with training days or twilight sessions being organised for individuals and staff teams. Participating in training at work with colleagues can be a great way to learn, as professional discussions take place and subject matter is directly related to practice within the setting. Learning within the workplace allows us to learn with peers and observe others within the context of the setting. This makes learning meaningful as it can be directly related to the ethos and unique circumstances of the setting and work team. Lemanski et al. (2011, cited in Alsop, 2013, p. 69) characterised work-based learning as:

- Learning *for* work – work experience and placements

- Learning *at* work – training organised by the organisation (often not assessed)

- Learning *through* work – on-site courses that are formally assessed and accredited

Coaching and mentoring

Coaching and mentoring are two useful methods of promoting both personal and professional development in the workplace. They both require a more knowledgeable or experienced member of staff to mentor or coach a newer or less experienced member of staff. There are some key differences in the two styles, however. Coaching is about skills and knowledge acquisition, whereas mentoring is transformational and involves much more than simply acquiring a specific skill or knowledge. For example, a manager of a youth club might coach another member of staff in managing the finances. A mentor, however, might build a relationship over time with a new volunteer, and help them to acclimatise into their new role. This is a very simplified explanation, and there are many different types of coaching and mentoring which are used for a multitude of scenarios (Figure 12.4).

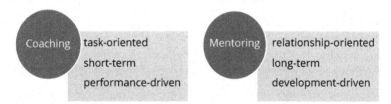

Figure 12.4 Coaching and mentoring

E-learning

Using e-learning allows us to use electronic technologies to access education and training online. This a very flexible and convenient method of learning for learners who are also working, as it is carried out in your own time at home. However, it is not an easy option, as learners have to motivate and organise themselves, without face-to-face interaction. Although the method suits some determined and enthusiastic learners very well, others may benefit from social interaction and learning from peers within a face-to-face group. Some courses use flexible and distributed learning, which includes e-learning, but also includes an element of taught classes too. This can be the 'best of both worlds', as much of the learning is very flexible, but there are some opportunities for peer support and face-to-face interaction.

Reading

Reading is a good way of continuing to learn and develop and to keep up to date with current topics related to your area of work. Regular journals and magazines will help you to keep informed with current practice and developments, and many companies provide these in staff rooms for staff break times. A good manager will share articles with staff and provide books for staff to borrow, but ultimately it is up to the individual to read if and when they want to do so.

Reading for a purpose is different from reading for pleasure. In reading for CPD purposes, it is rarely the case that a book will be read from cover to cover as when reading a novel. The following types of reading are useful;

- *Skimming* – this means going through the text of a book rapidly, 'getting the gist' of a book, skimming through the titles and contents page, reading the first couple of lines of paragraphs, to determine how useful it is likely to be and what the author's style is like. After skimming, you may choose to read certain sections more slowly and carefully.

- *Scanning* – scanning is used when you know the word or phrase that you are looking for. It is a quick scan though pages and paragraphs to find information on the subject.

- *Search reading* – looking for key words and phrases, after looking them up in the index. In search reading, it is important to consider that the author's keywords may be different from yours, so it is important to be flexible.

- *Receptive reading* – this involves paying close attention to what has been written, pausing to reflect and take in the meaning. This is often the next stage after skimming.

- *Reading with a pen* – whilst reading, it is useful to make notes. Always take down full details of the book/sources in case you need to come back to it. If you own the book, don't be afraid to make notes in the book with a pencil or highlighter. This does not come naturally to some people, as books are often treated as sacred and our parents and teachers always told us not to deface our books! But in scribbling notes, some useful thoughts can be captured before they disappear from your mind. If you really can't bring yourself to write on your books, Post-it notes on pages are a good alternative.

Social media

Social media can be a great way of keeping up to date with practice and developments. Many people prefer this method of keeping in touch; it is fast, lively and accessible to anyone with a smartphone, tablet or PC. Signing up for Twitter updates from noted leaders and academics in your field will keep you right up to date and joining groups of like-minded professionals on Facebook can be a great way of communicating with others in the field, having professional conversations and finding out about what is happening both nationally and internationally. Sites such as LinkedIn are a good way to widen your professional network. The level of involvement is a matter of choice, so it is possible to create conversations, join in with others or simply spectate.

Research

As well as engaging in secondary research by reading what others have written, primary research is essential in investigating your own setting. Research is not a separate activity; it is an integral part of practice. In work with children and families, whether we work in health, education or social care, we:

- question practice and processes
- read and talk to others to find out more
- 'try things out' and judge whether there has been an improvement
- share our findings with others.

Practitioner research, however small, can make an impact on others and can improve outcomes for children and families, as well as advancing our own practice. Research which happens within the workplace, carried out by practitioners themselves, proves a powerful and useful way to drive improvements and it impacts positively on professional growth and empowerment (Newman and Leggett, 2019, p. 121).

Time management and organisation

Personal organisation and time management are the keys to success in creating a work–life balance. When engaging in training it is important to set aside time to study and to read, but equally to make time for yourself, and for your family and friends. If you have other responsibilities, such as children or work, then it is important to acknowledge and decide how to organise these responsibilities. Identifying which tasks are urgent and which are important is essential in prioritising workload (Covey, 1999). Identifying specific dates to carry out tasks can also help with successful time management. Some students find that drawing up a plan of their week and identifying 'available time' can be useful, as was the case in Annabel's case study.

Case Study: Annabel Collins – Juggling work, family and study

I began my studies four years ago; my son had just moved up to high school, so after contemplating returning to studying for a while I felt that the time was now right and I would have a bit more time available to do this – how wrong I was!

Working and studying, both full time, was hard and I needed to learn how to use my time effectively and productively as an employee, student, mother and wife. Prior to studying, I had seen myself as an organised person and could manage my workloads both at home and in the office, but once on the course I needed to take this to the next level. My tutor suggested we create a plan to find out where in the week there would be times to study, write assignments and research. I worked out that I could do my entire studying etc. over evenings and weekends, excluding those days when I was being a taxi service for my son.

This seemed quite an easy task, until life throws in other unexpected situations, which then scupper the whole plan. In the end, I spoke to my husband and son and explained how much the course meant to me, and that I did need time away from the house to do all my studying and research. Things did become better and the feelings of guilt of not being there to do the usual household chores receded when I employed a cleaner!

Managing time effectively and productively is achievable; you need to have the focus and support to enable this to happen. I was asked how I managed to juggle work and studying and in all honesty, I do not know how I did it, but I did find a rhythm and system that worked for me. Finding the correct balance that works is key; whether this is studying in the morning alongside the dawn chorus or at night with the bats and owls, discover what works and use the time efficiently.

Case study reflections

- What can you learn from Annabel about organising study time?
- Would plotting free time on a calendar work for you? Why?
- Reflect on the importance of flexibility when, as Annabel says, 'life throws in unexpected situations'.

The learning journey

Reflection is important in all aspects of professional life, but particularly here in career development. It can be useful to look back at what has led you to where you are today, as this will help you to identify future developments.

Identifying the values you have, and the skills that you have developed, should help to inspire you for the future. In the diagram below, early years student Abi Broome has identified the factors that have influenced her development so far and the pressures that she has experienced along the way. Carrying out this reflective activity has helped Abi to identify her specific qualities as a practitioner and this should help to motivate her for the future (Figure 12.5).

Action planning helps to focus ideas and to aid decision making, based on steps that need to be taken to achieve particular goals. For the action plan to be useful, it should include SMART targets (Specific, Measurable, Achievable, Realistic and Time-based). It can be useful to have a goal in mind to aim for, which will include specific steps forward in order to reach the goal. Staff appraisals and professional discussions with peers can be helpful in focusing future plans.

Motivation

In order to make changes and improve things, we need to be motivated. In the case study within Chapter 9, you will see that Adam was motivated by his concern for his own grandchildren to try and change provision for young people within the community. There are many theories of motivation, but each individual has his/her own motivating factors. For some, it will be earning money, for others it will be in order to 'make a difference'. Work with children, young people and families is rarely motivated by money, as it tends to be relatively low paid, so there will generally be, for most people, a desire to improve the lives of others in some way. Here are just a few of the many motivation theories developed and some key questions based on each theory which may be useful in determining what motivates you (Table 12.2).

Personal development and self-appraisal

Self-appraisal, also known as self-assessment or self-evaluation, is a reflective process; whereas a staff appraisal by a line manager enables feedback from another person's point of view, managers are unlikely to be aware of, or to remember, every success or accomplishment of each member of staff. This reflective process can also help the individual to provide detailed information for the setting management, but also to clarify things for yourself. Self-assessment can prevent us from 'going through the motions' and getting stuck in a rut. We can learn from things that went well and from things that went wrong. It is OK to make mistakes, as this means that we are moving forward and taking risks. There is a famous quote (author unknown, but it has been attributed to Einstein, Henry Ford and Mark Twain), which states that; 'If you always do what you've always done, you'll

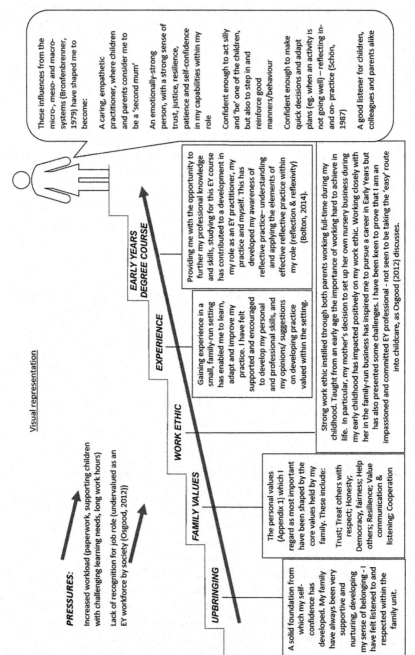

Figure 12.5 Abi's reflective journey

Table 12.2 Motivation theories

Writer	Ideas	Key Questions
Porter and Lawler (1968)	*Expectancy theory* – Effort, performance and satisfaction	What sort of reward would prompt you to make the most effort? Do you feel that you are adequately rewarded for your performance at work?
Maslow (1970)	*Hierarchy of human needs* – When each level of need is met, higher level needs emerge. The ultimate aim is self-actualisation.	Are all of my physical needs met in my place of work? Do I feel emotional safe, secure and valued? Do I have opportunities to build my confidence and try new things? Do I feel fulfilled?
McClelland (1988)	*Need theory* – Identification of three needs – achievement, affiliation and power	How important to you is achievement? How important to you is power? How important is it to have acceptance and approval from others?
Locke and Latham (2002)	*Goal-setting theory* – five goal-setting principles: 1. Clarity 2. Challenge 3. Commitment 4. Feedback 5. Task complexity	Set out some goals for your future. Are your goals: Clear? Challenging? Do you have commitment from your team? Have you planned how you will gain feedback? Have you ensured that your goals are not too complex/demanding?
Pink (2009)	*Internal motivation (drive)* – human motivation is intrinsic. It does not need reward or punishment. Three aspects are: • Autonomy • Mastery • Purpose	Are you able to direct yourself? Do you feel the urge to master new skills? Are you doing something that is meaningful and important?

always get what you've always got'. So, we need to make changes and try new things in order to improve outcomes, for our children, families, clients, patients and ourselves. A professional development plan can be an effective way to motivate us to continue to move forward with our learning and our career progression.

Acknowledging the importance of self-care and self-knowledge means that we must prioritise the development of our values and personal dispositions just as much as we do our professional skills. Personal development, collaboration skills and social/emotional competence are important areas to reflect on and develop (Malm, 2009, pp. 80–82). As we develop professional skills, we must be careful not to undervalue the personal competencies that we are also developing.

An important element of personal development should be about happiness within the workplace. It is important to have job satisfaction and a happy workforce is a productive and successful one; Google even employs a Chief Happiness Officer to develop the happiness of its workers. With benefits such as free food and classes, gyms, leisure activities, slides instead of stairs and bringing your dog to work, Google claims to have increased employee satisfaction by 37 per cent, with a 12 per cent rise in productivity (Krapivin, 2018). Whilst having a good work–life balance has always been an attractive goal, work should also make us happy and those people who are lucky enough to love their work will go the extra mile because they gain such satisfaction. People who are passionate about their work and can't imagine doing anything else are fulfilled and enriched, claims Sir Ken Robinson. In his book *The Element* (2009), he tells stories of many people who have 'found their element' and found happiness and success in their work. Robinson advises that we should identify our own personal talents and passions and use these in our work. This is what Abi did in her visual representation in this chapter; she identified the specific aspects of the work that she does well and this has helped her to find her place within her staff team, and to feel that she is fulfilling her potential.

Seligman (2011) identified five building blocks to well-being, which spell out the acronym PERMA: positive emotion, engagement, relationships, meaning and accomplishment. Having all of these aspects should result in a fulfilled working life. Ask yourself the following questions:

Positive emotion – am I happy at work?
Engagement – am I busy and involved at work?
Relationships – do I have good relationships with the people I work with?
Meaning – am I satisfied that my job is meaningful and important?
Accomplishment – do I feel that I am achieving? That I am fulfilled and feel useful?

Do you agree?

Case Study: Mandy Ajmal – The joy of learning

I began my educational journey five years ago, cautiously signing up to study for a level three teaching assistants' course. It had been 26 years since I left school with one GCSE to my name, but even then, I dreamed of one day earning a degree. Yet I was incredibly uncertain as to whether I was capable of studying at level three. Through wonderful support and intense interest in the subject, I gained my certificate. I continued to pursue the next level and to my surprise, three years later, had completed a Foundation Degree. My eagerness to learn held no limits!

Having thoroughly enjoyed studying at my local college, I decided to continue my education at university. It was here I undertook a BA (Hons) top-up degree. I studied alongside, and learned from, peers hailing from various walks of life. Although I had previously learned a great deal studying for a foundation degree, I hadn't really applied my new knowledge to practice. As a teaching assistant, I lacked a great deal of confidence in having the courage to implement change and build upon the good practice already existing within my setting. Now, I carried all this rich information back with me into my setting, with a greater understanding of holistic approaches to children.

The degree completely changed my confidence levels. The expanse of teaching covered across the three informative and fascinating modules, coupled with my choice of dissertation, illuminated my mind and opened it up to investigating new paths of inquiry. My thought processes were guided in directions I could never have imagined. The diversity of lecturers was outstanding, each with very individual teaching techniques and all incredibly approachable. They worked hard on our behalf, ensuring we felt comfortable and confident every step of the way. Their life experiences shone through their lectures and every class was fun, interactive and inspiring.

I now had an immensely improved knowledge of multi-agency practice, the pitfalls and its benefits. The most impressive aspect of this was that it was no longer theoretical as I now confidently implemented these elements into daily practice. Family and friends have commented on the positive change in me and that is due to the impact this course has had on my life. It is such a unique course, that regardless of where my career path takes me, the skill set I have acquired at university will be applicable wherever I go. In this past year, I have gained so much; a new-found confidence in working with others, self-trust and a new realisation of my capabilities that I had previously lacked.

My time at university not only strengthened my theoretical knowledge, but greatly impacted upon my practice too. As a result, I completed my course and was immediately offered a graduate position within my setting, working with children experiencing adverse mental health issues. I hope to now continue studying a master's degree and look forward to increasing my knowledge and experience in a specialised field. I would certainly encourage anyone to take up the fabulous opportunity to attend university. It will change you!

Case study reflections

- Mandy's feelings about her emotional learning journey shine through in the piece that she has written. Reflect on your own feelings about learning.
- Mandy gained much more than subject knowledge at university. What else is important in a learning experience?
- Which is the most important motivator for you, regarding CPD opportunities? Consider whether it is improving your skills in practice, increasing your self-esteem by gaining qualifications, or improving your career and life chances? What motivates you?

Career development and employability in the twenty-first century

The world of employment has changed significantly over past decades and changes will no doubt continue into the twenty-first century. People no longer expect to find a 'job for life' when leaving education. Arnold (1997, p. 16) describes a career as 'the sequence of employment-related positions, roles, activities and experiences encountered by a person'. This is an interesting definition which includes four viewpoints; personal, subjective, sequential and employment-related (Figure 12.6).

All sorts of things can impact on our careers; see Sophie Reid's case study on page...., Chapter 2. Sophie's career has been influenced by her education and training but also by volunteering, part-time bar work and even

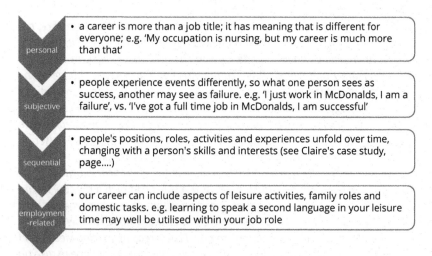

Figure 12.6 Career development

travelling. Careers are also transformed in unseen ways, for example 'conditions, conflicts, strategies and impacts' (Moen, 2017, p. 498). Experiences will have an impact on our career progression, whether they seem significant at the time or not.

Career development is valuable for everyone, regardless of age; although priorities will change throughout one's working life, career development impacts on staff satisfaction and retention. In a study by Health Education England (Foster, 2017), researchers found that, although nurses had different priorities, there were some generic themes that applied to all respondents, across generations, from newly qualified staff to those nearing retirement. Themes were:

- Supportive working conditions, e.g. work–life balance, childcare support, teamwork

- Systems of governance, e.g. administration and paperwork

- Acceptable pay, status and security

- Meaningful recognition – celebrating success, respect and value

- Growth and advancement – succession planning, career and professional development opportunities

- Professional autonomy, professional voice, and responsibility. (Foster, 2017, p. 67)

In the following case study, Claire describes her career progression, from children's nurse to primary school teacher.

Case Study: Claire Ashforth – A change of career

Having always wanted to work with children, I began my career as a registered sick children's nurse, but following the birth of my two children, I found it difficult to fit shift work into family life so I worked as a school nurse for eight years. However, I began to feel less and less job satisfaction as I did not believe I was making the difference I have always sought to achieve within any of the roles I have undertaken. I took a break from work to concentrate on my family and to consider my career options and it was at this point I began to consider primary teaching as a real possibility. I believed this could give me the fulfilment I'd felt was lacking in my school nursing role. After investigating the various routes into teaching, I settled on applying for a PGCE course that would see me qualified within 12 months. At the same time, I began a term of voluntary work within a mixed Year 1 and 2 class at a local primary school. Although I had spent some time in schools in my nursing role, this had not been classroom based and so this was the first time I had experienced school since my own primary education and how things had changed! Teaching was so fast-paced, with such a depth of learning, an array of different subjects and a range of activities forming part of an average school day. Some of the skills I had gained as a nurse were invaluable to me, particularly my skills in communicating with children and parents. There was a bigger emphasis upon supporting children with social and emotional needs than I had anticipated. This was linked closely to the need for an inclusive approach to education, and this was an aspect I had experienced within my nursing role when I would provide one-to-one support to children in both primary and secondary education. Also, my skills gained as a working parent were invaluable as the level of organisation and prioritisation of workload was something above and beyond any previous role I had undertaken.

My PGCE course was an intense year with what felt like unending assignments, tasks and presentations to complete alongside the planning and assessments of my school experience placements. I did not especially enjoy the academic side of the course as the qualification was more of a necessary means to an end as opposed to something I was choosing to complete for personal satisfaction. Furthermore, I did not find my university days were particularly helpful in preparing me for my role as a teacher. My preparation for teaching rested, in the main, with my school experience placements and I was extremely fortunate in the mentors I was allocated in the two different schools I trained in. However, the course provided me with an excellent network of support, both from my fellow students who were all encountering similar experiences, and the lecturers who were extremely knowledgeable and ready to offer whatever level of support was required.

At present, I do not plan to undertake any further academic qualifications as I do not feel this will enhance my ability to be an effective primary school teacher. I am, however, always looking for ways to improve my practice, either by partaking in subject-specific courses, from wider reading or from observing colleagues. I strive to be the best teacher I can, providing the children in my class with the best education I am able to offer, and this is what contributes to the fulfilment I achieve from having the most satisfying job I have ever undertaken.

Case study reflections

- Claire identifies many transferable skills here; list skills that you have developed in past roles and consider how these may be useful in other job roles.
- This case study illustrates Claire's view that she has learned more from her experiences and from observing others than in formal learning. Is this the case for everyone? Or does this depend on the person's individual learning style? Reflect on your own experiences.
- Look at Foster's career priorities for nursing; which of these can Claire expect to experience in her teaching role? Which are most important to her? And to you?

Internationalisation

In CYPF professions, we are working with families from a wider range of countries than ever before; the number of displaced families is at its highest, with 70.8 million people around the world forced from their homes, 25.9 million living as refugees and over half of these refugees under the age of 18 (UNHCR, 2019). There is, therefore, a need to identify needs, create resources and build awareness, thus fostering an 'empathic global community' (Lee, 2019).

The children who have been arriving in the UK in the past few years, and who have often experienced war zones, treacherous journeys and cramped, unsanitary refugee accommodation, exhibit a multitude of specific needs:

> The mental and emotional impacts caused by trauma, loss, and ongoing stress are profound. Strong personal social and emotional development is promoted by access to a safe, loving, and caring environment, which provides effective opportunities to develop physical skills and abilities. 'Typical' camp conditions do not support this requirement and, where a child's basic needs are not being met, higher functioning levels of development will be challenging to achieve. (Harvell and Prowle, 2018, p. 174)

The transition into UK schools, therefore, for these children is very challenging. Practitioners working with migrant children and their families will need to have good understanding of the complexity of their needs and they will need to provide a secure environment where children feel safe. Mental health support is crucial and so practitioners will need to fully utilise the skills they have developed. Personal skills such as empathy, compassion and emotional intelligence are crucial, as are many of the other skills discussed in this book (reflection, communication, collaboration, empowerment, etc.)

Working with migrant families is more widespread in the UK today, but there are other forms of internationalisation that are significant to careers. In the twenty-first century, more people will be working for organisations that have no boundaries and that are constantly changing and developing. Technology has transformed the way that we work and communicate with each other (Trought, 2017, p. 34) and, despite the current Brexit crisis in the UK, this has meant that having a global perspective is desirable. Diamond et al. (2008, cited in Trought, 2017, pp. 36–37) conducted research into what international recruiters look for and identified a list of ten 'global competencies'. These are additional to the usual employability competencies. Interestingly, none of the companies involved identified speaking another language or knowledge of processes and policies in other countries as being important. Crucial skills appear to be mostly related to openness and an ability to learn and adapt (Table 12.3).

Table 12.3 Global competencies

Importance	Global Competence
1st	Ability to work collaboratively with others from a range of backgrounds
2nd	Excellent communication skills
3rd	High degree of drive and resilience
4th	Ability to embrace multiple perspectives and challenge thinking
5th	Capacity to develop new skills and behaviours
6th	High degree of self-awareness
7th	Ability to negotiate and influence others
8th	Ability to form professional global networks
9th	Openness to, and respect for, a range of perspectives
10th	Multi-cultural learning agility

Conclusion

In this chapter, we have explored the importance of continuing professional development in CYPF careers, in order to keep us up to date with current trends and changes, and to develop our skill set. We have examined a range of methods that could be employed in continuing to learn. The choice of learning activity/development will be dependent on availability, time and need, but there will always be ways of continuing to learn and develop.

Although some professions have mandatory CPD, for others it is important to motivate ourselves to advance our skills, so we have looked at a range of motivation theories which may give you some ideas about what motivates you in particular. A major factor in motivation is self-appraisal; being aware of yourself, your strengths, your needs and your preferred way of learning will enable you to choose development activities which are well suited to you. Development which is based on both professional and personal growth brings the optimum success.

Career development in the twenty-first century is very different to that of our parents' and grandparents' generations. Careers are much more fluid and adaptable, and opportunities more accessible. The future is likely to be ever-changing, with new technology and more integration and inclusion, so it is more important than ever that we regularly upskill the workforce so that we are ready for the challenge!

Further reading

Alred, G., Garvey, B. and Smith, R. (1998). *Mentoring Pocketbook.* Alresford: Management Pocketbooks. Available at: https://www.sheffield.ac.uk/polopoly_fs/1.110468!/file/cipd_mentoring_factsheet.pdf [Accessed 11 August 2019].
  – Practical advice on mentoring.
Newman, L. and Leggett, N. (2019). Practitioner research: With intent. *European Early Childhood Education Research Journal*, 27(1), 120–137.
  – This journal article outlines the benefits to practitioners of conducting research in order to construct knowledge and identify strengths.
Robinson, K. (2009). *The Element: How Finding your Passion Changes Everything.* London: Penguin.
  – In this inspirational book, Robinson advises people to use their natural talent and personal passion to create a fulfilling working life.

References

Alsop, A. (2013). *Continuing Professional Development in Health & Social Care: Strategies for Lifelong Learning*, 2nd ed. Chichester: Wiley-Blackwell.
Arnold, J. (1997). *Managing Careers into the 21st Century.* London: Paul Chapman.
ATL (2015). *CPD: How to Access It and Why It's Essential.* Available at: https://www.atl.org.uk/Images/worklife_campaign_cpd_factsheet.pdf [Accessed 9 August 2019].
Bubb, S. and Earley, P. (2013). The use of training days: Finding time for teachers' development. *Educational Research*, 55(3), 236–248.
Covey, S. (1999). *Seven Habits of Highly Successful People.* London: Simon & Schuster.
DfE (2016a). *Standard for Teachers' Professional Development.* Available at: https://www.gov.uk/government/publications/standard-for-teachers-professional-development [Accessed 8 July 2019].
DfE (2016b). *Letter from Teachers' Professional Development Expert Group.* Available at: https://www.gov.uk/government/publications/standard-for-teachers-professional-development [Accessed 8 July 2019].
Fleming, N. D. (1995). I'm different; not dumb. Modes of presentation (VARK) in the tertiary classroom. In Zelmer, A. (ed.) *Research and Development in Higher Education.* Proceedings of the 1995 Annual Conference of the Higher Education and Research Development Society of Australasia (HERDSA), HERDSA, Volume 18, pp. 308–313.
Fleming, N. D. (2011). *Teaching and Learning Styles: VARK Strategies.* Christchurch: IGI global.
Fleming, N. D. (2012). The case against learning styles: 'There is no evidence…'. Available at: http://vark-learn.com/wp-content/uploads/2014/08/The-Case-Against-Learning-Styles.pdf [Accessed 25 October 2019].
Foster, S. (2017). Career development for all ages. *British Journal of Nursing*, 26(1), 67.

Frost, D. and Titchen, A. (2010). Understanding and developing our professional artistry: A critical creative journey towards reciprocity in the supervisor–student relationship. *Conference: Enhancing Practice 10*, at Belfast, UK.

Gardner, H. (1983, 2003). *Frames of Mind: The Theory of Multiple Intelligences*. New York: Basic Books.

Harvell, J. and Prowle, A. (2018). *Refugee Education: Integration and Acceptance of Refugees in Mainstream Society*. Innovations in Higher Education Teaching and Learning, 11. London: Emerald Publishing Limited, pp. 171–184.

Honey, P. and Mumford, A. (1982). *Manual of Learning Styles*. London: P. Honey.

Knipe, C. and Speck, M. (2005). *Why Can't We Get it Right?*, 2nd ed. London: SAGE Publications Ltd.

Kolb, D. A. (1984). *Experiential Learning: Experience as the Source of Learning and Development*, Vol. 1. Englewood Cliffs, NJ: Prentice-Hall.

Krapivin, P. (2018). How Google's strategy for happy employees boosts its bottom line. *Forbes.com*. Available at: https://www.forbes.com/sites/pavelkrapivin/2018/09/17/how-googles-strategy-for-happy-employees-boosts-its-bottom-line/#6441990b22fc [Accessed 17 July 2019].

Lave, J. and Wenger, E. (1990). *Situated Learning: Legitimate Peripheral Participation*. Cambridge: Cambridge University Press.

Lee, F. (2019). Cultivating a culture of peace and empathy in young children while empowering refugee communities. *Childhood Education*, 95(1), 16–23.

Lightfoot, S. and Frost, D. (2015). The professional identity of early years educators in England: Implications for a transformative approach to continuing professional development. *Professional Development in Education*, 41(2), 401–418. https://doi.org/10.1080/19415257.2014.989256.

Locke, E. and Latham, G. (2002). Building a practically useful theory of goal setting and task motivation: A 35-year odyssey. *American Psychologist*, 57(9), 705–717.

Malm, B. (2009). Towards a new professionalism: Enhancing personal and professional development in teacher education. *Journal of Education for Teaching*, 35(1), 77–91.

Maslow, A. H. (1970). *Motivation and Personality*. New York: Harper & Row.

McClelland, D. (1988). *Human Motivation*. Cambridge: Cambridge University Press.

Moen, P. (2017). Redesigning careers and care for the twenty-first century. *Community, Work & Family*, 20(5), 497–499.

Newman, L. and Leggett, N. (2019). Practitioner research: With intent. *European Early Childhood Education Research Journal*, 27(1), 120–137.

Newton, P. and Miah, M. (2017). Evidence-based higher education – Is the learning styles 'myth' important? *Frontiers in Psychology*, 8, 444.

Osgood, J. (2010). Reconstructing professionalism in ECEC: The case for the 'critically reflective emotional professional'. *Early Years*, 30(2), 19–133.

Pink, D. (2009). *The Surprising Truth About What Motivates Us*. New York: Riverhead Books.

Porter, L. W. and Lawler, E. E. (1968). *Managerial Attitudes and Performance.* Homewood, IL: Richard D. Irwin, Inc.

Rogers, C. (1951). *Client-Centered Therapy.* Boston, MA: Houghton Mifflin.

Schon, D. (1987). *Educating the Reflective Practitioner.* San Francisco: Jossey Bass.

Seligman, M. (2011). *Flourish: A New Understanding of Happiness and Well-Being.* London: Nicholas Brealey Publishing.

Trought, F. (2017). *Brilliant Employability Skills: How to Stand Out from the Crowd in the Graduate Job Market,* 2nd ed. New York: Pearson Education.

UNHCR (United Nations Refugee Agency) (2019). *Figures at a Glance: Statistical Yearbooks.* Available at: https://www.unhcr.org/uk/figures-at-a-glance.html [Accessed 20 July 2019].

INDEX

A

Ability model, *see* emotional intelligence 77–9

Abuse
  child abuse 14, 50, 85
  domestic abuse 21
  sexual abuse 142, 54, 87
  substance abuse 14, 21, 57

Active listening 53, 54, 95–6, 98, 105, 140, 149, 165

Activism, *see* child activism; reflective activism

Adaptability 8, 19, 66, 74, 149, 150, 153, 189

Adversity 13–15, 24–5, 31–3, 39–42, 83, 85, 112, 145, 148; *see also* multiple adversity

Advocacy 23, 45–60
  culture of 51–3
  skills 53
  types of 46–7

Affiliative leadership 66

Agent of Change 47, 62–74; *see also* child agency; multi-agency

Ambition 51, 63, 72, 165, 174

Anti-discriminatory practice 137

Anti-oppressive practice 147

Anti-social behaviour 14, 57

Anxiety 3, 7, 68, 79, 156, 164

Appraisal
  self-appraisal 170, 181, 190
  staff appraisal 94, 181

Assertiveness 46, 53, 82, 89, 114

Assumptions 17, 52–3, 65, 94, 99, 111, 134, 143, 148

Asylum seeker 18–19, 141

Attachment 4–5, 31, 104, 131, 142

Austerity 109, 155

Authentic leadership 66

Authenticity 17, 52, 96, 127, 132

Authoritarian 65

Autonomy 68

B

Barriers 36–7, 71
  barriers to communication 95–6, 99, 149
  barriers to empathy 6
  barriers to engagement 16–18, 143–45
  psychological barriers 15

'Bearing the unbearable' 34–5

Behaviour 8–9, 14, 17–18, 37, 40, 57–8, 82, 87, 124, 138, 141–2, 155

Beliefs 8, 17, 33, 36–8, 85, 95, 111, 122–9, 141, 145

Bereavement 35, 70, 164

Blue sky thinking 73, 110–1

Body language 3, 77, 94, 149

Boundaries, professional 1, 19, 33, 67, 83, 85

Bowlby, John, Richard 4

Brookfield's lenses 17, 129, 130, 132–4

Buddha, Buddhism 153, 158

Bureaucracy 115–8, 155

Burnout 7, 32, 34–5, 84, 153–55, 158, 165, 167

C

Cain, Susan 64, 92

CAMHS 41

Career 170–2, 185–6
  21st century 186–7, 190
  in CYPF 190
  development 180
  international 189
  progression 184, 186–8

Carer, *see* foster carer; kinship carer; foster carer; sibling carer; parents/ carers

Caring 1, 7, 9, 34–5, 49, 155, 165–6

Catalytic leadership 70

Printed by Printforce, United Kingdom